The Elohist

The Elohist

A Seventh-Century
Theological Tradition

Robert Karl Gnuse

CASCADE *Books* • Eugene, Oregon

THE ELOHIST
A Seventh-Century Theological Tradition

Copyright © 2017 Robert Karl Gnuse. All rights reserved. Except for brief quotations in critical publications or reviews, no part of this book may be reproduced in any manner without prior written permission from the publisher. Write: Permissions, Wipf and Stock Publishers, 199 W. 8th Ave., Suite 3, Eugene, OR 97401.

Cascade Books
An Imprint of Wipf and Stock Publishers
199 W. 8th Ave., Suite 3
Eugene, OR 97401

www.wipfandstock.com

PAPERBACK ISBN: 978-1-4982-9541-3
HARDCOVER ISBN: 978-1-4982-9543-7
EBOOK ISBN: 978-1-4982-9542-0

Cataloguing-in-Publication data:

Names: Gnuse, Robert Karl, 1947–.

Title: The Elohist : a seventh-century theological tradition / Robert Karl Gnuse.

Description: Eugene, OR: Cascade Books, 2016 | Includes bibliographical references and index.

Identifiers: ISBN 978-1-4982-9541-3 (paperback) | ISBN 978-1-4982-9543-7 (hardcover) | ISBN 978-1-4982-9542-0 (ebook)

Subjects: LCSH: Bible. O.T. Pentateuch—Criticism, interpretation, etc. | Bible. Pentateuch—Criticism, redaction. | E document (Biblical criticism).

Classification: BS1181.2 G58 2017 (print) | BS1181.2 (ebook).

Manufactured in the U.S.A. FEBRUARY 8, 2017

Dedicated to
Beth, Becky, Chris, Jake, Adam, and Riley

Contents

Acknowledgments ix
List of Abbreviations xi

1 Introduction 1
2 Scholarly Research on the Elohist 11
3 Critics of the Elohist and My Response 29
4 Prophetic Narratives in Samuel and Kings 44
5 The Social and Theological Setting of the Elohist 62
6 Theology of the Elohist 80
7 Commentary on Elohist Texts 99
8 The Modern Relevance of the Elohist 136
9 Conclusion 151

Bibliography 155
Scripture Index 163
Subject Index 173
Name Index 184

Acknowledgments

IN THE CREATION OF any book credit is due to many people who surround an author. Special credit goes to my wife, Beth, for patience while this book manuscript was generated both at home and at the office since 2010. I would like to thank Loyola University New Orleans for the sabbatical in the fall 2010 semester, when the bulk of this manuscript was written. I would like to thank the Interlibrary Loan Department of Loyola University for obtaining many volumes for me over the years, for this and for other projects. I would like to thank the library staff at New Orleans Baptist Theological Seminary for the use of their facilities for many years. Finally, I would like to thank Wipf and Stock for the willingness to publish this work.

I would like to thank Nicole Tilford, Production Manager of the Society of Biblical Literature Press, for permission to reprint an expanded version of my article, "Redefining the Elohist: 'Pools of Oral Tradition,'" *JBL* 119 (2000) 201–20, in chapters 2 and 5. I would like to thank Jürgen van Oorschot, editor of *Zeitschrift für die alttestamentliche Wissenschrift*, for permission to reprint my article, "Northern Prophetic Traditions in the Books of Samuel and Kings as a Precursor to the Elohist," *ZAW* 122 (2010) 374–86, in shortened form as chapter 4. I would like to thank David Bossman, editor of *Biblical Theology Bulletin*, to reprint my article, "The Elohist: a 7th Century BCE Theological Tradition," *BTB* 42 (2012) 59–69, in an expanded version in chapter 6.

Biblical texts quoted in this volume come from the New Revised Standard Version translation of the Bible, and specifically from *The New Oxford Annotated Bible: New Revised Standard Version*.

Robert Gnuse
James C. Carter, SJ/Bank One Distinguished Professor of the Humanities
Loyola University New Orleans
Spring 2016

Abbreviations

AB	Anchor Bible
ABD	*Anchor Bible Dictionary*, 6 vols., edited by David Noel Freedman. New York: Doubleday, 1992
AGJU	Arbeiten zur Geschichte des antiken Judentums and des Urchristentums
APS	American Philosophical Society
ATANT	Abhandlungen zur Theologie des Alten und Neuen Testaments
AUSS	*Andrews University Seminary Studies*
BASOR	Bulletin of the American Schools of Oriental Research
BIS	Biblical Interpretation Series
BJS	Brown Judaic Studies
BTB	*Biblical Theology Bulletin*
BZ	*Biblische Zeitschrift*
BZAW	Beihefte zur Zeitschrit für die alttestamentliche Wissenschaft
CBQ	*Catholic Biblical Quarterly*
CurrTM	*Currents in Theology and Mission*
EBib	Etudes bibliques
EvT	*Evangelische Theologie*
FAT	Forschungen zum Alten Testament
FOTL	Forms of the Old Testament Literature
HSM	Harvard Semitic Monographs

Abbreviations

HSS	Harvard Semitic Studies
IDBS	*Interpreter's Dictionary of the Bible, Supplement*, edited by Keith Crim. Nashville: Abingdon, 1976
Int	*Interpretation*
JANES(CU)	*Journal of the Ancient Near Eastern Society (Columbia University)*
JAOS	*Journal of the American Oriental Society*
JBL	*Journal of Biblical Literature*
JNES	*Journal of Near Eastern Studies*
JSOT	*Journal for the Study of the Old Testament*
JSOTSup	Journal for the Study of the Old Testament Supplement Series
JSPSup	Journal for the Study of the Pseudepigrapha Supplement Series
LHBOTS	Library of Hebrew Bible/Old Testament Studies
NCB	New Century Bible
OBO	Orbis biblicus et orientalis
OBT	Overtures to Biblical Theology
OTL	Old Testament Library
QD	Questiones disputatae
SBLDS	Society of Biblical Literature Dissertation Series
SBLMS	Society of Biblical Literature Monograph Series
SBLSymS	Society of Biblical Literature Symposium Series
SBLSS	Society of Biblical Literature Semeia Series
SWBA	Social World of Biblical Antiquity
TDOT	*Theological Dictionary of the Old Testament*
TZ	*Theologische Zeitschrift*
VT	*Vetus Testamentum*
VTSup	Vetus Testamentum Supplements
WBC	Word Biblical Commentary

ABBREVIATIONS

WMANT	Wissenschaftliche Monographien zum Alten und Neuen-Testament
ZAW	*Zeitschrift für die alttestamentliche Wissenschaft*

1

Introduction

IS THERE HIDDEN WITHIN our present Old Testament the words of a great theologian or theologians, who spoke a powerful religious message to people in an age of great turmoil and need? I believe so. Can the words and the message of this theological tradition be recovered for us? I hope so. This theologian, called the Elohist, lurks like a shadow in our Pentateuch. Some scholars have isolated the texts, dated them, and exposited their meanings. But scholars disagree on the texts, on the social setting of the theological tradition, and dates for the tradition range over five different centuries. Other scholars deny the existence of this source, maintaining it is a figment of our imagination and nothing more than a supplement to another tradition, the Yahwist. Still other scholars will admit to the existence of this tradition but maintain the fragmentary and limited nature of the Elohist texts in the Pentateuch make it unrealistic to speak meaningfully of this tradition and its message. In this work I shall attempt to recover the so-called "Elohist" texts, situate them in a different social context than usually has been done in the past, and most importantly, speak about the theological message and relevance of this shadowy literary and theological tradition in the Bible.

In the history of scholarship the Elohist was discerned to be a viable, albeit fragmentary tradition until the challenges issued in the 1930s by Paul Volz and Wilhelm Rudolph.[1] But even they admitted that certain texts such as Genesis 20 and 22 could not be easily dismissed. Thus, later critics of the source, especially John Van Seters, characterized the Elohist as simply small fragments used by the Yahwist Historian along with other sources,

---

1. Volz and Rudolph, *Elohist als Erzähler*; and Rudolph, *Elohist*.

but not sufficiently substantial to merit consideration as a source.[2] That is the point I wish to emphasize: the Elohist's existence is not really denied, but rather it is deemed too insubstantial to merit consideration along with the Yahwist, Deuteronomists, and Priestly editors. I therefore respond that if the few Elohist texts that we have can be used to reconstruct a theological perspective, they are sufficient to merit our consideration. I speak as a biblical theologian. If the Elohist texts can be used to craft an Elohist biblical theology, and if they in turn can also inspire a significant theological message for our modern audience, they are worthy of our consideration both as a pedagogical model in our textbooks and a source of inspiration for our theology.

My previous writings have been criticized for being somewhat backwards in methodological approach. It has been pointed out that I spend more effort crafting the message of the Elohist passages in order to observe their coherence rather than defending their cohesiveness on literary grounds.[3] That is a valid criticism. But I must respond by saying that the very fragmentary nature of the Elohist repository of texts makes it exceedingly difficult to substantiate literary coherence. Rather, I seek to discern overarching religious themes and idioms that betoken that once there existed an intellectually coherent tradition or at least several closely related cycles of tradition. The point at which I enter the debate is where critical scholars have stated that Elohist texts are too insubstantial to merit consideration as a source. My goal is to demonstrate that they are sufficiently substantial in order to perceive a coherent religious message, and for that reason I have chosen this methodological approach.

My Proposals

In the past I have argued for the existence of the Elohist, but I admit the cogency of the contemporary scholarly critique that questions the existence of the Elohist by pointing to the limited number of texts and the fragmentary nature of the texts. Thus, I speak of "pools of Elohist tradition" that may never have precipitated into written form before their use by the Yahwist in the exilic period, and they may never have been organized together into one coherent epic. I have suggested that such Elohist "pools of tradition"

---

2. Van Seters, *Prologue to History*; Van Seters, *Pentateuch*; and Van Seters, *Yahwist*, are works in which he distinctly made such observations.

3. Baden, *Reaction of the Pentateuch*, 189.

Introduction

may have arisen after the fall of Samaria and may have developed during the seventh century in the north, partially as a theological response to the crisis caused by the destruction of the state of Israel.[4] Then in the exile, or later, the Yahwist used this material. I have suggested also that some of those "pools of Elohist tradition" may have been the early prophetic legends in the books of Samuel and Kings, which may have inspired the creation of the later Pentateuchal Elohist narratives.[5] There may have been separate pools or cycles of tradition concerning the patriarchs, exodus and the wilderness, the mountain experience, the conquest, and the prophets.

If the Elohist arose as a response to the crisis caused by the destruction of Samaria in 722 BCE, then it attempted to give a meaningful religious message to Israelites taken into exile in Assyria as well as Israelites who still remained in the land of Israel. Those who remained in the land were far more numerous than those who went into exile. The Elohist proclaimed, among other things, that Elohim/Yahweh was to be exclusively worshipped by the Israelites, and that they should "fear God" and "obey" the divine will, especially as it was mediated to them through charismatic prophets. God was portrayed as a transcendent and awesome God, yet at the same time this deity accompanied them wherever they traveled in the world, including exile. This deity remained high and distant, yet was revealed through dreams, angels, a voice from heaven, fire, and above all, through prophetic mediators. God was distant, yet present for people who believed and obeyed.

The traditions were organized at the shrine of Bethel, hence, the importance of that shrine in the patriarchal stories. With the destruction of Samaria, and perhaps some destruction at Bethel, this shrine emerged as the center of Israelite religious hope and identity. The religious intelligentsia at the shrine condemned its previous cultic activity, the veneration of the calf, a cult sponsored by kings. The Elohist tradition thus condemned kings and the calf cult. It is not incongruous that religious intelligentsia at Bethel would condemn previous religious activity at Bethel, for the same phenomenon would occur later with Jerusalem in the rhetoric of the Deuteronomic Theologians. Jerusalem would be proclaimed as the religious center for the future, but the pre-exilic cultic activity there would be condemned in the Deuteronomistic History and also by a prophet/priest like Ezekiel. Thus,

---

4. Gnuse, "Dreams in the Night"; and Gnuse, "Redefining the Elohist," which provides the template for much of this volume.

5. Gnuse, "Northern Prophetic Traditions."

the Elohist tradition may have envisioned Bethel as a new center for hope and identity, once it was purified from the sins of its past.

The "pools of Elohist tradition" may have included at least two or more cycles of stories. Old prophetic tales were gathered together, perhaps loosely. Stories about Samuel, Elijah, and Elisha, as well as other prophetic tales found in the books of Samuel and Kings were collected. The Elisha tales influenced the shape of the Elijah stories, and perhaps in later years the Elijah stories, as we now have them, were further edited when the Deuteronomistic Historians drew upon these Elohist prophetic tales. Many of these tales may have been old when the Elohist circles collected them and shaped them into one or more "pools of tradition." Whether they were all connected is difficult for us to say, because the later Deuteronomistic Historians may have left out many of the accounts collected by the Elohist editors.

Elohist accounts in the Pentateuch were, for the most part, shaped and generated by the religious intelligentsia at Bethel in those years after 722 BCE. Prophetic accounts may have influenced the way in which Pentateuchal accounts were articulated. In my subjective opinion the prophetic narratives appear to be less theologically developed than the Pentateuchal Elohist traditions. These Pentateuchal accounts may have been brought together in separate cycles, or they may have been one continuous narrative. Yahwist editorial use of these Elohist accounts in the late sixth century was selective, leaving it impossible for us to determine the shape of these traditions. Hence, it can be argued whether the Elohist materials were separate, disconnected cycles of tales, or whether there was a unified narrative. Though I favor the former option, I am open to the possibility of theorizing the latter option. Either way, the important task is to draw forth the theological message from these accounts.

Michael Goulder had a similar theory. He believed that the Asaph Psalms, Psalms 50, 73–83, describe indirectly the events in the 730s and 720s BCE that led to the fall of Israel in 722 BCE. These Asaph Psalms also refer to the great traditions of the people: creation (Psalm 74), exodus (Psalms 77, 80), plagues, wilderness, and settlement (Psalm 78), testing at Meribah (Psalm 81). He believed these Psalms also helped give rise to the Elohist traditions at the shrine of Bethel. He pointed out that the Asaph Psalms do not know about Sinai. Thus, he regarded the psalms in the same way that I treat the prophetic traditions, as traditions that existed prior to the fall of Samaria, and he also hypothesized the later development of

INTRODUCTION

Elohist Pentateuchal traditions. He believed there was a fluid oral Elohist tradition at Bethel that evolved into one central narrative and which spoke of events from creation down to Solomon in 1 Kings 5, stressing the exodus. It was written down once the epic was taken to Jerusalem in Hezekiah's age.[6] Eventually this Elohist tradition would be taken up and used by the Yahwist tradition in the late sixth century.[7] I believe his suggestions have merit, for these psalms could reflect an earlier version of the Elohist traditions that I believe arose after 722 BCE under the influence of prophetic stories. His theory shares much in common with mine, especially in terms of the locus of the Elohist traditions and their later usage by the Yahwist.

Therefore, I theorize that there may have been at least two cycles of Elohist tales (prophetic and Pentateuchal), but very likely several separate cycles probably contained the stories (my ideas are similar to those of Yoreh, whom we shall discuss later). The Deuteronomistic Historians, either in late pre-exilic times or in the exile, drew upon the prophetic Elohist accounts, and the Yahwist Historian, in the Babylonian Exile or more likely after the Babylonian Exile, drew upon Pentateuchal Elohist tales. (For example, I believe that the Yahwist account in Genesis 11 knows of the fall of Nabonidus in 540 BCE, for the Tower of Babel parodies his unfinished ziggurats at Ur, Haran, and Teima, and the journey of Abraham into the land follows the route taken by returning exiles from Babylon, thus making the Yahwist post-exilic.[8]) In both instances the Elohist tales were used partially by the Deuteronomistic Historians and the Yahwist Historian, leaving us to debate endlessly on how unified the Elohist narratives may have been.

What I therefore suggest is that Elohist stories may be understood better as a message to exiles from the northern state of Israel. This has been proposed already by Hans-Christoph Schmitt (whom we shall discuss later). I believe that the Elohist is prior to the Yahwist, and that the Yahwist used Elohist narratives, sometimes re-crafting them in a form that contains both Yahwist and Elohist language. This is what gave us the impression that there was a JE redactor; it was the material that reflected the style of both traditions. Thus, the sequence of the traditions might best be understood simplistically as EDJP. What I propose ultimately is that all of the Pentateuch and the Deuteronomistic History may be understood as a message to people whose group identity has been destroyed and many of whom have

---

6. Goulder, *Psalms of Asaph*, 190–210; and Goulder, "Asaph's History."
7. Goulder, *Psalms of Asaph*, 200–209, 251, 330–31.
8. Gnuse, "Tower of Babel."

been sent into exile. I would observe that it really makes sense for great literature to be generated only in such a crisis, and at such a time, when people were in danger of losing their identity. This great literature was created primarily to preserve that identity by bringing their attention to focus upon some form of exclusive devotion to their group's deity.

I am not the first to assume a late date, a date after the 722 BCE fall of Samaria. These other scholars, however, addressed the issue of a late date in passing references, so no detailed argument was presented for a post–722 BCE date. Scholars, who did assume this late date, discussed the Joseph stories as part of the greater Elohist narrative. I do not make that assumption; I date the Joseph narrative in the post-exilic era and I really do not view it as part of the Elohist tradition. Commentators often point to the Joseph dreams and connect them with the dreams in the patriarchal narratives. But they are different kinds of dreams; the Joseph dreams have more in common with other post-exilic symbolic dreams, like those in Zechariah and Daniel. So other scholars, who date the Elohist late, do not address the same issues I approach, as I consider the epic texts in Genesis, Exodus, and Numbers.

I believe the Elohist religious intelligentsia gathered together old prophetic narratives that we now read in the books of Samuel and Kings and these tales inspired the later Pentateuchal Elohist tales. If so, the Elohist must be dated at least after 800 BCE. A comparison of Elohist dream reports and Mesopotamian dream reports points even later to the seventh century as the more likely time when these narratives were created. The Elohist message appears to address the needs of exiles, after their kingdom had been destroyed. For me, the last exposition is the most convincing in terms of determining the origin and provenance of the Elohist.

Elohist Themes and Texts for Consideration

In my selection of texts, I have been inspired by several recent scholars, but most notably Joel Burnett. In his study of the name, *'elohim*, he gave consideration to the Elohist tradition. His cautious delineation of those texts that may be assigned to the Elohist tradition with certitude provides foundation for my selection of texts. He concluded that the Elohist was unified intellectually, but highly fragmented. The Elohist proclaimed Elohim was Yahweh and people must choose to worship Yahweh. After Burnett cautiously determined which texts were Elohist, he discussed themes rooted in

Introduction

those texts. His core texts were Gen 20:1–17 (Abimelech's court), 21:9–21 (Hagar's flight), 21:22–32 (covenant with Abimelech), 31:1–42 (Jacob and Laban), 31:43–54 (covenant with Laban), and 35:1–7 (Jacob's journey to Bethel). He added further texts deduced to be Elohist because of similarity with the core texts. These were: Gen 28:10–12, 17–21a, 22 (theophany at Bethel), 30:1–23 (Jacob's children), 46:1–7 (theophany at Beersheba), and 48:8–22 (blessing of Ephraim and Manasseh). From these texts he spoke of the following themes: 1) use of Elohim for the name of God, 2) pronounced ethical sensitivity, 3) remoteness of the deity and revelation through dreams and angels, 4) association with northern cult sites, and 5) how Elohim accompanies the patriarchs in their travels.[9]

Building upon Burnett's method, I have chosen texts which appear to have the following themes: 1) use of Elohim, 2) reference to "fear of God," 3) distant deity, 4) auditory message dream format, 5) importance of prophets, 6) reference to angel or angel of God, 7) God speaks from heaven, 8) fire is mode of revelation or form of divine punishment, 9) reference to northern cult shrines, Bethel, Beersheba, and Shechem, 10) interest in the establishment of ritual pillars, 11) Joshua is important as a "minister" to Moses, 12) importance of Moses as leader and because he is the greatest prophet, 13) use of the idiom "king of Egypt" instead of pharaoh, 14) concern with the calf cult, 15) the tent of meeting is outside the camp, 16) reference to the pillars of fire and cloud, 17) interest in traditions of the Transjordan conquest, 18) moral sensitivity, 19) tendency to portray biblical figures in positive fashion, and 20) divine testing of people and their response of obedience. I have chosen these characteristics because they generally occur together in the same stories and provide an overall character and personality to those accounts. There are some motifs and vocabulary, which have been attributed to the Elohist over the years by scholars, which I feel do not occur with sufficient frequency to use as important or serious indicators of the Elohist texts (i.e., maidservant, congregation). Nor do they seem to indicate anything of significant import in reference to the particular theology of the Elohist.

I will use a number of texts that appear to meet these criteria. Some of them appear Elohistic to me; others are a little more dubious. These include: Gen 15:12–21 (Abraham's vision), Gen 20:1–4a, 5–17 (Abimelech's court), 21:2–8 (Isaac's birth), 21:9–21 (Hagar's flight), 21:22–31 (covenant with Abimelech), 22:1–13, 19 (sacrifice of Isaac), 25:21–34 (twins born),

---

9. Burnett, *Biblical Elohim*, 27–50, 127–50.

The Elohist

28:10–12, 16a, 17–21a, 22 (theophany at Bethel), 29:1–30 (meeting Rachel), 29:31–32; 30:1–24a (Jacob's children), 31:4–42 (Jacob and Laban), 31:43–49a, 50–55 (covenant with Laban), 32:1–2 (Mahanaim), 32:3–21 (journey to Esau), 32:22–32 (Penuel), 33:1–17 (meeting Esau), 33:18–20 (Shechem), 35:1–7 (journey to Bethel), 35:8–15 (Bethel), 46:1–4 (theophany at Beersheba), and 48:8–22 (blessing of Ephraim and Manasseh), 50:15–21 (Joseph's brothers), Exod 1:8–10, 15–21 (midwives), 3:1, 2b, 3, 4b–6, 9–15, 18–22 (burning bush), 4:17–18, 20 (Moses leaves Jethro), 5:3–4 (Moses before pharaoh), 13:17–22 (Joseph's bones), 14:5a, 7, 19–20, 24 (exodus), 15:20 (Miriam as prophet), 15:25b–26 (testing), 16:4–21 (manna and quail), 17:1–7 (testing), 17:8–16 (Amalek), 18:1–27 (Jethro), 19:2b–6 (eagle's wings), 19:16–19 (cloud on mount), 20:1–4a, 7–8, 12–17 (Decalogue core, maybe), 20:18–21 (people's response), 24:1–2, 9–15 (elders and Joshua on mount),[10] 32:1–10, 15–24 (golden calf), 33:7–11 (cloud), Lev 10:1–3 (Nadab and Abihu, reworked by Priestly Editors),[11] Num 11:1–3 (Taberah fire), 11:11–12, 14–17, 24b–30 (elders prophesy), 12:1–15 (identity of Moses), 14:13–16 (cloud), 21:4–9 (bronze serpent), 21:21–33, 35 (Sihon), 22:1–7, 9–13a, 14–17, 20–21, 36–40; 23:1–2, 18–21a, 22–24, 27–30; 24:2–6a, 6c–11a, 14–25 (Balaam), Deut 31:14–15 (pillar of cloud), 34:5, 10–12 (praise of Moses). These are chosen because they share themes with Burnett's core texts, and they have a consistent set of vocabulary and images throughout. In a later chapter I indicate which texts I feel might be more probable as Elohist texts than others.

The core vocabulary includes a number of words that occur in Elohist texts with a high degree of frequency, which means that there is a complex of words that occur together in select texts. This set of words is what has attracted the attention of commentators over the years and led them to isolate a source called the Elohist. The name, Elohim, frequently appears in these texts, thus giving its name to the source. But the use of Elohim outside the Elohist passages and the appearance of Yahweh in the Elohist passages preclude us from being too absolute in using this to isolate Elohist texts. The core vocabulary are as follows: 1) The specific word for dream, *hlm*,

---

10. Sommer, "Reflecting on Moses," 605–6, saw these Elohist passages designed to temper the image of an angry Moses in the rest of the chapter. This implies to me that the Yahwist inserted Elohist fragments for a theological reason.

11. The names of these sons of Aaron remind us of Jeroboam's sons, Abijah and Nadab (1 Kgs 15:25) and since both Aaron and Jeroboam built golden calves, we suspect Elohist theological agenda, Aberback and Smolar, "Golden Calves"; and Sweeney, *I & II Kings*, 184.

occurs in noun form only six times outside the Joseph narrative (Gen 20:3, 6; 31:10, 11, 24; Num 12:6) and in verb form only once outside the Joseph narrative (Gen 28:12). All of these texts are included among my Elohist passages. In the Joseph narratives of Genesis 37, 39–42 the word occurs twenty-eight times in noun form (Gen 37:5, 6, 8, 9 [twice], 10, 20; 40:5 [three times], 8, 9 [twice], 16; 41:7, 8, 11 [twice], 12 [twice], 15 [twice], 17, 22, 25, 26, 32; 42:9) and thirteen times in verb form (Gen 37:5, 6, 9 [twice], 10; 40:5, 8; 41:1, 5, 11 [twice], 15; 42:9), so that scholars who include the Joseph narrative in the Elohist can count a great number of references to the word for dream exclusively used in the Elohist passages. The word is not used elsewhere in the first four books of the Pentateuch, and that is most significant. 2) The word for "pillar of cloud" is found nine times in the Pentateuch (Exod 13:21, 22; 14:19, 24; 33:9, 10; Num 12:5; 14:14; Deut 31:15) and all are included in my Elohist passages. 3) The word for "pillar of fire" occurs four times in the Pentateuch (Exod 13:21, 22; 14:24; Num 14:14) and all are included in my Elohist passages. 4) God is revealed in fire in four different passages in the Pentateuch (Exod 3:2; 19:18; Num 11:1–3; 16:35) and three of them are included in my Elohist passages. 5) Joshua is called a "minister" to Moses three times in the Pentateuch (Exod 24:13; 33:11; Num 11:28) and all of them occur in my Elohist texts. 6) The word for "ritual pillar" or *maṣṣebah* occurs ten times in the first four books of the Pentateuch (Gen 28:18, 22; 31:13, 45, 51, 52 [twice]; 35:14, 20; Exod 24:4) and eight of them appear in my Elohist texts. 7) The expression "angel of God" appears five times in the first four books of the Pentateuch (Gen 21:17; 28:12; 31:11; 32:1; Exod 14:19) and all of them occur in my Elohist texts. 8) The expression "king of Egypt" is used thirteen times in the Pentateuch (Exod 1:8, 15, 17, 18; 2:23; 3:18, 19; 5:4; 6:11, 13, 27, 29; 14:5) and eight of them are included in my Elohist passages. There is a high degree of coincidence between these nine expressions and Elohist texts. Critics might say that I have a circular argument of texts and vocabulary, but I respond by noting that these words occur with each other and do not appear outside of this select collection of Elohist texts, and the vocabulary appears to be theologically congruent. Truly it would seem that this vocabulary constitutes a distinct indicator of Elohist texts as a separate corpus of literature. Those scholars who include even more Elohist texts might make the number of occurrences even higher.

It would be valuable for us to review those scholars who have analyzed the shape and theological identity of the Elohist tradition, as well as those who deny its existence. I shall respond to those latter critics in order to defend the Elohist's existence. This shall be the focus of our next two chapters.

2

Scholarly Research on the Elohist

History of Research on the Elohist Tradition

IN THE FINELY CRAFTED literature of the Pentateuch there appear to be various traditions or sources that have been woven together masterfully by the final authors or editors of the sacred text. For years commentators and scholars have noted these sources. Martin Luther (1483–1546) noted that Moses clearly used pre-existing sources in writing the Pentateuch. Baruch Spinoza (1632–1677), otherwise known for his philosophy, also made critical observations about the biblical text, and he was the first to suggest that the so-called "sources" may have arisen after the time of Moses. By the eighteenth century, critical thinkers were looking closely at the biblical text to determine which passages belonged to each particular "source." There are a number of fine histories of critical biblical research that detail the efforts of scholars up until the modern era.[1] For our purposes the efforts of those who evaluated the source called the "Elohist" merit our attention.

The quest to discover the Elohist passages in the Pentateuch was a fascinating journey for scholars over the past three centuries.[2] The Elohist source was recognized as a distinct entity first in 1753 by Jean Astruc (1684–1766), a medical doctor in Paris, who delineated two sources by their

---

1. Hahn, *Modern Research*, 1–43; Kraus, *Historisch-kritischen Erforschung*, 152–63, 242–74; Clements, *Old Testament Interpretation*, 7–30; Jenks, *North Israelite Traditions*, 2–18; Hayes, *Old Testament Study*, 115–20, 153–80; Blenkinsopp, *Pentateuch*, 1–28.

2. Jenks, "North Israelite Traditions," (diss.), provided much of the information on the early scholars.

use of the divine names, Yahweh and Elohim. Johann Gottfried Eichhorn (1753–1827), a professor at Jena University, developed this division by a more nuanced study of the sources. They both delineated a Yahwist and an Elohist source. In 1798 Karl David Ilgen (1763–1834), who succeeded Eichhorn at Jena, delineated seventeen different documents from three different writers (our Yahwist, Elohist, and Priestly Editors). He discerned two Elohist strands (our Elohist and Priestly Editors). In 1805 Wilhelm Leberecht de Wette (1780–1849) identified three strands in the Pentateuch, one of which he called the "prophetic strand" (our modern Elohist).

The "fragmentary" and "supplemental" theories of Pentateuchal evolution moved scholarship in a different direction for a time. Alexander Geddes (1737–1802) endorsed the "fragmentary" hypothesis, which suggested that Genesis arose out of many separate little traditions. Johann Vater (1771–1826) applied this fragmentary theory to the entire Pentateuch in 1802. Later, Heinrich Ewald (1803–1875) suggested that there were four such supplements or narrators, which ran from Genesis through Joshua. What he identified as the earliest strand or core narrative was a source he connected to the northern kingdom of Israel and prophets like Elijah and Elisha, which we would call the Elohist tradition.

Subsequently scholars, including Eduard Reuss (1851–1911), Wilhelm Vatke (1806–1882), and others turned to a source or documentary approach. Hermann Hupfeld (1796–1866) isolated an original priestly core of texts in Genesis, which used Elohim as the divine name and was separate from texts using Yahweh as the name. What he called the Elohist later would be recognized as both the Priestly and the Elohist traditions. His categories would be significant for later scholars who built upon his model. He ultimately delineated three sources: the older priestly texts (our Priestly texts), the younger priestly texts (our Elohist), and the Yahwist. All three were combined by a fourth person, a redactor. Essentially he did not believe that the younger priestly texts (Elohist) were combined with the Yahwist at some stage, but rather that all the sources came together at the same time. He also noted that the younger Priestly texts (Elohist) appear to be fragmentary remains of an older longer document that had a distinct theological identity. Karl Heinrich Graf (1815–1869) systematically extended these observations and clearly delineated the texts. He clearly placed the priestly texts later, after the Elohist and the Yahwist, for he felt that narratives were early, but laws arose later. He tended to treat the Yahwist and Elohist as though they were a single pre-exilic source. Abraham Kuenen (1828–1891) focused upon the laws to separate and date sources. He viewed the Yahwist and the Elohist as a unit because they shared stories and it was difficult to delineate them. His views were quite similar to those of Graf. August Dillmann (1823–1894) felt that the Yahwist used the Elohist, Priestly texts were separate, and one editor brought them together. He suggested (as do I) that the Yahwist had the Elohist text in front of him when crafting his narratives, which for Dillmann explained the narrative similarities in the two sources. Finally, the culmination of the work provided by these early authors came together in the writings of Julius Wellhausen (1844–1918) in writings published in 1876, 1877, and 1883. He separated Hupfeld's "E" material from the "P" material and decided that the "J" material (Yahwist) was the oldest. "D" material (Deuteronomist) was located in the former prophets primarily. He believed that the Elohist arose in the eighth century. However, he believed that it was very difficult to separate Yahwist and Elohist material because a redactor, called the Jehovist, wove the two together very thoroughly. He further believed that the Yahwist and Elohist went through several editions before the Jehovist reworked them, and that neither the Yahwist or the Elohist knew the other's work prior to their synthesis by the Jehovist. The Yahwist was prior to the Elohist due to the primitive nature of the Yahwist's thought in comparison to the Elohist. This became the theory used or debated throughout the twentieth century. Heinrich Holzinger (1863–1944) argued that the Yahwist and the Elohist were two separate sources independently based on a common original source (1893). Otto Procksch (1874–1947) in 1906 isolated two separate editions of the Elohist. These scholars laid the foundation for the ongoing debates in the twentieth century.[3]

Authors in the twentieth century refined Wellhausen's observations. Samuel Driver, Joseph Carpenter, John Hartford-Battersby, and Otto Eissfeldt especially provided extremely detailed divisions of the four literary sources in later years. Hermann Gunkel (1901) believed that the Yahwist and the Elohist were schools that produced several editions, or collections of oral stories; they were not the works of individual authors. He tended to view them together as an older stage in Israelite literature. Driver acknowledged the very fragmentary nature of the Elohist and viewed its existence as only probable and not assured (1913). Immanuel Benzinger (1921) believed that the Elohist could be traced from Genesis to 2 Kings 23 and was completed in 609 BCE. Gustav Hölscher (1923) believed that the Elohist

---

3. Nicholson, *Pentateuch*, 6–15; and Baden, *Redaction of the Pentateuch*, 13–40.

could be traced through 2 Kings 25 and was to be dated either to the time of Josiah (ending in 2 Kings 23) or the exile (ending in 2 Kings 25). Sigmund Mowinckel thought the Elohist was a revision of the Yahwist from around 800 BCE created over a number of years by scribes in the temple and court in Jerusalem.[4]

New directions were provided by Gerhard von Rad and Martin Noth, who characterized a well developed oral tradition which precipitated into written form to become the four sources, thus moving the Pentateuchal theories away from a written, "bookish" model, which had been assailed by several scholars. In von Rad's scheme the relationship between the Yahwist and the Elohist was not defined other than to imply that the Elohist was worked into the Yahwist at some point. Noth spoke of how both the Yahwist and the Elohist drew upon a common source, the oral or perhaps written *Grundlage*, but he did not define the relationship between the two sources.[5] Scandinavian scholars such as Johannes Pederson, Ivan Engnell, and Sigmund Mowinckel emphasized the oral formation and transmission of Pentateuchal traditions before their commitment to writing, and they critiqued early German scholars who spoke of the sources simplistically as written documents.[6] Thus, the models of von Rad and Noth which spoke of an oral pre-history of narratives before their commitment to writing in the four sources—Yahwist, Elohist, Deuteronomist, and Priestly Editors—provided a more sophisticated model of Pentateuchal evolution.

Throughout of all these theories, the Elohist source was isolated as a fragmentary and limited set of texts. It was seen as a parallel epic history to the Yahwist, and a reaction against the Yahwist. The model of von Rad and Noth placed the Yahwist in the southern kingdom of Judah in the tenth-century court of Solomon, while the Elohist emerged somewhere between the tenth and the eighth centuries in the northern kingdom of Israel. Both the Yahwist and the Elohist drew upon the same oral tradition, but presented and preserved it differently for their respective audiences. The Elohist was particularly dependent upon the already existent Yahwist. Noth articulated the minimalist view of the Elohist, declaring it to be preserved only in fragmentary form as the Jehovist editor left most of it out of the biblical narrative. The few texts isolated as Elohist gave commentators a

---

4. Nicholson, *Pentateuch*, 41–49; and Baden, *Redaction of the Pentateuch*, 40–48.

5. Von Rad, *Hexateuch*; von Rad, *Old Testament Theology*; and Noth, *Pentateuchal Traditions*, 1–259. See excellent observations by Baden, *Redaction of the Pentateuch*, 48–51.

6. See essays in Engnell, *Rigid Scrutiny*.

feeling for its theological perspective. But generally textbooks paid far less attention to the Elohist than they did to the other three traditions, especially when describing the theological significance of the four sources. For example, the Old Testament introductory textbook by Bernhard Anderson, which was the most extensively used text for a generation, devoted only two and half pages to the Elohist.[7]

Was the Elohist a minority report on the ancient Israelite traditions, a reaction to the Yahwist, or perhaps a complementary theological tradition as the later editors wove the Yahwist and Elohist together? The Elohist was described both ways. It was also popular among scholars to assume that an editor, the JE Redactor, wove the Yahwist and Elohist together around 700 BCE, favoring Yahwist texts over Elohist texts by a three to one ratio, leaving the Elohist as a vague and limited source among the Pentateuchal texts.

In the face of criticism concerning the Elohist's existence due to its fragmentary nature, rehabilitation of the Elohist was undertaken by Hans Walter Wolff.[8] He readily admitted the disconnectedness of Elohistic traditions by describing them as "Elohistic fragments," thus countering critics who took fragmentation as a reason to deny their existence altogether. Despite our inheritance of only parts of the epic, Wolff steadfastly defended the integrity of the Elohistic intellectual and theological tradition. He defended its unity by tracing the theological theme of the "fear of God" throughout the texts and he suggested that this was a defining concept for the tradition. The Elohist suffered vicissitudes at the hands of redactors, but missing plot lines could be intuited from the stories that remained and the theological themes that united them (especially the motif of the "fear of God"). Norman Whybray challenged the existence of the Elohist, but admitted that Wolff's analysis of the "fear" motif "is probably the most convincing argument yet advanced for a theology of E."[9] In a similar defense of the Elohist, Lothar Ruppert connected the Elohist tradition to the classical prophets in the eighth century.[10]

In a seldom-cited article worthy of attention, Joachim Schüpphaus delineated the themes that held the fragmentary Elohist accounts together. Since critics often declare that no unifying thread holds the Elohist narratives together, Schüpphaus's arguments are of value in the modern critical

7. Anderson, *Old Testament*, 267–70.
8. Wolff, "Elohistic Fragments."
9. Whybray, *Making of the Pentateuch*, 85.
10. Ruppert, "Der Elohist."

debate. He observed the value of Wolff's emphasis upon the "fear of God," and he elaborated upon it. He observed that the theme of fear is central to accounts about Abraham (Genesis 20, 22), Joseph (Genesis 42), midwives (Exodus 1), Moses (Exodus 3), and Israel (Exodus 20). Fear is the result of human response to the majesty of God, and in the Elohist narratives it leads to obedience and concretely results in the articulation of law in the Decalogue and the Book of the Covenant (Exodus 20–23, which he viewed as Elohist). Law, in turn, leads to the establishment of community, which for Schüpphaus, was a primary goal of Elohist texts. Another theme that unifies Elohist texts is God's faithfulness to the divine promise originally given to Abraham (Genesis 15), which is demonstrated in God's preservation of people at the time of the midwives, Joseph, and Balaam, all of whom are people used by God to protect and bless those who would become Israel someday. (I find these themes to be meaningful if they are addressed to seventh-century exiles.) The Elohist is a popular history, or "folk history," which recalls God's deliverance of Israel. Schüpphaus attempted to show that coherent themes connect the Elohist accounts.[11]

After the observations of Noth, Wolff, and others, textbooks throughout the 1960s and the 1970s presented a model of the four sources that suggested they were initially oral traditions that precipitated into written form and were complete by the fifth century under the Priestly Editors. The Elohist was clearly one of those four traditions, even though it received less attention than the other three. It was described as a northern tradition dating to the time of Elijah and Elisha in the ninth century or contemporary with the early classical prophets, especially Hosea, in the eighth century.

Elohist Themes and Theology as Hypothesized by Scholars

By the 1960s there was a general acceptance of the existence of the Elohist source, and a general consensus on what vocabulary, literary motifs, and ideological concepts could be found in this source. These characteristics are worth listing, because I find most of them still valuable in isolating Elohist texts.

Distinctive forms of divine revelation occur: dreams are a mode of divine revelation, and the word for dream is often *hlm* (Gen 20:6; 31:10, 11, 24; Num 12:6; discounting the use of the word repeatedly in the Joseph narrative). A voice from heaven is a mode of divine revelation (Gen

11. Schüpphaus, "Volk Gottes."

21:17; 22:11, 15). The "angel of God" is a circumlocution for God (Gen 21:17; 28:12; 31:11; 32:1; Exod 14:19). God appears in a cloud by the tent of meeting, which is outside the camp (for the Priestly tradition the tent is inside the camp). God descends in this cloud and meets Moses inside the tent (Exod 33:7–11; Num 11:16–17, 24b–30; 12:4–9), while in the Yahwist tradition the sacred place is the Ark of the Covenant. In the wilderness God does not lead the Israelites directly; rather, God sends a messenger to lead them (Exod 23:20–23a; 32:34) and only occasionally speaks to Moses in the tent of meeting, while in the Yahwist tradition Yahweh leads the people.

Thus, there is a high view of God, who is revealed only in the indirect modes listed above. Otherwise, when God is revealed, as at the mountain of God, it is very dramatic. God does not come down the ladder at Bethel in Gen 28:10–12, 17–18, 20–22, the Elohist text, for Jacob, but in the Yahwist passage in Gen 28:13, Yahweh stands by Jacob to speak. The Angel of God speaks to Hagar from the heavens in Gen 21:17 (Elohist), but the Angel of the LORD comes down to her in Gen 16:7 (Yahwist).

People are fearful of this awesome deity, so that at the mountain they are terrified (Exod 19:17; 20:18–21), unlike in the Yahwist accounts where they are attracted to the mountain (Exod 19:12–13, 21–24). Likewise, Moses is afraid of the burning bush (Exod 3:6).

Prophets are the representatives of God, including Abraham (Gen 20:7), Miriam (Exod 15:20), Moses (Num 12:6–8), seventy elders who receive the spirit (Num 11:16–17, 24b–30), Eldad and Medad (Num 11:26–29), and in Num 11:29, Moses declares that he wishes all God's people were prophets. Moses is portrayed as a powerful wonder worker in Elohist texts, more so than in the other traditions. In the Yahwist tradition the elders simply accompany Moses in Exod 24:1–2, 9–10 to experience the divine theophany.

Elohim is the usual name for God prior to the divine revelation of the name Yahweh in Exodus 3, and Elohim continues to be used in subsequent narratives thereafter. (Though one could theoretically construct an Elohist tradition without the sacred name Yahweh altogether.) Elohim may be understood as a generic way of referring to the significant deity, Yahweh; it is a way of referring to Yahweh before the time when the sacred name was revealed to Moses. To say it more clearly, Elohim is a very special title for God, not a proper name for God; Yahweh is the name, and that name is used cautiously by the Elohist.

The Elohist

There are distinctive ways for God to dialogue with people. When God speaks to a person, the verb form is "and he said" (Gen 20:11; 28:13; 31:12, 24; 46:2–3; Exod 3:5–6). God speaks to people with a double vocative (Gen 20:11; 46:2; Exod 3:4), and people respond to God by saying, "here I am" (Gen 20:11; 31:11; 46:2; Exod 3:4). God then speaks to people after they say, "here I am," by saying, "I am the God of XX," referring either to an ancestor or a site of revelation (such as Bethel) (Gen 28:13; 31:13; 46:3; Exod 3:6).

Certain vocabulary is seen as indicative of the Elohist. The verb *ht'* is the usual word for sin (Gen 20:9; 42:22; Exod 20:20). The word *'amh*, "maidservant," is occasionally used (Gen 20:17; 21:10, 12, 13; 30:3). The verb *yzh*, "to go out," is the word to describe the Israelite exodus (Exod 3:10, 12; 19:17). The verb *nsh* is the word for test or testing, as when God tests people (Gen 22:1; Exod 20:20). Sinai (the Yahwist name for the mount, Exod 19:11) usually is called "the mountain of God" (Exod 3:1; 18:5; 24:13) or occasionally Horeb (Exod 3:1; 33:6). Joshua is the "minister" to Moses (Exod 24:13; Jos 1:1). Residents of the land of Palestine are called Amorites (Gen 48:22), not Canaanites (Gen 12:6), as in Yahwist texts, although this is not consistent in the minds of some scholars. Jethro is the father-in-law of Moses (Exod 3:1; 4:18), not a priest of Midian (Exod 2:16), as in Yahwist texts. The ruler of Egypt is called "the king of Egypt" (Exod 1:8, 15, 17, 18; 3:18, 19; 14:5, though the Yahwist uses the term also). The expression "anger burns hot" is used to describe both God and people (Exod 32:10, 22). The expression, "God brought you up out of the land of Egypt" is found only in Elohist texts (Exod 18:1; 20:2; 32:1, 4, 7, 8, 11, 23).

Narrative technique in Elohist accounts is distinctive. Personages in the narratives are portrayed dramatically and often the narrative is terse, more so than Yahwist accounts. Things often come in pairs (two midwives in Exod 1:15–21; two servants accompany Abraham on the way to sacrifice Isaac in Gen 22:3; twice messengers go to the king of Edom in Num 20:14–20). There are more characters than in corresponding Yahwist narratives (Gen 21:9–21 has Abraham, Sarah, Hagar, Ishmael, and an angel messenger). Sometimes there is significant dialogue (as with Abimelech in Gen 20:9–16 and the Jacob/Laban interaction in Gen 31:1–54). Overall, there is a more dramatic narrative style.

The imagery of fire occurs in some narratives. Fire as a motif, often denotes the presence of God (Exod 3:2; 19:18; Num 11:1, 2, 3 [three times]; 16:35). There is reference to the pillar of fire (Exod 13:21, 22; 14:24; Num 14:14). There is reference to the pillar of cloud, which is the daytime equivalent of the fire pillar (Exod 13:21, 22; 14:19, 24; 33:9, 10; Num 12:5; Num 14:14; Deut 31:15).

A nexus of concepts are connected to describe appropriate human response to the distant and transcendent deity. The phrase "fear of God" is sometimes mentioned, but more often the implication is that people should have such fear (Gen 20:11; 22:12; Exod 1:17, 21). People are told to "fear not" by God (Gen 15:1; 21:17; Exod 18:21; 20:20), a popular prophetic phrase in both biblical and ancient Near Eastern texts. The Israelites are fearful at Horeb (Exod 19:16b–17). As a result, people should be obedient to God (by heeding the law and the spoken word of the prophets presumably). They should act with a high degree of morality.

The people are often tested (Abraham and Isaac, Genesis 22; the people at Horeb, Exod 20:19). The purpose of the testing is to insure their obedience and moral behavior.

There is a strong critique of the Israelite calf cult at Dan and Bethel as evidenced in the story of the golden calf in the wilderness (Exodus 32–33). This account is somehow connected to the story of Jeroboam's calves in 1 Kings 12.

There are references to a *maṣṣebah*, or "pillar," as a sacred object (Gen 28:18, 22; 31:13, 45, 51, 52 [twice]; 35:14, 20; Exod 24:4). Such pillars appear to be viewed positively in Elohist narratives. By contrast the Yahwist refers to altars in the narratives of Genesis.

Moses is important as a complete leader. God reveals the most sacred name of Yahweh to Moses (Exod 3:13–15); he is the commissioned representative of Yahweh before pharaoh (Exod 3:15; Exod 7:14–19). He leads the people out of Egypt, more so than God. Moses is willing to die for the people (Exod 32:32). Moses is an instrument of God, a miracle worker, who brings forth plagues in Exod 10:12–14 with his rod. The rod does miracles throughout the ministry of Moses, dividing the sea (Exod 14:16). In the wilderness Moses is the judge of the people (Exod 18:13–16), war leader (Exod 17:8–16), mediator of the covenant (Exod 19:2–9, 16–17, 19), and mediator during the crisis of rebellion against God (Exod 32:11–14, 30–34). Finally, God speaks to Moses "face to face" (Num 12:6–8). Moses' authority is established (Exod 19:9; 20:15), though sometimes the people doubt Moses' authority (Exod 32:1; Num 11:11–12, 14–15; 12:1–2; 16:1–2, 12–14, 28–30). In the Yahwist the people doubt Yahweh's leadership. When Moses ascends Horeb to obtain the laws, he is there for forty days (Exod

24:12–15a, 18b; 31:18; 34:1, 4, 5a, 28). Joshua serves Moses (Exod 24:13; 32:17; 33:11; Num 11:28–29), but the Yahwist does not recall Joshua at all.

By way of contrast, Aaron is portrayed somewhat negatively, for he creates the golden calf and is chastised for it, and he lies about its creation (Exod 32:24), implying that it came out of the fire on its own, thus insinuating that God made it (or perhaps insulting Moses' intelligence). He and Miriam challenge Moses' authority and are punished (Num 12:16). His sons die by fire sent forth by God (Lev 10:2). He may symbolize the priesthood with whom prophets have antagonistic relations. When Aaron is portrayed positively, scholars tend to assume we are reading Priestly texts.

Overall, the Elohist has a sensitive morality and piety. Stories reflect a high degree of moral behavior by the significant religious personages. When we have doublets and can compare Yahwist and Elohist accounts, we notice that the Elohist version portrays the biblical personage as acting with great integrity. Thus, Abraham does not really lie when he calls Sarah his sister (Gen 20:12), Abimelech does not touch Sarah (Gen 20:4, 6) as is implied in the earlier story (Gen 12:14–16, Yahwist account), Abraham prays for the women in Abimelech's household (Gen 20:17–18), Sarah sends Hagar away to protect Isaac (Gen 21:9–11), not out of jealously (as in Gen 16:5–6, Yahwist account), Abraham is distressed about Hagar's departure and he gives her provisions (Gen 21:11–14), and Jacob obtains Laban's sheep by divine will (Gen 31:6–12) rather than using his own cunning (Gen 30:25–43, Yahwist account).

After presenting this summary of motifs, I must acknowledge that in my more cautious approach I will not consider all of the aforementioned themes to be Elohist. There is reason to be cautious with using some of this imagery to delineate Elohist texts. Some of the vocabulary is simply not used very frequently, such as "maidservant." Some concepts can certainly be found in other texts. "Fear of God" is used also in wisdom literature, and thus some modern scholars call the Elohist wisdom literature or at least say there is wisdom influence in it. That is probably an unwarranted conclusion. However, the concept "fear of God" is a valid indicator of Elohist passages when it is intertwined with narratives that describe the majesty of God, the testing of people to insure obedience, and appropriate human response to God. The image of the "fear of God" is different in these ways from the expression found in other biblical literature.

Contemporary Defenders of the Elohist

Even though the existence of the Elohist has been challenged significantly since the 1970s, there are still those who defend the existence of the theological tradition. Theological themes delineated above likewise have been challenged, so that more recent advocates have pursued the discussion of specific and sometimes alternative themes.

Alan Jenks attributed numerous texts to the Elohist epic in his early monograph (1977) and later article in *ABD* (1992), suggesting that the Elohist was not a single author, but a school of thought, and the tradition emerged in the late tenth and early ninth centuries in the north. Jenks connected Elohist themes to northern Israelite prophetic traditions in insightful ways that may still be used for new points of departure, such as the concept of covenant (Exod 24:1–2, 9–11), which Jenks believed was important for the Elohist.[12]

Terence Fretheim provided a detailed and expansive list of Elohist texts in the *Interpreter's Dictionary of the Bible Supplement* in 1976 when the Elohist was coming under serious criticism. He saw the Elohist as an independent theological tradition, which stressed how God's message is mediated through charismatic leaders and the human response to God's word should be continued obedience.[13]

Hans Klein hypothesized that the Elohist was a testimony to the origin and significance of Bethel as a shrine, and that the Elohist thus was a historian comparable to the later Roman historian, Pausanias.[14]

Karl Jaroš opined that the Elohist was written in the late ninth or early eighth century, after Elijah and Elisha but before Hosea, to address the issue of Israelite religious identity in the face of the Canaanite religious threat of syncretism.[15] He believed that the Elohist was tolerant of Canaanite religion but rejected Baal as a deity and the fertility customs that infringed upon Yahwism. Thus, the Elohist accepted dream revelations, the *maṣṣebah* as a symbol of a transcendent deity, sacred trees minus the fertility emphasis, sacred symbols like the bronze serpent, and even human sacrifice. The Elohist rejected the calf cult and the cult at Baal-Peor. Our modern perception that Israelites were largely polytheistic and essentially the same as the

---

12. Jenks, *North Israelite Traditions*, 1–129; and Jenks, "Elohist."
13. Fretheim, "Elohist."
14. Klein, "Ort und Zeit."
15. Jaroš, *Stellung des Elohisten*, 13–249.

Canaanites in their religious beliefs and practices throughout most of the pre-exilic era vitiates his thesis.

An excellent textbook by Richard Elliott Friedman, *Who Wrote the Bible*, reconstructed a theoretical model for the Elohist quite similar to Jenks.[16] In another work Friedman traced the Yahwist tradition as a unified source from Genesis 2 through 1 Kings 2, which convinced him that the Elohist likewise had a unified narrative of similar length, but it was cut apart extensively by the later editors. This editorial work has fooled us into thinking that the Elohist is not a true source.[17] In other publications Friedman decried our desertion of the traditional model so well defined after more than a century of scholarship.[18]

Sean McEvenue provided another fine textbook outlining the theology of the four sources, including the Elohist, as well as isolating some of the significant texts.[19]

Leslie Brisman endeavored to explicate from a literary, theological, and existential perspective how a Jacobic author (Yahwist) reworked the Eisaacic narrative (Elohist and Priestly narratives combined). He is similar to other contemporary scholars who view the Elohist material as a source used by the Yahwist, only he preferred to characterize the work of the Yahwist as editorial.[20]

Robert Coote, who explored the social and theological message of the Elohist, used the work of Wolff and Jenks. His radically different thesis suggested that the Elohist was a written supplement to the Yahwist created in the court of Jeroboam I of Israel (c. 920 BCE) to counter the Yahwist's legitimation of Solomon, and it contained stories concerned with succession (endangered youths, *maṣṣeboth* or stones dedicated to ancestors, and the rejection of infant sacrifice) which reflected Jeroboam's own anxiety about his possible successors. The Elohist scribe legimated the new tyranny of Jeroboam I.[21] Coote's reading of the text was rather political and negative, and it left the Elohist as a very unusable ideological tradition for modern theologians.

---

16. Friedman, *Who Wrote the Bible?*, 50–88, 246–55.
17. Friedman, *Hidden Book*, 348–62.
18. Friedman, "Recession of Biblical Source Criticism," 99.
19. McEvenue, *Pentateuch*, 88–115.
20. Brisman, *The Voice of Jacob*.
21. Coote, *Defense of Revolution*, 1–141.

Scholarly Research on the Elohist

Antony Campbell and Mark O'Brien provided a critical evaluation of all four sources in *Sources of the Pentateuch: Texts, Introductions, Annotations*. They envisioned the Elohist as a supplement or an editor of the older Yahwist tradition; the fragmented Elohist texts were designed to add further insight to the Yahwist narratives with numerous editorial additions.[22]

Even though David Carr sought to refute the traditional model of the Yahwist and Elohist as separate sources combined at some point by a redactor, he still provided a theory very similar to my own, and thus I mention his scholarship here. After removing the clearly identified Priestly additions, he found a "non-Priestly" narrative. After removing from this narrative those texts that appear to be Deuteronomic editing, he isolated a "proto-Genesis" narrative. "Proto-Genesis" used a number of "precursor texts," which he evaluated. Carr characterized the "precursor texts" as narratives that legitimated existing shrines and religious beliefs. Such texts were interested in angelic beings and dreams (Gen 28:10–22; 31:11–13; 32:22–32; 37:5–9, 40–41). "Proto-Genesis" texts emphasized divine promise with direct divine contact. Such texts pointed more to the future and perhaps gave hope to Jews in the Babylonian Exile.[23] His "precursor texts" include passages I deem to be Elohist, and his "proto-Genesis" narrative I would call the exilic Yahwist Historian, who I believe used and edited the Elohist texts. Carr sought to refute an old theory of separate Yahwist and Elohist sources because of problems with this old theory. But if we view the Yahwist as editing the old Elohist texts, as I do, many of Carr's reservations are addressed. Furthermore, when he listed linking texts that appear to unite "proto-Genesis," I notice that many of his links are Elohist texts referring to other Elohist texts, and this supports my model.

David Pleins evaluated the social ethics of the Elohist as ultimately addressing a post-exilic audience, in particular, the folk of Judah, prior to the reforms of Ezra and Nehemiah, even though he assumed the literature originated in the sixth-century exile. The tradition was interested in rebuilding the identity of the community by affirming life, moral integrity, and moral law codes. The tradition was interested in the north because it hoped that Judah might reclaim the north.[24]

Joel Burnett undertook an evaluation of the name 'elohim in the biblical text, and as part of his study he gave consideration to the Elohist

---

22. Campbell and O'Brien, *Pentateuch*, 161–93.
23. Carr, *Fractures of Genesis*, 306–7 et passim.
24. Pleins, *Social Visions*, 126–34.

The Elohist

tradition, which he viewed as a theologically unified but fragmented source in our biblical text. His cautious selection of texts provides foundation for my selection of Elohist texts. He used his limited number of texts to envision the Elohist's theology. Primarily the Elohist proclaimed that Elohim was Yahweh and should be worshiped as such. I discussed his core texts and themes in the previous chapter.[25]

Axel Graupner provided a very detailed analysis of the Elohist narrative with a focus on describing the theological message of the tradition. He believed the Elohist arose at the shrine of Bethel between the time of Elijah/Elisha and Hosea, most likely in the age of Jehu (845–838 BCE) to give hope to people in turbulent times when the kingdom of Israel was weakened before the Aramean threat. He believed that Elohist spoke of how a transcendent deity became present for people in a meaningful fashion, and it reflected the influence of early prophetic theology and wisdom thought.[26]

Hans-Christoph Schmitt initially defended the integrity of the Elohist tradition with his consideration of the Joseph narratives in Genesis. He believed an Elohist author in the sixth-century Babylonian exile worked together disparate pre-exilic sources, and this work was later supplemented by the Yahwist.[27] In later writings he placed the Elohist's origin in the early seventh century because the Elohist texts seem to be aware of Israel's potential destruction (Genesis 22; Numbers 22) and foreign rule in the land (Gen 20:1; 21:23, 34), which reflects knowledge of the destruction of Samaria in 722 BCE. He believed the tradition was quite developed and he provided a summary of significant theological themes in the Elohist, further suggesting that it was influenced by the wisdom tradition.[28] I concur with his insights concerning the dates of the Elohist.

In his excellent two-volume commentary on Exodus, William Propp maintained that the bulk of the narrative in the book of Exodus was Elohist and Priestly, even though Yahwist and JE redactor material may also be found. Though he did not list specifically his selection of Elohist texts, and he occasionally admitted that he was uncertain about some texts, he distinguished quite a few texts as Elohist.[29]

---

25. Burnett, *Biblical Elohim*, 127–50.
26. Graupner, *Elohist*, 37–39, 112, 394–95 et passim; and Graupner, "Erzählkunst."
27. Schmitt, *Josephsgeschichte*, 145–47 et passim.
28. Schmitt, *Alten Testament*, 223–33.
29. Propp, *Exodus 1–18*; and Propp, *Exodus 19–40*.

Scholarly Research on the Elohist

While discussing how attitudes toward the golden calf changed over the years, Youn Ho Chung paid attention to the Elohist tradition. He provided an excellent analysis of Exod 32:1–25, 30–35 as an Elohist text. He believed that an early acceptance of the golden calf as the perceived pedestal of Yahweh was replaced by later theological criticism, especially from Hosea, the Elohist, and the Deuteronomist, as eighth-century Israelites began to merge Yahweh and Baal and see the deity as present in the calf. Hosea and the Elohist condemned the calf as a foreign deity, while the Deuteronomist in later years condemned the calf as an image used to represent Yahweh. For Chung the Elohist was contemporary with Hosea in the eighth century.[30]

Tzemah Yoreh believed that the Elohist was the first Pentateuchal source written and contained five well-defined separate cycles of stories (Abraham, Jacob, Joseph, Moses, and Balaam), not connected to each other, but sharing themes and paralleling each other chiastically. The terse narratives focused upon human heroes so that the theological perspective stressed human actions over divine intervention. Thus, Moses was the savior of the Exodus. He reconstructed the narratives coherently by consistently using the name Elohim along with other vocabulary. He suggested that the five cycles did not transition into each other, thus giving the Elohist texts a fragmented appearance. He maintained that the Yahwist was a subtle theologian who edited these narratives by adding parallel narratives and editorial insertions to offer a different "spin" to the accounts. By assuming that the Yahwist added to an already existing narrative, he endeavored to solve many of the source critical dilemmas in of these texts. The name Yahweh was placed into Elohist accounts along with the name Elohim by this Yahwist editor. His description of separate Elohist cycles is comparable to my model of "pools of Elohist" tradition. I, too, believe that the Yahwist used the Elohist material and added significantly to it. However, I would prefer to say that the Yahwist used the Elohist as a source rather than to say the Yahwist merely edited the Elohist. My assessment is similar to his, except that I exclude the Joseph Novella and thus have a much smaller corpus of Elohist texts overall.[31]

Most recently Joel Baden has presented a very systematically reasoned argument for the existence of the Elohist, which proceeds on strictly literary analysis without recourse to discussing social or historical settings. He

---

30. Chung, *Sin of the Calf*, 16–18, 30–46, 119, 206–8.
31. Yorah, *First Book of God*.

argued that the sources should not be reconstructed on the basis of vocabulary and theological themes, since vocabulary and theological themes often are shared by sources, nor should writing style be used, for too often the difference in style is subjectively evaluated by scholars, and stylistic differences between the Yahwist and the Elohist often may not be truly significant. Baden reconstructed narrative plot lines and found the connections between stories across the Pentateuch, for each of the four sources can be reconstructed as a coherent narrative, if the individual accounts are aligned properly. A final compiler respectively wove all four literary documents together at some point. He assumed that only a few stories may have been left out by the compiler, so that the original sources can be faithfully recovered.[32] This removes his observations from critics who might dispute his presentation on the basis of when and where he situates the tradition. Baden discerned narrative continuities between texts often separated from each other in the text, and he discovered plot and vocabulary connections between these disparate accounts. (The vocabulary is not over-arching vocabulary through the entire Elohist often discussed by scholars in the past, but rather significant words that unite one or two stories in a logical narrative sequence.) I find this to be a good response to those who speak of the Elohist as being too fragmented to be described as a true source, and I will appeal to some of his arguments in the next chapter.

Very recently Jeffrey Stackert has defended the existence of the Elohist and observed that without the paradigm of the Elohist one cannot explain the theology of the tent of meeting.[33] He argued that one of the primary agenda of this late eighth or early seventh-century tradition was to portray Moses as the great prophet, who was also the last prophet, thus undercutting the legitimacy of the eighth-century prophets. The prophets spoke unreliably in riddles, but Moses spoke clearly through the Law. This legitimates the emergence of the textual word of the Law over the oral word of the prophets as a medium of divine revelation.[34] Though I concur with his dating, I do not accept his thesis.

---

32. Baden, *Composition of the Pentateuch*, 103–28.
33. Stackert, *Prophet Like Moses*, 71.
34. Ibid., 56, 62–63, 71–81, 92, 112–14, 117–19, 124.

Scholarly Research on the Elohist

Range of Dates Suggested for the Elohist

Scholars have proposed a wide range of dates for the provenance of the Elohist. Some suggested a late tenth-century date, maintaining that the tradition arose in the northern kingdom of Israel during the reign of Jeroboam I as a counter epic to the Yahwist epic, which they also dated to the tenth century. The Elohist tradition is portrayed as reflecting northern concerns in opposition to the values of Davidic Judah, and certain texts are seen to contain hints that point to this era. This suggested tenth-century origin has been put forward by Alan Jenks, Robert Coote, and most recently by Jules Gomes.[35]

A ninth-century date in the northern state of Israel was suggested by those who feel the tradition is co-terminus with Elijah and Elisha.[36] Some scholars assumed the tradition arose out of the context of the Elijah and Elisha prophetic ministries, but they placed it later, usually in the reign of Jehu or broadly between the time and Elijah/Elisha and Hosea.[37] Axel Graupner, in fact, dated it precisely between 845–838 BCE.[38]

Older German scholars, Martin Noth and Hans Walter Wolff, placed the tradition in the mid-eighth century, around the time of Jeroboam II.[39] Though Yoreh gave no dates to the Elohist in his work, he implied that the Elohist preceded the Deuteronomic Reform, which he located in the late eighth century in the days of Hezekiah, thus making the Elohist an eighth-century tradition.[40]

A few have suggested a date after the destruction of Samaria in 722 BCE.[41] Hans Jürgen Zobel and Karl-Martin Beyse proposed a date immediately after the fall of Samaria.[42] Jeffrey Stackert suggested the late eighth or early seventh century.[43] Rudolph Smend and Frank Zimmer dated the

---

35. Jenks, *North Israelite Traditions*; Jenks, "Elohist"; Coote, *Defense of Revolution*; and Gomes, *Sanctuary of Bethel*, 62–100.

36. Fretheim, "Elohist," 259–63; and Anderson, *Old Testament*, 289–90.

37. Klein, "Ort und Zeit," 247–60; Jaroš, *Stellung des Elohisten*; Friedman, *Who Wrote the Bible*, 50–88; and Zobel and Beyse, "Selbstverständnis Israels," 283.

38. Graupner, *Elohist*, 399.

39. Noth, *Pentateuchal Traditions*; and Wolff, "Elohistic Fragments."

40. Yorah, *The First Book of God*, 1–273.

41. Schmitt, *Alten Testament*, 228. See Graupner, *Elohist*, 37, for a listing of the scholars.

42. Zobel and Beyse, *Alte Testament*, 189.

43. Stackert, *Prophet Like Moses*, 72.

Elohist in the early seventh century, a generation after the fall of Samaria.[44] Their dating corresponds to mine.

David Pleins suggested the audience was initially sixth-century Judean exiles in Babylon and he discussed various texts that addressed the concerns of landless people. Later the tradition spoke to the needs of returning exiles in the fifth century.[45] The sixth century was proposed also by Gustav Hölscher, Donald Redford, and Hans-Christoph Schmit.[46]

Otto Kaiser gave several arguments for a late date for the Elohist, but he dated all the sources late and even placed the Deuteronomist a century after the Elohist. He believed that the Balaam Oracles with their triumphalistic hope implied an exilic audience, and the interest in dreams is both an exilic and post-exilic phenomenon.[47] In a later work, he decidedly dated the Elohist to the post-exilic period.[48]

In conclusion, the Elohist source has been a topic of scrutiny among Old Testament scholars for many years. Its existence has been affirmed by many, but it has been declared to be nonexistent or so fragmentary as to render it no longer worthy of consideration. In the next chapter we need to consider the views of the naysayers and respond to them in some fashion.

---

44. Smend, *Hexateuchs*, 37; and Zimmer, *Elohist*, 307.

45. Pleins, *Social Visions*, 126–34.

46. Hölscher, *Geschichtsschreibung*, 188–90; Redford, *Joseph*, 208–10; and Schmitt, *Josephsgeschichte*, 145–47 et passim, both of whom spoke from the perspective of the Joseph narrative.

47. Kaiser, *Old Testament*, 99–100.

48. Kaiser, *Grundriss*, 70.

3

Critics of the Elohist and My Response

Recent Challenges to the Existence of the Elohist

SOME SCHOLARLY DISSENTERS DISCOUNT the existence of the Elohist altogether by suggesting it was figment of the scholarly imagination. In the 1930s Paul Volz and Wilhelm Rudolph declared that Elohist texts were a supplemental variation on the Yahwist tradition, and their origin was in the south among sophisticated intellectuals, not the north. As fragmentary traditions the Elohist could never have functioned as an independent source ("kein Erzähler"). It was simply a later supplement in an ongoing Yahwistic tradition in Judah. They did admit that passages in Genesis 20 and 22 could lay claim more than other texts to a real Elohist identity. However, they felt that two accounts could not justify speaking of a theoretic source.[1] (I believe that if you concede the existence of only two narratives, you vitiate your claim to deny the existence of the Elohist.)

In the 1970s serious doubts about the existence of the Elohist began to arise as some scholars began to challenge the tenth-century date of the Yahwist and suggest it arose after the Deuteronomistic History.[2] A. D. H. Mayes, John Van Seters and Martin Rose saw the process as one of a DJP sequence, since both the Yahwist and Priestly traditions were seen to have

---

1. Volz and Rudolph, *Elohist als Erzähler*, 1–183; and Rudolph, *Elohist*, 1–281. See critical observations by Baden, *Redaction of the Pentateuch*, 54–60.

2. Winnet, "Re-examining Foundations"; Van Seters, *Abraham*; Van Seters, *Prologue to History*; Van Seters, *Pentateuch*; Van Seters, *Yahwist*; Schmid, *Der sogenannte Jahwist*; Rose, *Deuteronomist und Jahwist*; Blenkinsopp, *Pentateuch*; and Levin, *Jahwist*. A good summary is provided by Knight, "Pentateuch."

emerged in the exile, and for them the Elohist was subsumed primarily into the Yahwist as fragments. These fragments were not worth treating as a separate source.[3] Joseph Blenkinsopp postulated a DPJ sequence, emphasizing the priority of Priestly narrative that subsequently was augmented by the Yahwist (and for him also E seems to be absorbed mostly by J or D).[4]

Even more dramatic was the denial of the Yahwist tradition. If the existence of the Yahwist is not assumed as a well-defined source by an author, then the Deuteronomist is seen as having drawn all these little fragments into a unified history.[5] Well-defined epic sources were denied altogether. Rolf Rendtorff suggested that the various cycles of narrative tradition arose independently from smaller form-critical units and that vocabulary differences are insufficient criteria by which to delineate sources.[6] Erhard Blum believed that the Deuteronomic tradition ultimately created the Pentateuchal tradition with subsequent Priestly editing. In reference to texts formerly considered Elohist, he believed that the Jacob cycle (Genesis 25–33) was formed at the time of Jeroboam I, since Penuel and Bethel were sanctuaries under him, and the Abraham-Lot cycle arose in the seventh century.[7] David Carr believed that a "proto-Genesis" author wove loose oral fragments together into a unified work, and no organized Yahwist or Elohist existed in a self-contained form. (Although I believe his work does, in fact, support a Yahwist and Elohist model).[8] Christoph Levin likewise viewed these Elohist texts as either fragments collected together by the early sixth-century Yahwist editor (who was not an author), or they were later midrash on those Yahwist texts that were placed into the narrative, but they never had any unified existence.[9]

---

3. Van Seters, *Abraham*; Van Seters, *In Search of History*; Van Seters, *Prologue to History*; Van Seters, *Life of Moses*; Van Seters, "The Pentateuch," 3–49; Rose, *Deuteronomist und Jahwist*; and Mayes, *Story of Israel*, 139–49.

4. Blenkinsopp, *Pentateuch*, 1–243.

5. Whybray, *Making of the Pentateuch*, 11–116.

6. Rendtorff, *Problem des Pentateuch*; Rendtorff, "'Yahwist' as Theologian?"; Whybray, *Making of the Pentateuch*, 43–131; and essays in Dozeman and Schmidt, *A Farewell to the Yahwist?*

7. Blum, *Vätergeschichte*; and Blum, *Pentateuch*.

8. Carr, *Fractures of Genesis*.

9. Levin, *Jahwist*, 171–80, 216–64. Cf. Levin, "Yahwist and the Redactional Link"; and Levin, "Yahwist."

CRITICS OF THE ELOHIST AND MY RESPONSE

My Response

All of these scholars admitted to some degree that the texts formerly called Elohistic do have a somewhat different identity or distinctive personality, though many they deemed to really be Yahwist texts. John Van Seters best typifies this approach. He viewed the Yahwist as a sixth-century historian who used prior sources in the same way that Greek historians crafted their works. He acknowledged that the Yahwist used "northern Israelite stories" of Jacob and Joseph, and in particular he considered Gen 22:1–19 (sacrifice of Isaac), 25:21–34 (Jacob and Esau), 29:31—30:24 (genealogy of Jacob's family), 46:1–5 (Jacob's dream at Beersheba), and 48:8–22 (blessing of Ephraim and Manasseh), as well as other narratives, to be sources that were used by the Yahwist, which at times even appear to be intrusions into the text. Though he did not mention them, I will list other accounts associated with the Elohist, that I assume would be considered fragments also picked up by the Yahwist historian, using his model. These include: Gen 48:8–22 (blessing of Manasseh and Ephraim), Exod 17:8–16 (Amalek), 18:1–27 (Jethro), Num 11:11–12, 14–17, 24b–30 (elders prophesy), Num 12:1–5 (Miriam and Moses), and Num 21:21–33, 35 (Sihon), all of which are unique to the so-called Elohist tradition in my opinion and in the eyes of Joel Baden.[10] Yet Van Seters maintained that such sources are too few evaluate as a literary or theological tradition, and so he denied the existence of the Elohist.[11] Personally, I believe that Van Seters' observations actually support my overall theory, for he acknowledged that such "north Israelite traditions," as he called them, had a prior existence to the Yahwist. I would simply depart from his views by saying the "north Israelite traditions" or the "Elohist" can be worthy of theological reflection even if the texts are limited. Essentially, I believe that I build upon Van Seters' model, for I believe that the Elohist was finally absorbed into the Yahwist's historical narrative.

Another significant critic of the Elohist's existence was Norman Whybray, who raised a number of questions concerning the integrity of such a source. He maintained that we cannot distinguish Elohist texts by isolating parallel words, such as Amorites (E) and Canaanites (J) or Jethro (E) and Reuel (J), when there are too few examples of such words and the great possibility exists that an author may have simply have engaged in

---

10. Baden, *Composition of the Pentateuch*, 107, 126.
11. Van Seters, *Yahwist*, 43, 46, 54, 125–26, 262.

an "apparently motiveless and inexplicable alternation" between words.[12] Whybray was somewhat correct in this criticism, especially when seldom used words are found in isolation in the text. However, as noted earlier, I have chosen select words that have been used more frequently and occur in conjunction with each other in the same texts. Whybray suggested that perhaps biblical authors casually used different words unconsciously, which deceives source critics into separating out two or more sources on the basis of vocabulary. But I cannot believe that a scribe would unconsciously use differing words in a casual fashion when so often the words of the biblical narrative are chosen with clever thought to achieve great literary artistry, as so many modern literary critics have observed in so many texts. Also, these casual choices of vocabulary seem to sort out consistently together in the same narratives, which leads me to assume their occurrence is more than accidental. Ultimately sources are not delineated by vocabulary alone, as so often critics of the source critical method seem to imply, but rather the differentiation of sources occurs because of vocabulary, theological theme, and coherence of narrative plot line. To put it negatively, sources are delineated when tensions, contradictions, and parallel narratives in the text appeal to one's common sense and demand the separation into separate sources.[13]

Furthermore, Whybray and other critics of source criticism assault the theory that assumes a JE Redactor combined separate Yahwist and Elohist sources, for source critics cannot explain why a redactor would engage in merging two such works and radically edit the Elohist in the theoretic manner that is suggested. In addition, opponents of source criticism are rightly suspicious even more when they see Yahwist language in Elohist stories.[14] But I work with a different theory: the Yahwist has used Elohist material in a Yahwist History and has partially rewritten Elohist accounts, supplemented Elohist accounts, and omitted some accounts to give us that confused and blurred appearance in Elohist narratives. (I often like to point out that one may observe how the gospel of Luke reused the gospel of Mark, sometimes adding accounts, changing vocabulary, rearranging stories, and omitting accounts. The Yahwist simply was more extensive in this revision of the Elohist than Luke was with Mark.) Two sources are not being merged

---

12. Whybray, *The Making of the Pentateuch*, 57.
13. Ibid., 57, 72.
14. Ibid., 120–23.

together by a redactor in my theory, but rather, it is the Yahwist using Elohist materials in piecemeal fashion.

Whybray also observed that the name Elohim appears in Elohist texts after the name Yahweh has been revealed.[15] But if Burnett was correct in assuming that the Elohist sought to impress upon the audience that Elohim was Yahweh, the continual use of both names makes good sense. I believe, in general, that we have taken the criticism of the existence of the Elohist too naively and have not counter-critiqued the critics sufficiently.

From a broader perspective Whybray also assailed the entire working methodology of source criticism. He believed it is absurd that at times source critics separate texts due to identical or parallel statements that are repeated in a narrative, while at other times sources are separated because contradictory vocabulary and ideas occur.[16] But this separation of narrative is indeed logical depending upon the stories you are reading. Parallels are meaningful for division into sources when the separate sources produce common sense clarity in a reading of the story; in other words, parallels are meaningful for a source critic when they are combined with the observation of narrative inconsistency in our present text. It is inappropriate to criticize one aspect of the source critical method when usually several different aspects (vocabulary, narrative consistency, and message) are used by source critics.

Whybray's criticism is in the abstract; it sounds good in theory without actual recourse to observing the narratives. He spoke of words apart from actual narratives. The direct reading of stories elicits a common sense analysis that observes sometimes different stories exist because they are indeed parallel versions of the same narrative and sometimes in those parallel narratives you will naturally have the repetition of a similar plot-line as well as the differences that stand in tension so as to demand that the biblical author respectively retain both narratives. For example, Whybray observed that there are frequent repetitions of words and expressions, especially in the flood narrative, which do not demand the separation into sources, while at other times such repetitions justify source division.[17] But again, we have to use our common sense. The reading of the narratives will indicate when there is literary repetition for effect, and when there appear to be separate plot lines with different theological assumptions. Criticism of the source

15. Ibid., 67.
16. Ibid., 74.
17. Ibid., 83.

critical method or supplementary method in analyzing the biblical text has been hyper-critical, and it sounds good in theory, but an actual consideration of the biblical text leads one back into the assumption that in some way there are sources or at least fragments that have been woven together. (In all fairness to Whybray and his brilliantly written volume, I must admit that he was critical of the concept of sources, but more receptive to the idea that fragments were woven together by biblical authors. We may not be that far apart in our assessment of individual texts.) I have chosen to respond in detail to Whybray's assessment, because his is one of the best critiques of the source critical method.

In the light of criticisms raised against the concept of an Elohist source, I have chosen to proceed somewhat cautiously in selecting the texts that were listed in the previous chapter. Some texts I have adapted with hesitancy because Elohist themes do not seem too readily apparent. These texts may have been Elohist passages, but perhaps the Yahwist Historian rephrased the text so as to make Elohist characteristics less readily apparent. The image I prefer to use is that Elohist language has been melted into the Yahwist version of the narrative like hot wax. I have listed such passages in the commentary with the word "perhaps." However, I feel it is necessary to list these texts because of the possibility that they might be Elohistic, and because other commentators have sensed the presence of Elohist thought in them.

In addition, there are numerous accounts where one may observe fleeting Elohist imagery or vocabulary in the narrative. Often in the past scholars have delineated the presence of such imagery with the inclusion of single verses, or partial verses (i.e., v. 9aβ) in their list of Elohist texts. I try to avoid listing such allusions as much as possible. I suspect that the Yahwist Historian may have been influenced by the rendition of some Elohist accounts, so that an occasional phrase or expression from the Elohist vocabulary may have been used, when, for the most part, the Yahwist Historian did not use that particular Elohist account.

Another indication of the legitimacy of an Elohist tradition is the presence of references in certain Elohist accounts to other Elohist accounts, and references to narrative that seem to be missing in our present biblical text. Both of these phenomena imply that a unified narrative once existed at least for a significant sequence of narratives. For example, Genesis 28 contains a significant revelatory experience for Jacob, and Gen 35:1, 3, 7 refers back to the revelation he had while fleeing Esau. Golden rings looted from the Egyptians are anticipated in Gen 15:14 and Exod 3:22, and said to be used in making the golden calf in Exod 32:2. Joseph desires that his bones be taken back to Canaan (Gen 50:25), and the later Israelites do that (Exod 13:19). Other examples exist that imply narratives have been lost. In Gen 46:4 Jacob is told that Joseph will close his eyes when he dies, but we lack that account, implying that it has been edited out. In Gen 42:21 we are told that Joseph pleaded with his brothers to spare him and now they regret not having listened, but we have no such narrative of Joseph's pleas. Again in Gen 50:16–17 we are told that Jacob earlier told his sons to bring a message to Joseph seeking forgiveness for them, but this story is lacking.[18] (Though I will suggest that the Joseph novel does not really evidence significant Elohist materials, this post-exilic novel may have used a few Elohist fragments.) The account of Isaac's birth in Gen 21:2–8 logically follows after the Elohist narrative of how Abraham almost lost his wife in Genesis 20. The allusions to Joseph's bones in Exod 13:19 may connect exodus traditions to patriarchal traditions. Thus, we have further indications that our present Elohist texts were part of a longer narrative. Perhaps there was an epic tradition that included the stories of the patriarchs, exodus, wilderness wanderings, Sinai, and conquest. Or perhaps, as I have suggested, these cycles might never have been merged, but rather there may have existed only "pools of Elohist tradition." If the latter paradigm is correct, this would indicate why our Elohist narratives give the additional impression of being fragmentary in the final Pentateuchal accounts.

Continuity in the Elohist Texts

Critics of the Elohist say that there is no continuity between the texts in terms of narrative plot, and common vocabulary is insufficient to demonstrate the existence of an integral source. I would respond by saying, even though our texts are limited, there are hints of connective narrative in the various stories. If, indeed, the Yahwist used the Elohist as a source and chose material selectively, the presence of any connection between texts, limited though they might be, is indicative that there once was a greater narrative tradition that was either unified or at least unified within the "pools of tradition" that I have characterized. Let us then consider some possible unity or connections in the isolated Elohist narratives.

18. Graupner, *Elohist*, 9; Jenks, "Elohist," 479; and Baden, *Composition of the Pentateuch*, 122–24.

The Elohist

Genesis 20:1–4a, 5–17; 21:2–21; Genesis 22:1–13, 19

To begin, there are parallels between the accounts of Hagar's expulsion in Gen 21:9–21 and the sacrifice of Isaac in Gen 22:1–13, 19: 1) In both accounts a child's life is placed in jeopardy, but he survives. 2) Abraham arises early to carry out the command given to him (Gen 21:14; 22:3). 3) A journey occurs (Gen 21:14; 22:4–8). 4) The child is about to die (Gen 21:16; 22:10). 5) An "angel of God" saves the child (Gen 21:17–18; 22:11–12. 6) The "angel" speaks from heaven (Gen 21:17–18; 22:11–12). 7) The "angel" refers to "fear" (Gen 21:17; 22:12). 8) The "angel" gives a command that saves the child's life (Gen 21:17–19; 22:12–13). 9) Promise of future greatness is made (Gen 21:18; 22:17). 10) Hagar and Abraham "see" the solution to saving the child (Gen 21:19; 22:13).[19]

Sean McEvenue saw a common format in all three accounts in Genesis 20–22 (patriarch's wife, Hagar's expulsion, test of Abraham): 1) God directs Abraham to wander (20:13), expel Hagar (21:12), or sacrifice Isaac (22:2). 2) Abraham obeys (20:1–2; 21:14; 22:3). 3) Bad things happen: Sarah is abducted and disease affects women (20:2, 18); the child almost dies (21:16); and Isaac almost dies (22:9–10). 4) God intervenes: Sarah is returned and women are healed (20:6–7, 17); the angel discloses location of the well and child is blessed (21:19–20); and the angel prevents sacrifice and reveals a ram (22:11–12).[20] All three of these Elohist accounts are connected by a similar dramatic plot line.

Genesis 28:10–12, 16a, 17–21a, 22

This account may be the beginning of an Elohist Jacob cycle that concludes with the account of Jacob's return to Bethel to bury the idols in Genesis 35. In Gen 35:1, 3, 7 God refers to the revelation Jacob experienced at Bethel. Throughout the narrative of these chapters, there are allusions to the eventual return of Jacob to Bethel and especially the building of an altar there (Gen 28:20; 31:13; 35:1, 3, 7).[21]

---

19. Wenham, *Genesis 16–50*, 99–100; and Carr, *Fractures of Genesis*, 198.
20. McEvenue, *Pentateuch*, 99–100.
21. Gomes, *Sanctuary of Bethel*, 64–76.

Critics of the Elohist and My Response

Genesis 31:4–42

When Jacob speaks to his wives, he refers to Genesis 28 when he identifies the deity as the "God of Bethel" to whom he anointed a pillar and swore an oath (v. 13). When God prevents Laban from hurting Jacob, God thus keeps the promise of guidance and protection given at Bethel in Gen 28:20–21. Jacob then alludes to this promise in Gen 31:42. A *maṣṣebah*, or pillar, is erected by Jacob in Gen 28:18, alluded to in Gen 31:13, and then Jacob and Laban build a pillar at their meeting place, mentioned in Gen 31:45, 51, 52 (twice). The sacrifice and a sacred meal in Gen 31:54 foreshadow the Elohist narrative of the trip to Bethel in Genesis 35.

Genesis 35:1–7

Gen 35:1–3, 7 refers to how Jacob has a revelation at Bethel while fleeing Esau. In Gen 28:18 Jacob builds an altar and pours oil on it. In Genesis 35 Jacob builds an altar (vv. 3, 7), pours out a drink offering (v. 14), erects a pillar (v. 14), and gives an oblation of oil (vv. 7, 14).

Since the rejection of the idols occurs at Bethel, we usually assume this is criticism of the old calf cult at Bethel. The notable reference to earrings that are disavowed in v. 4 may foreshadow the use of earrings by Aaron to make the golden calf in Exod 32:2–3, another Elohist text.

Genesis 46:1–4

In this narrative Jacob is named Israel, a reference to either Jacob's struggle at Penuel (Gen 32:22–32) or his naming at Bethel (Gen 35:10). In this text and in Gen 15:5–6, 13–14 there are promises to the patriarchs. Both narratives are dream theophanies that contain the imperative "do not fear" (Gen 15:1; 46:3), a promise of descendants to the patriarch, and a promise of return to the land. Reference to the return to the land and the dream format makes these accounts unique, and these themes create a connecting link between Elohist narratives. I believe a similar theophany to Isaac was lost.[22]

---

22. Baden, *Redaction of the Pentateuch*, 243–46.

The Elohist

Exodus 1:8–10, 15–21

Joel Baden believed that in these Elohist texts there are connections with other Elohist texts. In this story the Egyptians "mistreat" or kill the Israelites in Egypt, but they do not enslave them. He quoted what he believed to be Elohist laws in Exod 22:20 and 23:9 that demand Israelites not to "mistreat" foreigners in their midst because they were mistreated in Egypt. The non-Elohistic traditions describe the Exodus experience as enslavement. Baden observed the continuity between Gen 50:23 and Exod 1:15 by noting that Joseph is alive to see his children born in Egypt to the third generation, and only after his death, in the fourth generation, does pharaoh mistreat the Israelites. Another Elohist text in Gen 15:16 says that the Israelites would be in Egypt for four generations. Further Elohist continuity may be observed in the fulfillment of the divine promise of descendants, for Gen 28:3; 35:11, 48:4 all promise descendants in the Elohist tradition, and the failed attempt to kill the babies because of their increased number in Exodus 1 shows the fulfillment of that promise.[23]

Exodus 3:1, 2b, 4b–6, 9–15, 18–22; 4:17–18, 20

The call of Moses at the burning bush has a number of allusions that connect it to other Elohist accounts. These allusions have been excellently delineated by Ludwig Schmidt: 1) Exod 3:4b, 6b contains the double vocative and reference to the ancestors found in Gen 46:2–3. 2) Exod 3:10 speaks of bringing the people out of Egypt as promised in Gen 46:4. 3) Exod 3:9–12 alludes to taking the people away from pharaoh, as is mentioned in Exod 14:5a. 4) Exod 3:12b speaks of worshipping God after leaving Egypt, which occurs in Exod 18:12. 5) Exod 4:18 speaks of the people coming out to meet Jethro, which happens in Exod 18:1–2.[24]

Exodus 13:17–22

This passage concerning taking Joseph's bones to Canaan connects to Gen 50:25–26, and may indicate a connection between Elohist patriarchal accounts and the exodus narrative.

---

23. Baden, "From Joseph to Moses," 138–40, 147–55, 155–56.
24. Schmidt, "Berufung des Mose," 352–53.

CRITICS OF THE ELOHIST AND MY RESPONSE

Exodus 19:16–19

This narrative may share continuities with the account of the meal eaten by king Ahab and Elijah on Mount Carmel after Elijah has defeated the prophets of Baal in 1 Kgs 18:41.[25] I believe the prophetic narratives in Kings may precede the creation of this pentateuchal narrative and may have influenced its formation.

Exodus 19, 20, 24, 31–34; Num 11–12, 16

Baden discerned a unified Elohist narrative about the Israelites at Mount Horeb in Exod 19:2b–9a, 16 (except "on the morning of the third day"), 17, 19; 20:1, 18–22; 20:23–23:33; 24:3–8, 11b–15a, 18b; 31:18a (only "he gave him the two tablets of the covenant"), 32:1–25, 30–35; 33:4, 6–11; 34:1, 4 (except "early in the morning and went up to Sinai"), 5a, 28; Num 11:11–12, 14–17, 24b–30; 12:1–15; 16:1b–2a, 12–15, 25, 27b–34. In this narrative at Horeb, Baden found consistent historical claims. The mountain is called Horeb (Exod 33:6) or the Mountain of God (Exod 24:13), Moses' authority is established (Exod 19:9; 20:15), the Israelites exhibit fear (Exod 19:16b–17; 20:18–22), Yahweh sends a messenger to lead Israel and Yahweh only occasionally speaks to Moses (Exod 23:20–22; 32:34; Num 11:17, 25; 12:5, 9), the covenant is rooted in laws (Exod 20:23–23:33), the covenant is ratified in a ceremony (Exod 24:3–8, 11b), Moses breaks the tablets and receives the commands a second time, spending forty days on the mountain in each instance (Exod 24:12–15a, 18b; 31:18; 32:1–25, 30–35; 34:1, 4, 5a, 28), the tent of meeting is outside the camp where Yahweh descends and meets Moses inside the tent (Exod 33:7–11; Num 11:16–17, 24b–30; 12:4–9), Joshua serves Moses (Exod 24:13; 32:17; 33:11; Num 11:28–29), the people doubt Moses' leadership (Exod 32:1; Num 11:11–12, 14–15; 12:1–2; 16:1–2, 12–14, 28–30), and the seventy elders are chosen to receive the spirit (Num 11:16–17, 24b–30). For Baden these texts appear to present a coherent, consistent, and unified narrative that differs in numerous ways from the corresponding Yahwist version.[26]

---

25. Roberts, "God, Prophet, and King."
26. Baden, *Composition of the Pentateuch*, 117–18.

The Elohist

Exodus 32:2

In Exod 32:2 Israelites build the golden calf with gold rings. In Gen 15:14 Abraham is promised that his children will have great wealth when leaving Egypt, and in Exod 3:21–22 Moses is told that Israelites will despoil the Egyptians and put silver and gold ornaments on their sons and daughters. Aaron then directs the sons and daughters of Israel to take off those silver and gold ornaments to make the calf in Exod 32:2.

Exodus 32:1–10, 15–24

Youn Ho Chung observed narrative continuity between Exodus 19, 24, and 32. In Exod 19:5 there is reference to the covenant broken later by the creation of the golden calf in Exodus 32 (reference to tablets of the covenant are in Exod 32:15). In Exod 24:12–14 Moses and Joshua are told to go up the mountain to receive the tablets of stone, and in Exod 32:15–16, 19 Moses is up on the mountain with the tablets of stone. Exodus 32 assumes that the people have accepted the Decalogue and the Book of the Covenant (which Chung viewed as Elohist texts). The role of Moses as intercessor and mediator is dominant in Exod 32:7–14, 30–34, as in other Elohist texts (Exod 3:10, 12; 20:19, 21). Thus, the core narrative in Exodus 32 is essential for the overall Elohist plot line.[27]

Exodus 33:7–11

The reference to the "pillar of cloud" (v. 9), the reverence of the people (v. 10), and the description of Joshua as "minister" (v. 11, found also in Exod 24:13; Num 11:28; Josh 1:1) imply some narrative continuity. In this narrative, the tent of meeting appears to be the site of prophetic revelation, if we view Moses as a prophet receiving the divine messages from God. Comparable passages about the tent of meeting include Num 11:16–17; 12:4–10; and Deut 31:14–15. The tent of meeting is located outside the camp, as is also the case with the Elohist account in Num 11:16–17, 24b–30.[28] This portrayal of the tent diverges from those priestly texts that place the tent inside the camp and emphasize the holiness of the tent (Lev 16:2; Num 3:7–10, 38). The prophetic portrayal views God as coming down from the

---

27. Chung, *Sin of the Calf*, 32–35.
28. Sommer, "Reflecting on Moses," 605.

CRITICS OF THE ELOHIST AND MY RESPONSE

heavenly realm to reveal a message, thus emphasizing the transcendence of God; while the priestly portrayal views God as present in the midst of Israel, as the temple was in the midst of Jerusalem, thus emphasizing the immanence of God. This prophetic portrayal of Moses reflects Elohist thought wherein God affirms the prophetic leadership of Moses after people doubt him, and does so with the coming of the cloud (Exod 19:9; 20:16; 32:1; Num 11:12, 14–15; 12:1–2; 16:1–2, 12–14, 28–30).[29]

Numbers 11:11–12, 14–17, 24b–30

In these passages Moses must "bear the people" and this "burden is too much" for him, so seventy elders must be appointed to assist Moses.[30] It appears that this frustration of Moses would follow logically after the story of the golden calf. Also, the Lord comes down in the cloud (v. 25), as in Exod 33:9–10, Joshua appears as Moses' assistant or "minister" as in Exod 33:11, and the tent of meeting is outside the camp as in Exod 33:7–11. This is one of four texts in which the tent of meeting is associated with prophetic revelation (the others are Exod 33:6–11; Num 12:4–10; Deut 31:14–15).[31]

Elohist and Deuteronomy

A most interesting argument for the integrity of the Elohist was provided by Baden, who maintained that Deuteronomy 1–9 quotes Elohist texts as an entity separate from Yahwist texts. He observed that this implies no JE combined epic was created before the exile. This would certainly also imply the integrity of Elohist traditions. If I date the Yahwist to the late sixth century and the Deuteronomistic History to the late seventh century, it would be quite possible for the Deuteronomist to use Elohist material before the Yahwist absorbed those traditions into his history. If Baden's observations are cogent, this supports my reconstruction of the pentateuchal traditions immensely, for I suggest the sequence of EDJP. Baden, however, believed that the Yahwist, Elohist, Deuteronomistic, and Priestly traditions were all brought together for the first time in the days of Nehemiah (Neh 8:8–9, 14–15), for the Priestly traditions do not directly use the Yahwist or Elohist

---

29. Knohl, "Two Aspects of the 'Tent of Meeting.'"
30. Baden, *Composition of the Pentateuch*, 85–94.
31. Yoreh, *First Book of God*, 255; and Baden, *Composition of the Pentateuch*, 98–101.

traditions.[32] I could accept his theory as an alternative model to mine own, for it still implies the priority of the Elohist over the Yahwist.

Baden observed how the texts in Deuteronomy that refer back to the experiences of the Israelites in the wilderness quote or paraphrase Elohist narratives and lack familiarity with the Yahwist narratives, even when the Yahwist and Elohist narratives are interwoven in our present narrative. Examples he adduced include: Moses returning with the second inscription on the two tablets after forty days (Deut 1:1–4 used Exod 34:1, 27–29a), the complaint of Moses (Deut 1:9–12 used Num 11:11–12, 14–15, 17), the appointment of judges (Deut 1:9–18 used Exod 18:25–26; Num 11:14, 17), Israelites avoid Seir (Deut 2:2–6 used Num 20:14–21), Israelites cross the Zered and the Arnon (Deut 2:13, 24 used Num 21:12–13), defeat of Sihon (Deut 2:26–37 used Num 21:12–31), defeat of Og (Deut 3:1–7 used Num 21:33–35), distribution of the land in the Transjordan (Deut 3:12–20 used Num 32:1–2, 4–5a; 32:5b, 6a, 6b, 16a 17a, 18–19, 20a, 20b, 22aβ, 24b–27, 32–33, 39–42), general references to Horeb (Deut 4:10–14; 5:2–5, 19–28; 9:8–21, 25–29; 10:1–5 used Exod 19:16–17, 19; 24:18b; 31:18; 32:7–13, 15, 19b–20; 34:1–5, 28), the mountain enveloped in fire and a black cloud (Deut 4:11 used Exod 19:16–17), Moses on the mountain for forty days without food or water (Deut 9:9 used Exod 24:18b; 34:28), the tablets made by the finger of God (Deut 9:10 used Exod 31:18; 32:16), God angry with the people after they make the calf (Deut 9:12–14 used Exod 32:7–10), Moses smashing the tablets (Deut 9:17 used Exod 32:19), Moses pleading for the Israelites (Deut 9:26–27 used Exod 32:11–13), second set of tablets (Deut 10:1–5 used Exod 34:1–5, 28), the earth swallowing Dathan and Abiram (Deut 11:6 used Num 16:30), and even Deuteronomy's use of the Elohist Decalogue (most of Deut 5:6–21 used most of Exod 20:2–17). Baden also noted the similarity of Deuteronomic Laws with narrative material: Moses as the great prophet and intercessor (Deut 18:15–22 used Exod 18:16), exclusion of Ammon and Moab (Deut 23:4–5 used Num 20:14–21, 22–24), the skin disease of Miriam (Deut 24:8–9 used Num 12:10–15), and the hatred of Amalek (Deut 25:17–19 used Exod 17:8–16). This established that at the time when Deuteronomy was written, the Elohist had not yet been merged with the Yahwist tradition.[33]

---

32. Baden, *Redaction of the Pentateuch*, 197–207, 258–60, 311–12.

33. Ibid., 106–107, 137–172, 183, and *Composition of the Pentateuch*, 128, 133–37.

Conclusion

Scholars who maintain that so-called Elohist texts are insufficient to merit treating as a source are voicing a rather subjective opinion. In my opinion they have not refuted the existence of the Elohist, but rather have conceded its existence in a rather begrudging fashion. One could maintain, as other scholars have done, that our present Elohist texts are all that remain from a larger corpus of literature after the biblical authors mined that literature to create our present biblical text. That, too, is a subjective opinion. For the analysis of the biblical text is an art, not a science. I prefer the latter opinion that the Elohist texts in our present Bible did first arise in a larger corpus of narratives, some of which have been lost. For me the indication that these texts have a separate identity worth discussing can be found in the consistency of the theological message in those texts.

There are a number of significant expressions and terms that have a high incidence of occurrence in the same texts. Critics have said that using vocabulary to identify a source is a circular argument. They have said that once certain texts are related to each other arbitrarily, the vocabulary they share becomes a self-serving argument to bind them together. This, however, overlooks the fact that a significant number of terms and expressions occur "together" in these same texts and not in other texts. The emphasis is upon how these terms are "together" with each other and not found or rarely found elsewhere. This is not arbitrary association of random texts; this provides a high statistical probability that somehow these texts were connected with each other at some point in time. Furthermore, these expressions all relate to each other in a theological sense, they support the same worldview. Critics of the Elohist's existence have not shown that the "so-called" classic vocabulary of the Elohist is internally contradictory. If critics wish to truly refute the existence of the Elohist, they need to show that Elohist thought is incoherent because the language is discordant. No one, to my knowledge, has done that. But then most of the critics of the Elohist's existence are looking at the literary dimensions, not the theological or intellectual dimensions, for it is in the latter sphere rather than the former, that greater coherence may be found for the texts.

4

Prophetic Narratives in Samuel and Kings

PROPHETIC NARRATIVES IN THE books of Samuel and Kings appear similar to Pentateuchal texts usually associated with the Elohist. If we combine these texts with the Pentateuchal Elohist narratives, we would have sufficient passages in the greater Elohist tradition to give it consideration as a theological source. Furthermore, imagery, themes, and theological expressions in those prophetic stories appear to be prior to comparable imagery in the Pentateuchal stories, which provides a major argument for dating Elohist texts after 700 BCE.

The Elohist and Prophetic Traditions

Consideration of prophetic texts in the Deuteronomistic History, especially narratives about Elijah and Elisha, may help us locate the Elohist tradition in its social and theological context. Similarities between these prophetic narratives and the Pentateuchal Elohist traditions have been noted by scholars in the past, but because we assumed that the Elohist was prior to or contemporary with the times of Elijah and Elisha in the ninth century, the prophetic narratives were viewed to be dependent upon Elohist traditions. However, my dating the Elohist to the seventh century raises a radical possibility for reconstructing the evolution of the Pentateuch. For example, Jenks viewed the prophetic traditions as arising a century or two after his proposed date for the Elohist in the late tenth century, and the former were inspired by the latter.[1] However, if we date the Pentateuchal Elohist

---

1. Jenks, *North Israelite Traditions*, 83–111.

accounts to the seventh century, imagery in the prophetic narratives could have inspired the Pentateuchal texts. Van Seters suggested a similar paradigm when he postulated that narratives in the Deuteronomistic History inspired accounts in the Pentateuch, especially in the Moses traditions.[2] I parallel Van Seters by suggesting that northern prophetic texts in Kings arose in some early Elohist or proto-Elohist circles and later inspired Elohistic accounts in the Pentateuch. Theological themes and literary motifs in the prophetic narratives in Kings may be isolated to show their affinity with and possible influence upon later Elohist texts in the Pentateuch.

Prophetic narratives in the books of Kings seem to have their own distinct style, which has led scholars in the past to characterize them as north Israelite traditions. Some suggested that there was a source used by the author of Kings (and somewhat by the author of Chronicles), which appears for us as the bulk of the narrative between 1 Kings 17 and 2 Kings 10.[3] I am tempted to suggest that this source comes from one of those early "pools of Elohist tradition" in the north, and that the Deuteronomistic author of Kings selected portions and fragments, which would explain the fragmentary nature of the overall narrative plot line, abbreviated narratives, and why the Elijah traditions in particular seem to begin *in medias res* with no memory of how Elijah became a prophet or his early ministry.

The prophetic passages, I believe, that merit comparison with Pentateuchal Elohist texts include the following: 1 Sam 1:1–28 (Samuel's birth), 2:11–36 (Samuel at Shiloh), 3:1–21 (Samuel's dream), 9:1–10:16 (Samuel and Saul), 15:1–35 (Saul's rejection), 16:1–13 (Samuel and David), 19:18–24 (prophetic ecstasy), 25:1 (Samuel's death), 1 Kgs 11:29–40 (Ahijah of Shiloh), 13:1–32 (man of God from Judah), 14:1–18 (Jeroboam and Ahijah), 17:1–24 (Elijah and the Widow), 18:1–46 (Elijah on Mt. Carmel), 19:1–21 (Elijah at Horeb), 20:13–22, 35–43 (prophets and Ahab), 21:1–29 (Naboth's vineyard), 22:1–40 (Ahab and Micaiah-ben-Imlah), 2 Kgs 1:1–18 (Elijah and the soldiers), 2:1–25 (Elijah's ascent), 3:4–27 (war with Moab), 4:1–44 (Elisha and the widow), 5:1–27 (Naaman), 6:1–7 (ax floats), 6:8–23 (defeat of Arameans), 6:24–33, 7:1–20 (siege of Samaria), 8:1–6 (Shunammite woman), 6:7–15 (Elisha and Hasael), 9:1–13 (Jehu anointed), 13:14–21 (Elisha dies). I am aware that parts of these narratives include Deuteronomistic editing, especially the story of Naboth's vineyard, but to

---

2. Van Seters, *Life of Moses*.

3. Auld, *Kings Without Privilege*; and Bernhard Lehnart, *Prophet und König*, who included accounts of Samuel, Elijah, and Elisha in this source.

enter into that debate to isolate the proto-Elohist material in the accounts is beyond the scope of this work. For example, scholars for years have suggested that the Elijah traditions may have been inspired by and patterned after the Elisha traditions, and more recently some also have observed the possible influence of the Nathan traditions upon the Elijah stories.[4] The Elijah traditions probably existed in some form before the Deuteronomistic Historians began to shape them into the form we now have. This is evidenced by the disjointed plot line of the Elijah accounts. They begin with no real introduction of Elijah's origins, and parts of the plot line are out of sequence. Elijah is informed by Obadiah of one hundred hidden prophets (1 Kgs 18:13) before his lament to God in which he complains that he alone is left, and then is told, apparently for the first time, that seven thousand people are still faithful (1 Kgs 19:18). Why does he run to Horeb in despair in 1 Kings 19, saying that he alone is left, when he has just won the contest on Carmel? This disjointed narrative sequence resembles the story of Moses, who defeats the Egyptian magicians and then goes to the mountain to receive the Law. Someone made Elijah appear like Moses and thus placed Elijah traditions out of sequence chronologically. The Elijah traditions have been reworked extensively, and we shall not enter into that complex discussion. We shall simply examine the prophetic stories for themes in their present canonical form, isolating such themes as they appear to stand out in the accounts. We shall compare the themes with texts in the Pentateuch that have been viewed as Elohist by various scholars over the years.[5]

The Imagery of Fire

The motif of fire is a striking image, especially since fire so often symbolizes the presence of the divine, not only in the Bible, but also in many religious traditions. Fire as a motif occurs often in Pentateuchal Elohist texts, so its occurrence in these prophetic texts is significant.

Fire sometimes comes from the sky. Elijah engages in a contest with the prophets of Baal on Mt. Carmel in 1 Kgs 18:19–40, and he wins when fire comes down from the divine realm to consume the sacrifice (v. 38). At a later time King Ahaziah sends three companies of soldiers to bring Elijah before him (2 Kgs 1:9–14). The captains of the first two companies demand

---

4. White. *Elijah Legends*, 12–15.

5. The following material is an expanded version of a discussion taken from my article, "Northern Prophetic Traditions," 374–86.

Elijah to come down from the top of a hill, so Elijah calls fire to come down and destroy both companies. (They should have said please!) The captain of the third company asks more courteously and so Elijah complies. In both stories the image of fire that comes from the divine realm is a powerful symbol of divine power. One gets the impression that the Lord sent the fire on Mt. Carmel, but in the second account Elijah is able to call it down himself.

Fire is one of the three natural phenomena at Mt. Horeb in which God is said not to be present (1 Kgs 19:12), the other two being wind and an earthquake. We are reminded of how God was present in fire in the theophanies that occurred on Mt. Sinai for Moses. In Elijah's experience the fire is indeed a theophanic element, which is now highlighted as a way in which God will not appear to Elijah and perhaps this implies that God will no longer be revealed in natural phenomena for the prophets in the future, but rather in the still, small voice of the prophetic word. Thus, fire is an important element insofar as it is being transcended as a mode of theophany.

Chariots and horses of fire also come from the divine realm. As Elijah and Elisha walk together on the other side of the Jordan River, a chariot and horses of fire come down and separate the two of them, so that Elijah may ascend into heaven in a whirlwind (2 Kgs 2:11–12). Strangely Elisha recognizes this phenomenon, for he screams, "the chariots of Israel and its horsemen!" (v. 12). We are probably missing some stories that could explain this imagery and why Elisha so quickly recognizes it. When Elisha is threatened by the soldiers sent by the king of Aram, he is protected by horses and chariots of fire on the mountain (2 Kgs 6:17). When the Aramean soldiers advance, they are struck blind (maybe by a bright light like fire) and are led to Samaria by Elisha (2 Kgs 6:18–19). When King Joash of Israel comes to see the dying Elisha, he declares, "My father, my father! The chariots of Israel and its horsemen!" (2 Kgs 13:4). Though fire is not mentioned, we suspect that this is another reference to the chariots and horses of fire. It appears to be a recurrent theme in the Elijah and Elisha narratives, and we wish we knew more about it.

Numerous accounts in the Pentateuch Elohist texts allude to fire, especially fire on the sacred mountain that indicates the presence of God. The most notable is the appearance of God to Moses in a burning bush (Exod 3:1, 2b, 4b–6). God is dramatically perceived as being revealed in the fire. This, of course, contrasts with 1 Kgs 19:12 where it states that God was not in the fire on Mt. Horeb for Elijah, an allusion that sets up Elijah for a new revelation which moves beyond the imagery of Sinai and Moses' experience.

On the return trip to the mountain, Moses and the Israelites again experience God in a theophany involving fire. People see thunder and lightning (and a thick cloud in addition) on the mountain at one point in their sojourn there (Exod 19:16), and the lightning might loosely be considered fire. Subsequently the narrative says that God comes down upon the mountain in fire and thus covers the mountain in smoke (Exod 19:18). God is present in the fire, and this is the text that contrasts with Elijah's experience on Mt. Horeb.

Fire imagery occurs in other texts that sometimes have been defined as Elohist. In the theophany to Abraham in Genesis 15 the appearance of God is described as "a smoking fire pot and a flaming torch" (v. 17), and the word "fire" is directly used.

One of the ten plagues is fiery hail from heaven (Exod 9:23), a passage often considered to be Elohist (though not included in my list). God is not revealed in the fire, but it is fire from heaven comparable to the fire that consumed the sacrifice on Mt. Carmel (1 Kgs 18:38), the fire called down by Elijah against the soldiers (2 Kgs 1:9–14), and the fiery chariot that comes down and ascends with Elijah (2 Kgs 2:11–12). Fire comes out of the sky in various forms in these accounts, and they all manifest the power of God.

In the wilderness God is in a "pillar of fire." During the night Yahweh leads the Israelites by a "pillar of fire" (Exod 13:21–22). At the sea crossing Yahweh looks out at the Egyptians from a "pillar of fire" (Exod 14:24). When the Tabernacle is set up in the wilderness, the cloud covers it during the day and at night the cloud has the "appearance of fire" (Num 9:15–16), and the image seems to be dependent on the prior image of the cloud by day and the "pillar of fire" by night leading the Israelites. (In its present form, the text in Num 9:15–23 has been reworked by Priestly Editors.) Later Moses reminds the Lord of how the Israelites are led by a "pillar of fire" (Num 14:14). These texts share the concept that God is present in the fire either in the sky or on a mountaintop, which is like being in the sky.

Other texts have the imagery of fire as a significant motif. In what traditionally is defined as a Priestly text, we are told of how Nadab and Abihu, sons of Aaron, offer strange fire, and are killed by fire that comes out from the presence of the Lord (Lev 10:2). We do not know what the presence of the Lord means. We note, however, that the names of these sons of Aaron are similar to the names of Jeroboam's sons, Abijah and Nadab

(1 Kgs 15:25) and that both Aaron and Jeroboam built golden calves.[6] We suggest that this text has an origin prior to the Priestly Tradition's use of it, for the Priestly Tradition would not invent such a story that told about the death of priests and especially Aaron's sons.[7] Perhaps, the Priestly tradition used this old Elohist allusion for some inscrutable reason. At Taberah the people complained and as a result the fire of the Lord burned against them and consumed outer parts of the camp (Num 11:1–3). It is not clear whether God was in the fire, nor does the story explain how this happened so as to burn part of the camp and not all of it, or where the fire came from. A ballad that speaks of war in Num 21:27–30 refers to fire going forth to destroy cities. Fire comes from Heshbon to destroy Ar of Moab, and the fire also spread to Medeba. It is strange that this ballad of non-Israelite war is included here, and we cannot tell what the image of fire refers to. All of these stories appear to be fragmentary references and so they appear rather strange to us. We are reminded of a number of comparable stories in the prophetic traditions in Kings. Perhaps, these north Israelite proto-Elohist traditions in both the Pentateuch and the book of Kings have been cannibalized by later Yahwist, Deuteronomistic, and Priestly traditions to the point where they are somewhat vague.

In the prophetic accounts fire comes from God to accomplish the divine will, but in the Pentateuchal narratives God is sometimes in the fire. This would seem to make the Pentateuchal accounts appear more theologically dramatic, for the theme is used to emphasize the majesty of God. It would seem that the Pentateuchal accounts have developed later than the prophetic accounts.

The Angel of God

As in Elohist Pentateuchal texts, there are references in the prophetic narratives to an intermediary figure from the divine realm called variously the "angel" or the "angel of God." The old prophet from Bethel tells the "man of God" that an "angel" spoke to him saying that the "man of God" could eat at his home (1 Kgs 13:18). We assume he was lying about the angel, since the "man of God" dies for his disobedience. An angel tells Elijah to eat a cake and drink some water (1 Kgs 19:5), then later orders him to continue his journey to Horeb (1 Kgs 19:7), and in this second reference the

---

6. Aberback and Smolar, "Golden Calves"; and Sweeney, *I & II Kings*, 184.

7. Nicholson, *Pentateuch*, 211.

messenger is called an "angel of the Lord." Elijah is told by the "angel of the Lord" to meet messengers from Ahaziah after the king's injurious fall (2 Kgs 1:3), and a little later, after Elijah has roasted two companies of soldiers, an "angel of the Lord" tells him to go with the third company (2 Kgs 1:15). Commentators have connected the "angel of the Lord/God" in the books of Kings with the Elohist tradition in the past, and usually suggested that both literatures arose in the eighth century.[8] It is interesting that Elijah is told to go somewhere in three of his experiences. (It is also interesting that the expression, "angel of the Lord" is used, which we otherwise expect to be a Yahwist expression. Perhaps the idiom was modified by the Deuteronomistic Historians, or perhaps early Elohist traditions did not avoid the sacred name of God in the prophetic traditions.)

In Elohist texts the expression "angel of God" is an indirect way of speaking about God when the biblical author wishes to be very circumspect and not make God appear in a fashion that is too anthropomorphic, unlike Yahwist imagery. (As Elijah is told to go somewhere, in the Elohist dream reports in Genesis the human recipient is often on a journey or told to go somewhere.) In the Pentateuch we have several comparable references to the "angel" personage. After Hagar is sent away by Abraham she hears the "angel of God" (Gen 21:17) promise her that Ishmael will be the father of a great people. The "angel of the Lord/God" prevents Abraham from killing Isaac and promises him many offspring (Gen 22:11). The "angel of God" goes before and then follows the Israelites as they flee toward the sea crossing (Exod 14:19). The expression, "angel of God," does not occur frequently, but it does seem to be a significant marker of Elohist texts, and thus this phrase appears to be a common link between Pentateuchal and prophetic texts in Kings.

In the prophetic texts the angel is a being apart from God, but in the Pentateuchal passages the angel personage is really a circumlocution for God. This implies a move in a somewhat monotheistic direction, for the persona of the angel is absorbed into the oneness of God. But the angel persona also functions to portray God as more transcendent and majestic, for the angel is like a mask for God, so that God can remain distant while the angel persona becomes the mode for revelation. This is yet another indication that the Pentateuchal texts are later than the prophetic texts.

---

8. Gray, *I & II Kings*, 463–464; and Jones, *1 and 2 Kings*, 378.

Mountains

Mountains, or at least large hills, seem to be important in the plot line of these stories. Obviously, the most important mountain top experience was Elijah's encounter with the divine on Mt. Horeb (1 Kgs 19:1–21). His experience clearly parallels that of Moses on Mt. Sinai. Which of the two memories may have influenced the other is a matter of debate, but it appears to most scholars that the Elijah narrative depends upon the Mosaic texts.[9] The significance of the theophany on Mt. Horeb demands familiarity with the theophany on Sinai, since God is no longer present in the natural phenomena, such as fire, that occurred for Moses at Sinai, but now for Elijah God appears in the "sound of sheer silence" (1 Kgs 19:12). Furthermore, the placement of Elijah's victory over the prophets of Baal on Mt. Carmel (1 Kings 17) appears as though it should follow the Horeb theophany (1 Kings 19), but its prior location may be meant to remind us of sequence of narrative in the Moses traditions, for therein Moses defeats the magicians of pharaoh before taking the people out into the wilderness to Sinai. This does, of course, pose a major problem for a theory suggesting that the prophetic narratives precede the Pentateuchal accounts, unless we posit some further redaction of the Elijah traditions by later Elohistic and Deuteronomist editors make the text in Kings provide subtle reference to the texts in the Pentateuch.

The other significant mountain top experience is the contest between Elijah and the prophets of Baal on Mt. Carmel when fire comes down and consumes the sacrifice (1 Kgs 18:19–40). Yahweh's supremacy over Baal is accomplished in a region that would have been considered part of Baal's territory. We are reminded of Moses' confrontation and defeat of the magicians in pharaoh's court in the book of Exodus.

A third mountain top experience occurs when soldiers of Ahaziah come to get Elijah, and fire comes down the mountain and destroys them (2 Kgs 1:1–17). In all three of these mountain top experiences the element of fire plays a very important role. Maybe we really should speak of the theme of fire on the mountain. Fire is a powerful symbol of the divine presence, and it is frequently associated with mountains, which are often the abode of the divine.

---

9. White, *Elijah Legend*, 5–6.

Finally, an allusion to Mt. Carmel occurs in 2 Kgs 4:25, 27 when we are told that the Shunammite woman seeks Elisha and finds him at Mt. Carmel where she asks him to help her deceased son.

In the Pentateuch all the traditions view Moses' mountaintop experience as crucial, for that is where the Law is revealed. There is the narrative of the near sacrifice of Isaac, which occurs upon a mountain (Gen 22:1–13, 19). There God also speaks directly to Abraham as a voice from the heavens, which is a significant revelation. The image of the mountain as an abode for the divine presence and the source of great revelation appears to be a theme in the prophetic traditions of Kings as well as the Pentateuchal Elohist.

Excluding the account of Elijah's experience on Mt. Horeb, which may be a late narrative, the other mountain experiences in the prophetic accounts appear less dramatic and thus earlier than their Pentateuchal counterparts. While Mt. Horeb is named in the prophetic accounts, the mountain in the Elohist narratives often is called the "mountain of God" (except Exod 3:1 calls it Horeb), so that it usually seems to be symbolic without specific location. This appears to be a later and more theologically profound symbol of a mountain wherein the human and the divine realms intersect.

Dreams

The only dream report in the north prophetic traditions, I believe, is the account of the little boy Samuel in 1 Samuel 3. I have argued in the past that the narrative contains the component parts of an ancient Near Eastern auditory dream message, even though the word dream is not used, in addition to containing elements of a prophetic call narrative.[10]

Scholars have often suggested that the high and majestic view of God in the Elohist led to the portrayal of God as distant and communicating through indirect means, such as fire, the voice from the heavens, the angel, dreams, and most importantly, prophets, as opposed to the more anthropomorphic mode of revelation found in Yahwist texts.

Dream reports are found in the following Elohist texts: one for Abimelech (Gen 20:3–8), two for Jacob (Gen 28:12, 16a, 17–21a; 31:10–13), one for Laban (Gen 31:24), one for Jacob/Israel (Gen 46:2–4), and two for Balaam (Num 22:9–13, 20–21). The Pentateuchal dream reports have a more stereotyped formulaic structure which can be summarily rendered as

10. Gnuse, "1 Samuel 3," 379–90; and Gnuse, *Dream Theophany*, 119–77.

thus: "God or the angel of God came to so-and-so in a dream by night and said, 'Behold I . . .'" These elements appear to be most similar to Assyrian and Chaldean Babylonian dream reports of the seventh and sixth centuries.

I believe an earlier less developed formula in the prophetic traditions, connected to Samuel, has become more stereotyped in the later Pentateuchal Elohist texts. (I also see the relationship between the Pentateuchal Elohist texts and the Assyrian and Chaldean dream reports as a significant indicator for a seventh to sixth-century date for the Elohist.) But I must also acknowledge that I have only one narrative in the prophetic traditions, 1 Samuel 3, for such comparison.

Magical Striking with a Special Object

Another small motif is the image of striking something to produce results magically. Twice the Jordan River is parted by a prophet, once by Elijah (1 Kgs 2:8) and once by Elisha on the return trip (1 Kgs 2:14), both using the prophetic mantle of Elijah. We recall how Joshua stops the Jordan River for his army to cross into the land and the crossing of the sea in Exodus 14–15, wherein Moses parts the water. In another magical act of striking, King Joash strikes the ground three times with arrows in the presence of Elisha (2 Kgs 13:18–19) to determine the number of victories over the Arameans.

When Moses parts the sea with his staff (Exod 14:16), he uses an object that may have prophetic symbolism, as the prophet's mantle has for Elijah and Elisha. The use of the staff by Moses in Exod 14:16 is considered an Elohist or a Priestly motif, which contrasts with the Yahwist motif of Moses' hand (Exod 14:16, 21, 26–27). (I did not include Exod 14:6 because of the ambiguity of Elohist or Priestly origin here.) Moses also uses his staff to bring plagues to Egypt. In the reports of the plagues, Moses strikes the water before pharaoh to turn it into blood (Exod 7:17–20), Aaron stretches out his hand and staff to bring forth frogs from the water (Exod 8:5–6), Aaron strikes the dust with his staff to bring forth gnats (Exod 8:16–17), Moses stretches forth his staff to the heavens to bring hail and fire down (Exod 9:23), and Moses stretches forth his staff to bring locusts (Exod 10:13). Not all of these passages obviously are seen as Elohistic, but some are, and originally Elohist texts may have been reworked radically by Yahwist or Priestly traditions.

The image of the prophetic figure using an object, be it a prophetic mantle or a prophetic staff, to part waters seems to connect the crossing

The Elohist

of the Jordan by the Elijah and Elisha and the crossing of the sea under Moses. If we include the story of Moses striking the Nile to turn it into blood, we have several stories where the prophet uses an object to affect water significantly.

The theme of striking is found in both the prophetic traditions and the Elohist traditions. In the latter it is more uniformly associated with the prophetic staff, and perhaps that might imply later development. Since a staff can also be a priestly symbol, one could assume that it became more symbolically significant for prophets in later years, thus implying once more that the Pentateuchal Elohist material comes after the prophetic traditions.

Themes of Prophetic Identity

In the prophetic narratives we observe many fascinating characteristics of the prophets. Discussion of such details is worthwhile, since there are hints of continuity with Pentateuchal stories. The old prophetic traditions in Samuel and Kings tell us much about prophets, including: 1) their baldness or tonsure (1 Kgs 20:35–43; 2 Kgs 2:23–24) (Sweeney additionally points out that one shaves the head to mourn the dead [Lev 21:5; Deut 14:1; Isa 15:2; Jer 16:6; Ezek 7:18; 27:31; Amos 8:10; Mic 1:16], or to mourn for a "dead" god of vegetation like Baal or Tammuz [Deut 14:1; 1 Kgs 18:28]. "Korah" means "bald" and may thus describe Levitical priests in Psalms 42, 44–49, 84–85, 87–88. He creatively suggests that prophetic tonsure may have been a characteristic of a holy man in the Transjordan.[11]); 2) "companies of the prophets" or "sons of the prophets" under Samuel (1 Sam 10:5–6, 10–13; 19:20–24) and Elisha (2 Kgs 2:3–7, 15–18; 4:1, 38; 5:22; 6:1; 9:1); 3) ecstasy (1 Sam 10:5–7, 9–14; 19:20–24); 4) connection to special trees, like an oak or a broom tree (1 Kgs 13:14; 19:4–5); 5) food wondrously provided for helpless people through the efforts of the prophets (1 Kgs 17:6, 14–16; 19:5–6; 2 Kgs 2:18–22; 4:1–7, 38–41, 42–44); 6) prophets helping women in distress with wondrous signs (1 Kgs 17:13–16, 17–24; 2 Kgs 4:1–7, 17, 18–37); 7) prophets consulted for illness (1 Kgs 14:1–18; 17:17–24; 2 Kgs 1:1–17; 4:18–37; 5:1–19; 8:7–15) (McKenzie notes that in three of these accounts the prophet declares that the king or a member of the royal house will die, be it Abijah [1 Kgs 14:1–18], Ahaziah [2 Kgs 1:1–17], or Ben-Hadad [2 Kgs 8:7–15]. This would be strong comment by the seventh-century Elohist of the authority of prophets over kings.); 8)

---

11. Sweeney, *I & II Kings*, 275.

Prophetic Narratives in Samuel and Kings

clairvoyance with Samuel (1 Sam 9:6), Ahijah (1 Kgs 14:6), Elijah (1 Kgs 18:43), a nameless prophet (1 Kgs 20:13, 22), Micaiah ben-Imlah (1 Kgs 22:17), and especially Elisha (2 Kgs 4:16; 6:16–17; 7:1; 12:17–19); 9) stories with anonymous prophets (1 Kgs 13:1–32; 20:28; 20:35–43; 2 Kgs 9:1–13); and 10) occasional odd behavior, exemplified by Jehu's passing reference to the prophet as crazy (*mešugga*).[12]

In general, the reader cannot help but notice the overarching theme in the books of Samuel and Kings that prophets are portrayed as the intermediaries between God and the kings, so that in a certain sense the authority of the prophet is greater than that of the king.[13] Samuel makes both Saul and David king and unmakes Saul's kingship. Nathan's judgment oracle brings David to his knees. Later prophets dictate the future of dynasties, and in particular, Elijah forecasts the doom of the Omrides, and Elisha insures it by commissioning Jehu's revolution.

In the Pentateuchal Elohist, we do not see any real references to the prophetic identity in the stories. Personages are described as prophets: Abraham (Gen 20:7), Miriam (Exod 15:20), the seventy elders who prophesy (Num 11:25), and Moses (Num 12:6–8). Abraham's function as a prophet is his intercession for Abimelech (Exod 20:7, 17), the other personages are prophets because they speak in a prophetic manner, or in the case of Moses, God speaks to him. Like the prophets, Abraham helps women in Abimelech's courts by allowing their babies to be born (Gen 20:17–18). Elohist Pentateuchal texts speak of people as prophets, while the rest of the material in Genesis through Leviticus shows no interest in prophets, and this invites the observation that the prophetic narratives and the Pentateuchal Elohist are similar.

In the Pentateuch, people are sometimes associated with special trees. In a Pentateuchal Elohist narrative we are told Deborah, the nurse of Rebecca, is buried under an oak tree (Gen 35:8). Since we do not know the complete significance of such trees, we do not know whether this connection means anything. We also can note that Abraham passes by the oak of Moreh (Gen 12:6), settles by the oaks of Mamre (Gen 13:18), and plants a tamarisk tree (Gen 21:33), all of which are probably Yahwist texts that imply somehow these trees are significant.[14]

---

12. Ibid., 333–34.

13. Lehnart, *Prophet und König*; McKenzie, *Trouble with Kings*, 93.

14. Gomes, *Sanctuary of Bethel*, 77–78.

The Elohist

Ultimately, because the Pentateuch does not tell the stories of prophets, we have little to compare between the two corpora of literature. The best we can do is to compare Balaam to the northern prophets and observe that one text speaks of Balaam as experiencing ecstasy, perhaps (Num 24:16). Also, we can observe the use of similar formula. When God speaks initially to Samuel, the boy prophet says, "Here I am," (1 Sam 3:4-6) three times. Moses gives the same response at the burning bush in the Elohist version in Exod 3:4. These are tantalizing, but limited hints of similarities.

However, if we observe the texts from the vantage point of how the details in the lives of Abraham, Moses, Joshua, Samuel, and Elisha are presented, we observe interesting parallels—not necessarily prophetic characteristics, but more general similarities.[15] When all of the Pentateuchal and prophetic Elohist texts are considered, they appear to define the role of a prophet by attributing similar characteristics to various archetypal personages. In Gen 22:1; Exod 3:4; and 1 Sam 3:4 Abraham, Moses, and Samuel: 1) hear an auditory message from God, 2) in which they are called by name with a single or double vocative, 3) and they respond by saying, "here I am." Perhaps, this may have been a formula in some Elohistic prophetic call narrative, for these accounts function as such for both Moses and Samuel. As a result of their experience, both Moses and Samuel, in particular, are: 4) called to be prophets, 5) who deliver Israel from foreign enemies (Egyptians, Philistines), 6) and function in diverse roles as holy war leaders against Amalekites (Exod 17:8-16) and Philistines (1 Sam 7:3-14), judges, and covenant mediators. Presumably, we may have lost some stories because our present texts in this regard are sometimes non-Elohistic (1 Sam 7:3-14), so that the similarities that we may still observe are noteworthy.

Furthermore, we may point to interesting parallels between Elijah/Elisha and Moses/Joshua: 1) Elijah flees Ahab (1 Kgs 17:2-6) and Moses flees pharaoh (Exod 2:15). 2) Elijah receives bread and meat in the morning and the evening (1 Kgs 17:6); Moses and the Israelites receive bread in the morning and meat in the evening during the wilderness wanderings (Exod 16:8, 12). 3) Elijah lives with the foreign widow (1 Kgs 17:8-24) and Moses lives with foreign Midianites (Exod 2:16-22). 4) Elijah fights Baal and the Baal prophets (1 Kgs 18:20-40); Moses opposes the gods of Egypt and the magicians (Exod 7:8-13, 20-22) (though the magician motif may be Priestly in origin). 5) Both raise up a testimony of twelve stones

---

15. Jenks, *North Israelite Traditions*, 32-36, saw these similarities as evidence of a unified Elohist history.

as testimony to God (1 Kgs 18:32; Exod 24:24, as Joshua also does in Josh 8:8–9). 6) Both are commissioned to do the work of God at mountains: Elijah goes to Horeb (1 Kgs 19:1–18); Moses goes to Sinai (Exod 3:1—4:17). 7) Elijah parts the Jordan with his mantle (2 Kgs 2:8); Moses parts the sea with his staff (Exod 14:16). 8) Elijah passes authority to Elisha (1 Kgs 19:16–21; 2 Kgs 2:1–25), as Moses passes authority to Joshua (Deut 31:14; 34:9). 9) Elijah and Moses die or disappear at an unknown site in the Transjordan (2 Kgs 2:1–12; Deut 34:1–8). 10) Their successors, Elisha (2 Kgs 2:14) and Joshua (Josh 3:1–17), part the Jordan River to cross into the Cisjordan after they inherit authority and leadership (2 Kgs 2:14; Josh 3:1–17). 11) Both sets of tradition maintain the priority of prophets over rulers. And 12) both sets of tradition have a holy war ideology: Elisha leads the people against the Moabites (2 Kgs 3:9–27) and against Baal devotees (2 Kgs 9:7–13), as Moses leads the people against Amalek (Exod 17:8–16) and Joshua leads the people against the Canaanites.[16] Of course, a number of these parallels may have been generated by the Deuteronomistic Historians in regard to Elijah and Joshua, but nevertheless, a number of the parallels perhaps reflect Elohist origins, and the complexity of later revision by the Deuteronomistic Historians and Priestly Editors may render it impossible to determine how the motifs developed and influenced each other.

Food Provided to People as a Sign of Divine Fertility

There are numerous allusions to the food provided by Yahweh directly or through the agency of the prophets. This narrative technique, of course, contrasts Yahweh with Baal, the supposed god of fertility. Elijah is fed by ravens (1 Kgs 17:6) who bring him food rather than eating it themselves, a rather unusual action for birds of prey. According to the assurance of Elijah the widow's jars of oil and flour do not empty (1 Kgs 17:14–16). Elijah is supplied with a cake and a jar of water under a broom tree after an angel awakens him (1 Kgs 19:5–6). On several occasions Elisha directly provides food to others. Elisha makes water drinkable (2 Kgs 2:18–22), he makes a pot of stew edible (2 Kgs 4:38–41), and he feeds one hundred men with twenty loaves of bread (2 Kgs 4:42–44). Most notable is the account of how

---

16. Carroll, "Elijah-Elisha Sagas"; Jones, *1 and 2 Kings*, 172; and Jenks, *North Israelite Traditions*, 89–101; and Walsh, *I Kings*, 284–89, who additionally observed many vocabulary and stylistic parallels between the Moses and Elijah traditions.

Elisha provides a boundless source of oil for the widow so that she could pay her debts (2 Kgs 4:1–7).

The fertility imagery associated with the prophets is not found in the Pentateuch because of limited references to prophets. However, one can draw the parallel with the various references to the provision of manna and quail for the Israelites during their wilderness wanderings.

Immediate Divine Retribution

The entire Deuteronomistic History assumes divine retribution for human sinfulness, but these prophetic narratives have some classic examples of rather immediate retribution for failure to heed the prophetic word. When the "man of God" condemns Jeroboam I at the altar, Jeroboam reprimands him (in the same manner that Amaziah, the priest, responds to Amos in Amos 7:10–13). But Jeroboam's hand withers when he gives the order to seize the "man of God" (1 Kgs 13:4). When Jeroboam repents, his hand is healed (1 Kgs 13:6). Both events are quick responses of retribution and forgiveness. This same "man of God" disobeys his prophetic commission when he heeds the lying message of the prophet from Bethel, and as a result, a lion quickly kills him after he departs from his host's luncheon engagement (1 Kgs 13:24). The prophet who refuses to strike his prophetic colleague in response to the latter's word from God is also killed by a lion during the time of the battle between Ahab and Ben-Hadad (1 Kgs 20:36). Soldiers who rudely demand Elijah's presence before the king are consumed by fire (2 Kgs 1:9–14). The prophetic oracle of Micaiah-ben-Imlah (1 Kgs 22:17) is fulfilled shortly as the king dies in battle. The boys who mock Elisha are quickly consumed by bears (2 Kgs 2:23–24). Soldiers who threaten Elisha are struck blind (2 Kgs 6:18–20). Finally, the captain is trampled (2 Kgs 7:17) fulfilling the earlier hint of this retributional event (2 Kgs 7:2). It is fascinating how often animals serve God in bringing about such swift retribution.

In Elohist narratives in the Pentateuch there are examples of immediate retribution. When Abimelech takes Sarah into his harem, the wombs of his other women are closed (Gen 20:17–18). The sons of Aaron, Nadab and Abihu, are destroyed by fire for their inappropriate sacrificial behavior (Lev 10:2) in a Priestly story that may once have been Elohistic.

This theme may not be sufficiently distinctive to link both sets of tradition closely, for the concept of retribution is found elsewhere in the biblical text. But the dramatic immediacy of retribution in these particular stories provides an allusive link between the two sets of tradition.

Fear of God and Obedience

In other ways one could suggest that the overall theological style of the narrative in these prophetic traditions has contributed to the development of theology in Pentateuchal Elohist texts. This would include theological concepts such as the "fear of God" and "obedience." The "fear of God" as an expression occurs in Gen 20:11; 22:12; Exod 1:17, 21; 18:21; 20:20, all texts usually assumed to be Elohistic. Although the term is not a hallmark idiom in the prophetic narratives, certainly the reader gets the feeling that the "fear of God" characterizes what should be the appropriate response to the divine in those accounts. That appropriate response, of course, should be obedience to God. We only need recall how the "man of God" in 1 Kings 13, the unresponsive prophets in 1 Kings 22, the unfortunate soldiers in 2 Kings 1, and the rowdy boys in 2 Kings 2 so quickly perish as a result of standing in opposition to the will and prophetic word of God. Certainly such stories should inspire fear and obedience. I would suggest that the Elohist narratives in the Pentateuch, which more directly use the expression, "fear of God," might have developed at a later point in time than the prophetic narratives, for they have coined a particular expression to capture the feeling that was in those earlier prophetic accounts.

Fragmentary Nature of Many Accounts

There are a number of accounts that seem to be fragmentary; that is, it appears as if we have lost part of the plot line that would make the story more comprehensible.

In 1 Kgs 17:1 Elijah appears and we find ourselves in the middle of the plot, not knowing where he came from and how be became a great prophet. In 1 Kgs 18:17 Elijah is called the "troubler of Israel." How did he earn this reputation? What stories are we missing which would tell us of his prior prophetic activities? In fact, the Elijah narrative in its present form seems to have been re-arranged. Elijah's great victory on Mt. Carmel (1 Kgs 18:19–40) precedes his despair on Mt. Horeb (1 Kings 19:1–21). This is not logical; it should be reversed. Elijah discovers on Mt. Horeb that he has supporters. Logically he should then proceed with these followers to Mt.

Carmel, for there his followers ultimately kill the prophets of Baal. Placing the Mt. Carmel victory before the theophany at Horeb reminds us of the plot in the Moses stories wherein Moses defeats pharaoh's magicians with the plagues and then takes the slaves to Sinai to experience the theophany of God.

Elisha accompanies the kings of Israel and Judah on their invasion of Moab (2 Kgs 3:11–27). The war seems to end suddenly when the king of Moab offers his son as a sacrifice and this causes a "great wrath" to come upon the Israelites and Judahites (2 Kgs 3:27). What happened? Why did they leave Moab? Something has been left out, perhaps by the Deuteronomistic Historians, who may have been embarrassed by the fuller narrative involving successful human sacrifice.

The reference to Elisha, the boys, and the bears is altogether too brief (2 Kgs 3:23–24). Why did the bear eat the boys? What was their offense? Why was the explanation left out?

It is interesting that the prophetic narratives appear fragmentary, because by comparison the Elohist narratives in the Pentateuchal are fragmentary also. Every scholar has acknowledged that in some way Elohist accounts in Genesis, Exodus, and Numbers have been selected or edited, so that little of the overall plot remains. Perhaps some of the terseness found in these accounts both in the Pentateuch and the prophetic narratives is due to the Elohist style, or perhaps it reflects an editorial process in which narrative material was lost when Elohist stories were woven into longer narratives by the Deuteronomistic Historians, Yahwist Historian, and Priestly Editors.

Strangeness in the Narratives

In the subjective opinion of this author, many of the accounts contain strange images and ideas. Of course, the biblical narratives all record the miraculous, and we often hear narrative imagery that puzzles us. But the prophetic narratives in Kings seem to have more than would be expected in the short length of these texts. We have accounts of a withered royal hand, prophets eaten by lions, raven food delivery service, jars of food that never empty, fire from heaven to ignite sacrifice, children raised from the dead, revelation on mountain tops, fire sweeping down a hill to kill two companies of soldiers, a prophet going to heaven in a whirlwind, chariots of fire, prophets looking for Elijah in case his ascension to heaven did not succeed, pools of water in the desert, jars of endless oil, one hundred people fed with but a little food, leprosy cured in the Jordan River, leprosy transferred to a dishonest servant, an ax head that floats, armies that flee in the night, and invisible armies. Then there are some truly weird stories—bears eating boys, human sacrifice scattering a victorious army, and cannibalistic mothers. There are numerous miraculous elements, entertaining mythic elements, and truly bizarre scenes. These narratives have a personality of their own and appear distinctly different in some ways from Pentateuchal narratives. The Elohistic Pentateuchal narratives appear subjectively to me to be more sophisticated and from a later, more reflective era.

Conclusion

This comparison of prophetic traditions in Samuel and Kings with the Pentateuchal Elohist stories is not an absolutely convincing argument, but rather is suggestive. If it were more easily demonstrated that these prophetic accounts were prior to the Pentateuchal narratives, Julius Wellhausen would have suggested this in the nineteenth century. In my opinion certain themes in the prophetic narratives have inspired the later Pentateuchal Elohist accounts in regard to themes such as fire, the angel, mountain experiences, dreams, objects which strike water, fear, and obedience. In the Pentateuchal narratives they subjectively appear to have a more sophisticated theological meaning than in the prophetic narratives.

If I suggest that the prophetic narratives arose in the eighth century as a memory of the prophetic activity in the ninth century, and if I believe that the prophetic narratives influenced the Elohist accounts in the Pentateuch, then it becomes logical to date the Elohist Pentateuchal narratives to the seventh or sixth century. Furthermore, if I consider the Pentateuchal narratives to be influenced by the prophetic narratives, then it becomes advisable to consider all of these texts together in any theological evaluation. If I look at these texts as emerging in some coherent form after 700 BCE, distinctive theological themes begin to appear. Elohist texts, especially in the Pentateuch, deal with issues of foreign rule by the Assyrians in the north and the possible exile of people by the Assyrians. The later absorption of these texts by the Yahwist occurred because the Yahwist also wrote from the vantage point of exile in Babylon either in the sixth or fifth century, and so the earlier Elohist texts about exile became relevant once more.

5

The Social and Theological Setting of the Elohist

SITUATING THE ELOHIST IN a northern exilic situation produces a theological message that makes sense. When we release the texts from the ninth or the eighth centuries and locate them to a later date, we can view the texts with fresh eyes and find a different message, one that speaks hope to exiles from the northern state of Israel. This is a subjective argument. But I believe that this new construal is a cogent argument for locating the Elohist.

Suggesting that the Elohist tradition is prior to the Yahwist tradition also addresses many of the criticisms issued by scholars in the past. It explains, in part, why the Elohist plot line appears truncated at times; perhaps much of it has been edited out by the Yahwist Historian. It can explain why some texts appear Elohist, but the language is lacking. It perchance may be due to the Yahwist cannibalizing fragments of Elohist narratives in a new rewritten form that is primarily Yahwist in its personality. Such a theory also obviates the need for the so-called JE Redactor, since the Yahwist is that redactor. This theory would explain, for example, why the Genesis 28 vision of God to Jacob appears to be coherent in the Elohist version and fragmented in the Yahwist version; the Yahwist simply added language to a pre-existing Elohist narrative.

The Social and Historical Setting of the Elohist

After observing the relationship between prophetic narratives in the books of Samuel and Kings with the Pentateuchal Elohist material, I am drawn to conclude that those latter narratives arose after the fall of Samaria in

722 BCE. Are there other arguments that may be marshaled to indicate a similar date and setting for Elohist narratives?

Dream Reports

In my article, "Dreams in the Night—Scholarly Mirage or Theophanic Formula?," I suggested that dream reports in Elohist texts reflect a seventh- to sixth-century origin in comparison with Neo-Assyrian and Chaldean Babylonian dream accounts.[1] In "Redefining the Elohist" (portions of which have been expanded upon in this chapter) I suggested a late date on the basis of a comparison with the dream reports and the Deir 'Alla inscription, as well as with other inferential arguments.[2]

In quick summary the arguments in these articles were as follows:

The eighth-century Deir 'Alla plaster inscription, made available to scholars in the 1970s, describes Balaam as a significant Transjordanian seer.[3] If the inscription dates from the eighth century, maybe the actual Balaam persona might be dated historically a century prior to the plaster inscription. Then the Elohist memory of Balaam that surfaced in the biblical text of Numbers 22–24 may be a later reaction to these eighth-century Transjordanian traditions, coming either from the late eighth century or early seventh century.[4]

The Deir 'Alla inscription itself may also recall beliefs of Israelites in the Transjordan for whom Balaam was an acceptable prophet.[5] Perhaps Numbers 22–24 used language from the inscription, especially in the report of the dream theophany in Num 22:9–21.[6] But the Elohist most likely distanced Balaam from Israelite traditions by making him into a foreign

---

1. Gnuse, "Dreams in the Night."

2. Gnuse, "Redefining the Elohist."

3. Hoftijzer and van der Kooij, *Aramaic Texts*, 173–82; Hacket, *Balaam Text*, 1–125; Cross, "Notes on the Ammonite Inscription," 14; Cross, "Ammonite Ostraca," 12–17; and McCarter, "Balaam Texts."

4. Ahlström, "Another Moses Tradition," 69; McCarter, "Balaam Texts," 57; Rouillard, *Balaam*, 483–87; Coogan, "Canaanite Origins," 117–18; and Michael Moore, *Balaam Traditions*, 95.

5. Müller, "Die aramäische Inschrift," 239; Puech, "L'inscription súr plâtre," 362, connected it to the tradition about Jacob's encounter at Penuel; and Levine, "Balaam Inscription," 336–39, suggested the cult may be condemned by Hos 6:7–10; 11:11.

6. McCarter, "Balaam Texts," 57; and Gnuse, *Dreams and Dream Reports*, 58, especially pointed out these similarities.

enemy or a strangely ambiguous figure in contrast to Moses and other prophets in the Elohist narratives. Thus, those Tranjordanian Israelite traditions and concomitant piety were marginalized. Again, one would expect this kind of response after the fall of the northern kingdom in 722 BCE.

Even though the Transjordanian traditions may have been marginalized, recalling Balaam's blessing may be a form of concession to Balaam traditions among people who viewed themselves as Israelite in the Transjordan. But the way in which the Elohist traditions about Balaam ultimately took shape in Numbers 22–24 may have domesticated the memory of old prophetic practices by placing them somewhat outside the Israelite prophetic tradition.

The Elohist probably redefined the Balaam traditions around 700 BCE or thereafter, implying that Israelite intelligentsia envisioned prophecy as a response to the disaster of Samaria's fall in 722 BCE. This could be part of a larger endeavor in which the north Israelite traditions, especially traditions about Elisha, were brought together in some form or cycle of narratives. Prophetic opposition to the kings as evidenced in the accounts of Elijah and Elisha may have epitomized the feelings of religious intelligentsia about their former monarchy after the fall of Samaria.

There are biblical accounts about revelatory dreams received by the patriarchs and other important figures. Dream reports (Gen 15:12–21; 20:1–8; 28:10–22; 31:10–24; 46:1–7; Num 22:8–21; 24:2) appear in Elohist texts and related accounts (1 Sam 3:1–18; 1 Kgs 3:4–15) with a distinct form that is comparable to other ancient Near Eastern dream reports.[7] Dream reports with similarity to the Elohist dream reports are the Neo-Assyrian reports of Sennacherib, Esarhaddon, and Ashurbanipal in the seventh century and Chaldean Babylonian reports of Nabonidus in the sixth century. Reputedly dream interpretation became popular in Assyria because Esarhaddon's conquest of Egypt brought dream interpreters to Assyria from Egypt in the mid-seventh century. Sennacherib ruled Assyria prior to Esarhaddon, but his dream report was recorded by Ashurbanipal.[8] During the seventh century, the northern state of Israel was under Assyrian rule, as the Assyrian province of Samerina, and in the sixth-century Chaldean Babylon ruled all Palestine. Perhaps in the seventh century the

---

7. Gnuse, "Reconsideration"; Gnuse, *Dream Theophany of Samuel*, 11–177; and Gnuse, "Dreams in the Night."

8. Oppenheim, *Interpretation of Dreams*, 201–2; Bergmann et al., "ḥalam," 4:425; and Gnuse, *Dream Theophany of Samuel*, 31–32; and Gnuse, *Dreams and Dream Reports*, 49–50.

The Social and Theological Setting of the Elohist

Elohist used Mesopotamian dream formulas to recall revelatory experiences of great Israelite personages in the past.

Ancient Near Eastern dreams may be analyzed in the following forms:

1) *auditory message dream reports*, with theophany, recipient, dream reference, reference to night, message, termination of dream;
2) *visual message dream reports*, containing an image with a clear message;
3) *symbolic message dream reports*, containing bizarre visual images requiring a professional dream interpreter or dream book, such as the *Assyrian Dream Book*, to decode them; and
4) *psychological status dreams*, the ordinary and everyday frenetic dreams of common people, which may envision their personal future, and likewise require a professional interpretation to unravel the meaning and to remove the impurity that the dream might bring upon the dreamer.[9]

Most Assyrian and Chaldean dream reports were auditory message dreams, as were Pentateuchal dreams outside the Joseph Novella in Genesis 37–50.

Significant parallels exist between auditory message dreams of the ancient Near East and Elohist dreams. Elohist dreams may be outlined as follows: "and the angel of God or God came to so-and-so in a dream by night and said, ..." (Gen 15:12–21; 20:1–8; 28:10–22; 31:10–17; 31:24; 46:1–4; Num 22:8–13, 19–21). The formula would contain reference to the theophany of the deity ("God came" in Gen 20:3; 31:24; Num 22:9, 20; "angel of God came" in Gen 31:11; and "God spoke" in Gen 46:2), the recipient of the dream (Gen 20:3; 31:11, 24; 46:2; Num 22:9, 20), specific reference that the experience is a dream (Gen 20:3, 6; 31:10, 11, 24; in Gen 46:2 it is a "vision"), reference to night (Gen 20:3; 31:24; 46:2; Num 22:20), indication that the message is oral (Gen 20:3, 6; 28:13; 31:11, 12, 24; Num 22:9, 20), the message itself, a reference to the termination of the dream and/or the awakening of the recipient in the morning (Gen 20:8; 28:16, 18; 31:17), and reference to the subsequent fulfillment of the dream commands. The message would contain an introductory "Behold" (Gen 20:3) or a vocative (Gen 31:11; 46:2) wherein God addressed the dreamer, followed by divine self-identification (Gen 28:13; 31:13; 46:3), the imperative to "fear not"

---

9. Oberman, *How Daniel*, 1–30; Oppenheim, *Interpretation of Dreams*, 179–255; Oppenheim, "Mantic Dreams"; and Oppenheim, "New Fragments of the Assyrian Dream-Book"; Kammenhuber, *Orakelpraxis*, 7–183; and Sasson, "Mari Dreams"; as well as subsequent scholars.

(Gen 46:3), the promise of divine accompaniment (Gen 28:13–15; 46:2–3), directions for where the dreamer should travel (Gen 31:12; 46:2–3; Num 22:20), and warnings to the dreamer (Gen 20:3; 31:24). Human dialogue sometimes occurs (Gen 20:4–5; Num 22:10–11), although sometimes the human response is simply "here I am" (Gen 31:11; 46:2). If the dreams of Samuel and Solomon are included, this formulaic pattern seems even more established among biblical authors. This formula was lacking or only very partial in two dreams recalled by the Yahwist (Gen 26:2–6, 24–25).[10] The specific dependence of Elohist texts upon the Mesopotamian format implies a literary connection, for so many of these form-critical categories may be found in the Mesopotamian dreams. It should be noted that the biblical formula are fairly short and crisp compared to their Mesopotamian counterparts.[11]

Monotheistic Values

A more subjective argument considers the theological themes traditionally attributed to the Elohist for the past century by scholars. These make more sense to us if articulated in an era only somewhat earlier than the Babylonian Exile. Those classic themes of divine transcendence, fear of God, obedience to God, indirect revelation (dreams, the angel of God, fire, voice from the heavens, and prophets), and concern for morality have been characterized subjectively by scholars as fairly sophisticated concepts. This would make sense if the Elohist tradition is dated later. These concepts might appear to us also to be connected to an exclusive worship of God, perhaps even monotheism. Contemporary authors now suggest that monotheism emerged late, perhaps only prior to the exile or perhaps during the exile.[12] If so, the Elohist might have been part of religious developments prior to the exile who helped create the seedbed for the emergence of radical monotheism in the exile. Certain themes in Elohist texts might be perceived as reinforcing this assumption. Jenks suggested that Elohist

---

10. Gnuse, "Dreams in the Night," 39–40.

11. Gnuse, *Dream Theophany of Samuel*, 11–55.

12. To name but a few: Lang, "Yahweh-Alone Movement"; Vörlander, "Monotheism Israels"; Lohfink, "Alte Testament und sein Monotheismus"; Lohfink, "Cult Reform"; Lohfink, "Monotheismus im Alten Israel"; McCarter, "Origins of Israelite Religion"; and Smith, *Early History of God*; and Smith, "Yahweh and the Other Deities." A fuller explication of contemporary views is found in Gnuse, *No Other Gods*, 62–128.

texts sought to connect El traditions to Yahweh.[13] This would be part of the process of convergence of deities so aptly described by Smith.[14] The ridicule of the *teraphim* stolen by Rachel in Gen 31:25–42 might be polemic against other religious beliefs. The pilgrimage to Bethel undertaken by Jacob and his family in order to bury the idols (Gen 35:1–4) would certainly speak to a later generation and demand that they no longer worship the other gods. This encouragement to reject the other gods appears to be rhetoric that would emerge in the seventh century, when we find comparable rhetoric in Judah with Deuteronomic language (which, of course, may have received inspiration from this Elohist material). These observations are very hypothetical when used to date the Elohist to the seventh or sixth century, but in conjunction with other arguments, they may carry some weight. Kaiser has made similar observations to mine in this regard. He believes that the level of sophisticated and reflective thought in Genesis 20 and 22 betokens an exilic or even post-exilic setting for the origin of Elohist traditions.[15]

Additional Observations

Further hints may be provided by various texts to assist in locating the provenance of the Elohist. The ladder imagery in Genesis 28 appears to allude to a Mesopotamian ziggurat. Ziggurats were built as early as 2000 BCE, primarily in Babylon, but the time when Israelites might be familiar with them would be after the exile of Israelites in 722 BCE and the exile of Judahites in 586 BCE. This was because deportees from foreign countries often were conscripted to work on massive Mesopotamian building projects, such as ziggurats, and survivors back in the homeland probably would have been aware of what exiles were forced to do. Exiles from Israel after 722 BCE may have worked on the building projects of the Assyrian king Sargon at Dur-Sharrukin around 710 BCE. Jacob sees the angels ascending and descending a ladder to the divine realm, and the cognate word for ladder in Akkadian is an object used to descend to the underworld where Ereshkigal rules—an interesting coincidence. Since the dream format already reflects Mesopotamian influence, this additional language tempts us to locate the account in the seventh or sixth century. Work on the ziggurat and main temple complex in Babylon, the Entemenanki, was undertaken

---

13. Jenks, *North Israelite Traditions*, 124.
14. Smith, *Early History of God*.
15. Kaiser, *Old Testament*, 99.

especially by exiles from Judah in the sixth century. The phrase, "top of it reaching to heaven" (v. 12) may refer particularly to the temple of Marduk, the Esagila, in Babylon. The expression "gate of heaven" (v. 17) is like the name, Babylon, "the gate of the gods."[16]

The theophany at Bethel in Genesis 28 bears an unusual relationship to the account of the Tower of Babel in Genesis 11. Both are towers which seem to reach up into the heavens, both accounts mention the prior movement of people that brings them to this place, both accounts mention stones either as a building material or as a "pillow," and as Jacob views the ladder as a "gateway" to the divine realm, so the word "Babel" means gateway to the gods. The contrasts between the narratives also stand in tension. The Babelites seek to go up into the divine realm, but God comes down to Jacob. Human ambition is thus contrasted with divine initiative. Jacob receives a blessing, but the Babelites are scattered as perhaps a punishment. Jacob will continue his journey with purpose, the Babelites move in all directions. Jacob seems to go toward Mesopotamia, but the Babelites are leaving "Shinar" or "Sumer" behind. Could it be that the narrative in Genesis 11 is a Yahwistic judgment parable inspired, in part, by the Elohist narrative in Genesis 28?[17] The Tower of Babel narrative is universally seen as Yahwist. If Genesis 11 depends upon the old core of Elohist story contained in Genesis 28, later supplemented by the Yahwist, it implies the priority of the Elohist tradition. Elsewhere I have argued that the Tower of Babel narrative in Genesis 11 dates to the late sixth century from the Yahwist Historian after the time of Nabonidus of Chaldean Babylon.[18]

A subjective ideological analysis of Elohist texts by Z. Weisman led him to observe that the Elohist lacks a sense of state consciousness, unlike the Yahwist. He concluded that the Elohist was prior to the Yahwist, a conclusion that fits with my paradigm of dating the Elohist to the seventh or sixth century and the Yahwist to the late sixth or early fifth century.[19] Norman Gottwald and Hans-Jürgen Zobel likewise observed the Elohist's lack of consciousness of the state.[20]

Thomas Dozeman included Num 20:14–21 in the Elohist tradition, and then pointed out that the references to Edom in this text assume a

---

16. Hurowitz, "Babylon in Bethel," 437–41.
17. Sherman, *Babel's Tower*, 55–58.
18. Gnuse, "Tower of Babel."
19. Weisman, "National Consciousness," 67.
20. Gottwald, *The Hebrew Bible*, 138, 150–51; and Zobel, "Selbstverständnis Israels."

The Social and Theological Setting of the Elohist

seventh-century date for several reasons. Edom flourished from the eighth to the sixth centuries, the "King's Highway" mentioned in the text was an Assyrian road system created in the seventh century. Edom was west of the Arabah, and hence Israel's route of travel in this text could exist only in the seventh century.[21]

The reverence that Jacob renders to Esau in Gen 33:1-17 may be of particular value in helping to locate the time of this tradition. After 586 BCE Edomites were hated for their complicity in the destruction of Judah. One cannot envision a narrative in which the returning Jacob (Israel) bows to Esau (Edom) in the sixth century or later. This indicates that perhaps this narrative speaks to Israelite exiles in the seventh century, after the destruction of Samaria in 722 BCE, but not to exiles after the destruction of Jerusalem in 586 BCE. The general portrayal of Esau in other Elohistic texts (Gen 23:21-34; 32:3-21; 33:1-17) is not negative, implying a pre-exilic origin for all these stories. Goulder saw the ambivalent portrayal of Esau as reflective of seventh-century attitudes toward Edom.[22]

Allusions to shrines, such as Bethel and Beersheba, indicate no knowledge of centralization advocated by those religious leaders in Jerusalem. This implies a pre-Josianic date.[23] However, the Elohist may simply have chosen to ignore such centralization rhetoric from the south.

The Elohist has no primeval traditions, no traditions prior to Abraham, unlike the Yahwist tradition, which is strange if the Yahwist traditions were earlier than the Elohist and known to the latter. I am tempted to suggest that the lack of a set of traditions prior to Abraham indicates that the Elohist is earlier than the Yahwist. I would date the Yahwist to the late sixth century or early fifth century, after the initial return to Palestine under Persian rule, which could bring out a greater interest in the Mesopotamian traditions that surface in Genesis 1-11, which were not to be found in the earlier Elohist tradition.

Graupner's analysis adds an interesting but subjective observation. He discerned elements of prophetic thought, wisdom influence (such as the "fear of God" motif), and a well-developed concept of "salvation history" in Elohist texts, which implies a late date.[24] Late for Graupner meant the early eighth century, but I might suggest the presence of these themes, if

---

21. Dozeman, "Geography and Ideology," 184-85.
22. Goulder, *Psalms of Asaph*, 222.
23. Graupner, *Elohist*, 396.
24. Ibid., 394-95.

they are really there in the texts, could point to an even later date, such as the seventh or sixth century.

Setting for the Elohist

Overall, I suggest that the Elohist narrative or Elohist pools of tradition may have arisen after the fall of Samaria in 722 BCE in the city of Bethel. A number of years ago Klein likewise suggested that Bethel was the site where the Elohist was created, written by a historian who was comparable to the much later Roman Pausanias. The Elohist created this work as a guidebook to affirm the antiquity and importance of the Bethel shrine.[25] Schmitt also affirmed a seventh-century date by suggesting that Elohist texts allude to Israel's potential destruction (Genesis 22; Numbers 22) and foreign rule in the land (Gen 20:1; 21:23, 34).[26]

Suggesting that Bethel was the location for these emerging traditions acknowledges that the northern state of Israel was not emptied of people by the Assyrian deportations, for such deportations only affected urban centers and left the countryside with a significant population. Deportations removed most of the upper- and middle-class folk in order to destroy the group identity of a region. An outlying shrine like Bethel might have been less affected by deportation than the capital city of Samaria. The loss of Samaria and the royal court meant that the priests of Bethel were no longer under the authority of an Israelite king, thus permitting a new religious spirit of reform to emerge. This would be a perfect setting for the generation of Elohist literary traditions.

In past years scholars would not have suggested that Samaria or Bethel was the locus for the emergence of religious traditions, because they assumed that the extensive destruction and deportation of the people by the Assyrians was too great for any subsequent creative intellectual activity. We were reading 2 Kgs 17:24–41 too literally, as it described the destruction of the north, and we failed to realize that this portrayal of northern religious activity after 722 BCE was overtly negative because it was a southern perspective designed to discredit the Yahwistic religion practiced in the north. Modern critical historians inform us that Assyrian and Babylonian

---

25. Klein, "Ort and Zeit."

26. Schmitt, *Alten Testament*, 228. Though he did not date Elohist texts, Pleins, *Social Visions*, 126–134, evaluated the social ethics of the Elohist as ultimately addressing an exilic audience, in particular, the folk of Judah.

deportations removed only the populace of urban centers while other segments of the population remained in place. Archaeological evidence indicates that the Assyrians attempted to keep Israel in the north, the Assyrian province of Samarina, in a productive mode, and thus much of the north outside of Samaria remained a viable society.[27] Critical historians who build upon these archaeological findings admonish us not to overlook the significance of the land of Israel in this era. There was no break in cultural continuity, only 27,000 of the Israelites were exiled according to Assyrian records, and that only constituted one-fifth to one-fourth of the population.[28]

These newer historical perceptions make it very likely that a vibrant theological tradition could have emerged in the north after the 722 BCE defeat of the kingdom, and this theological reflection upon such a defeat could have created our Elohist tradition. Remaining folk included people in the highlands where the Yahwistic prophets had support, and some form of Yahwistic faith was revered. As a site apart from Samaria, the shrine at Bethel continued to function, and if we disallow the propagandistic nature of the Deuteronomistic message in 2 Kings 17, we should assume that religious activity there was closer to a traditional pre-exilic form of Yahwism than our Deuteronomistic authors might concede. Of course, the calf cult was practiced there, and any form of pre-exilic Yahwism in both Israel and Judah was far removed from the monotheistic faith that would emerge during and after the exile. So now we should assume that Yahwistic religious activity continued in Bethel, which perhaps sought to purify itself after the fall of Samaria, including the removal of the calf cult.

If Josiah believed it necessary to destroy shrines at Bethel and Samaria and kill the priests (2 Kgs 23:15–20), there must have been significant religious activity and devotion to Yahweh, which Josiah found to be unacceptable and a clear rival to the temple worship in Jerusalem. If this is true, there could have been centers in the north, such as Bethel itself, where prophetic traditions, including the Elohist, might have been remembered. With the importance of Bethel in Elohist accounts, one might suggest that the traditions emerged and were shaped in that center. We have not been inclined to suggest this because our present biblical text implies that the shrine at Bethel was a hotbed of pagan or syncretistic worship, which was the Deuteronomistic justification of Josiah's vengeful destruction of it and

27. Tappy, *Israelite Samaria II*; and Zertal, "Province of Samaria."
28. Knoppers, "In Search"; and Moore and Kelle, *Biblical History*, 305–9.

the murder of priests. Unconsciously we accepted the Deuteronomistic interpretation and assumed that no tradition found in our present biblical text could have originated in such a setting.

In the past when we wrote a history of Israelite religion, we did not reconstruct the religion of the northern state, Israel, as a distinct form of Yahwism different from that in Judah. We assumed that the religious piety of Israel should have been the same as that found in Judah, but that it was corrupted by foreign influence and syncretism after the division of the two kingdoms, thus it was outside the pale of true Yahwism. Now we sense that there were different Yahwisms, to be sure, all legitimate, all of which would flow into and be reformed by exilic and post-exilic Judaism. The Yahwism in Israel and the Yahwism in Judah were different, but these differences between Bethel and Jerusalem may have been less than the final edition of Kings implies when it characterizes the religion of the north as totally corrupt. Thus, it is possible that northern traditions from Bethel or other shrines in the north were cannibalized into the Pentateuch, especially by the Yahwist and Deuteronomistic Historians, because there was theological continuity in terms of basic religious beliefs. Of course, once the integration of northern traditions occurred, the origin of those northern traditions was forgotten with the final exilic or post-exilic editions of the Deuteronomistic History and Priestly redaction of the Pentateuch.

As Bethel continued to function as the religious center for what was left of Israel after Samaria's destruction, Elohist traditions may have been gathered and shaped there as a religious and ideological tool for reform and purification of the cult. This would explain the character of some of the narratives in the books of Leviticus and Numbers, which are viewed as Deuteronomistic or Priestly by us, but seem to have northern agenda that would fit with Elohist theology. Nadab and Abihu were priestly sons of Aaron who died for sacrificing with unholy fire (Lev 10:1–2). This passage is considered a Priestly text, but the two names are similar to the names of the two sons of Jeroboam I, and thus we suspect some northern Elohist agenda originally lies behind the story. Aaron and Jeroboam I both made golden calves, and the calf cult at Bethel may have been seen after 722 BCE as one of the reasons for the fall of Samaria. Hence, the death of Nadab and Abihu may be critical polemic against the calf cult. The rebellion of Korah (Num 16:1–35), often seen as a Deuteronomistic or Priestly account, might originally have been part of an Elohist critique of northern priests who supported the calf cult. An early version of this story may have contained veiled allusions to particular families who supported the royal house and the calf cult and were subsequently seen as responsible for bringing judgment upon the kingdom. Other allusions and narratives that vaguely recall the conflict between priestly families (Mushites and Aaronides) may reflect the conflict between reformers and others in the shrine at Bethel during the seventh century. As these accounts were absorbed into the southern Deuteronomistic and Priestly traditions, the agenda of those passages were forgotten and the feeling of that northern setting in Bethel was lost. Similarly, Baruch Levine suggested that stories in the book of Numbers often assigned to the Deuteronomist by contemporary commentators might originally have been Elohist accounts.[29]

Elohist traditions in those early years might have recalled stories about the patriarchs, especially Jacob, the exodus from Egypt, the wilderness wanderings, perhaps some legal materials, such as the Decalogue and the Book of the Covenant, which scholars over the years oft have attributed to the Elohist. If purification of the cult was important, perhaps material, which later came to be part of the Priestly legal material in the Pentateuch, might have originated there in Bethel also.

Aside from this discussion of the origin of Elohist traditions, other scholars have theorized that Bethel was a center of literary and theological activity after the destruction of Samaria in 722 BCE and continuing through the seventh century.[30] Some have further suggested that Bethel was a religious center for folk in Judah even after the destruction of Jerusalem in 586 BCE until at least 540 BCE. Only in the Persian period did Jerusalem finally surpass Bethel to become the religious center for the bulk of the population in Judah.[31] Scholars suggest that in spite of Josiah's destruction in 621 BCE, Bethel continued as a shrine,[32] but some even suspect that this destruction by Josiah may be a fiction and that Bethel was not destroyed at all.[33] The role of Bethel as a shrine for those in Judah is inferred on the

---

29. Levine, *Numbers 21–36*, 128.

30. Pfeiffer, *Heiligtum*; Rofé, "Ephraimite"; Guillaume, *Waiting for Josiah*; and Gomes, *Sanctuary of Bethel*.

31. Pfeiffer, *Heiligtum*; Guillaume, *Waiting for Josiah*, 152, believed this is the era in which the literature was bequeathed to Jerusalem; Blenkinsopp, "Judean Priesthood"; Blenkinsopp, "Bethel"; Amit, "Epoch and Genre," who believed Jerusalem and Bethel were rivals; Gomes, *Sanctuary of Bethel*; Knauf, "Bethel"; Knauf, "Archaeology of the Hexateuch," 277, 284; and Davies, *Biblical Israel*, 159–71.

32. Hurowitz, "Babylon in Bethel," 446.

33. Gomes, *Sanctuary of Bethel*, 217–22; and Guillaume, *Waiting for Josiah*, 152.

basis of texts in Jer 41:4; 48:13; Zech 7:2–3 that refer to people coming from Bethel to Jerusalem in the Chaldean period.[34] This might imply that Elohist traditions could have moved south to Jerusalem at some point after Josiah's destruction of Bethel during the sixth century. Thus, we must describe the parameters for the provenance of Elohist fragments to be both seventh and sixth centuries.

I suggest that the impetus for the emergence of Elohist traditions was the destruction of the northern state. It has been similarly suggested that the creation of the Psalms of Asaph was caused by the deterioration of the Israelite state in the 740s and 730s BCE.[35] So other literature may have arisen out of the same social and political chaos. When the Assyrians reduced the kingdom of Israel to an Assyrian province, Samerina, the loss of group identity led intelligentsia, especially religious leaders, to articulate a new self-identity built upon religious traditions rather than political, nationalistic values. The same process occurred two centuries later for exiles of Judah in Babylon and Palestine, and this resulted in Yahwistic, revised Deuteronomistic, and Priestly literature in the Pentateuch. Would it not be logical that literature could be generated by the same social-historical forces in the northern state in the seventh century and beyond? If intelligentsia in Judah and Babylon generated the Deuteronomistic History and the Priestly additions during and after the exile, we need to accept the possibility that a similar process of theological reflection may have occurred in the north, in Israel, during the seventh century. We simply have not really considered this as a viable option in the past, when it makes as much sense as our other paradigms of exilic behavior.

Critical scholars have suggested for years the similarity between the Elohist and the Deuteronomic traditions. Deuteronomic theology emerged before the exile and became more developed in the early years of the exile, according to some theories.[36] Emerging soon after the destruction of Jerusalem in 586 BCE, the final edition of the Deuteronomistic History placed a heavy emphasis upon warning about impending doom for the kingdom to explain why such horrible destruction befell the Judeans and Jerusalem. Later Yahwistic and Priestly traditions did not proclaim such a message of judgment and impending doom, but implied that there was grace, forgiveness, and future hope. The Elohist may be similar to the Deuteronomic

---

34. Knauf, "Bethel," 295, 319.
35. Goulder, *Psalms of Asaph*.
36. Cross, *Canaanite Myth*, 274–89; and Nelson, *Double Redaction*.

The Social and Theological Setting of the Elohist

traditions because of its initial emergence after the destruction of Samaria in 722 BCE. Both betray a stern religious character with the emphasis upon obedience to God and moral behavior. Also, if the Elohist traditions came south from Bethel to Jerusalem after Josiah's conquest of Bethel, the Elohist narratives may have directly influenced Deuteronomic thought.

As noted earlier, Joel Baden observed that Deuteronomy 1–9 appears to know Elohist texts as a distinct entity without Yahwist texts or redaction, so that, no so-called combined JE Epic existed prior to the Deuteronomistic History. Baden also indicated that the Deuteronomistic Historian was familiar with a separate Yahwist text, but used it seldom in contrast to the heavy usage of the Elohist tradition. He believed the Deuteronomistic Historian favored using the Elohist because of the prophetic role of Moses, the law codes in Exodus 20–23, and the wilderness traditions. Baden's argument reinforces my belief that the Elohist traditions were separate in the late seventh century, when the Deuteronomistic Historian would have used them, and they were not woven together with Yahwist traditions until the Yahwist Historian inherited them in the late sixth century.[37]

At the same time we need to account for some of the dissimilarities between the Elohistic and Deuteronomic theological traditions. The Elohist tradition respects dream revelation while the Deuteronomic tradition (Deut 13:2–6) and Jeremiah (Jer 23:25–32; 27:9–10; 29:8–9) condemn dreams as a mode of revelation. Scholars assumed that since the Elohist tradition arose earlier than these southern theologians, we were simply observing a historical evolution in which a once accepted mode of revelation simply was rejected in later years. Even I worked with this assumption.[38] But with this newer paradigm, it might be better to suggest that the Elohist was sympathetic to dream revelation at shrines, because that was a phenomenon which occurred at Bethel and other sites in the north, while the Deuteronomic tradition and Jeremiah opposed dream theophanies because they viewed the temple as the place where worship should occur, and dream theophanies were not a characteristic religious phenomenon there.[39] Thus, the opposition to dream theophanies may not be the result of religious development but rather regional theologies. This would then permit the Elohist to be contemporary with the greater Deuteronomic tradition.

---

37. Baden, *Redaction of the Pentateuch*, 106–7, 137–72, 197–207, 218–60, 311–12.

38. Gnuse, "Theological Significance," 166–71, *Dream Theophany of Samuel*, 57–118, and *Dreams and Dreams Reports*, 68–101.

39. Coote, *Defense of Revolution*, 112–13.

The Elohist

As this new model envisions a different relationship between Elohist and Deuteronomic traditions, it can suggest a different way of describing the relationship of the Elohist tradition to the prophet Hosea. Hosea's relationship to the Elohist tradition has occupied the attention of scholars in the past. For example, Procksch boldly declared that Hosea was exclusively dependent upon the Elohist.[40] However, Jenks critiqued Procksch's arguments and suggested that Hosea's connection to the Elohist was so minimal that the prophet may have had recourse to an oral tradition separate from both the Yahwist and the Elohist. To be sure, Hosea was familiar with Elohist stories, such as Jacob's birth, the flight to Aram, the Bethel revelation, service to Laban, and the confrontation at Penuel. But in Jenk's opinion both Yahwist and Elohist elements were found in Hosea's oracles only in rudimentary form. The only true continuity between Hosea and the Elohist include: 1) the characterization of Moses as a prophet (Hos 12:14), 2) the condemnation of the calf cult, and 3) an anti-royal bias.[41]

But let us reverse the order and place Hosea prior to the Elohist; it would explain why Hosea's knowledge and use of the Elohist is rudimentary. With the reversal, Hosea's motifs could be seen as the inspiration for the Elohist, and their simpler form, observed by Jenks, would be more logical.

Suggesting that the Elohist traditions arose in Bethel and that they sought to understand the destruction of Israel as punishment for the sins of the kings and the calf cult can explain the character of other texts. In the past those who described the theology of the Elohist noted that this tradition was interested in and supportive of northern cult shrines, such as Bethel. Yet the tradition was also very critical of the calf cult at Dan and Bethel. How do we explain this tension? If the tradition arose after the fall of Samaria, the Elohist supported the legitimacy of Bethel as a shrine, but declared that it was polluted by the calf cult and hence led to the punishment of the kingdom. Accounts of Aaron and the calf (Exod 32:1–29), and Jeroboam and his calf shrines at Dan and Bethel (1 Kgs 12:26–32), were remembered critically, even though Bethel was a revered shrine by virtue of the patriarch Jacob's connection to it (Gen 28:10–22; 35:1–15). This two-edged theological assessment, legitimation and condemnation, logically would be the portrayal we should expect soon after the fall of Israel and Samaria. The revered shrine of Bethel, polluted by the calf cult, in which Israelites too directly worshiped the calf, and thus, made it responsible, in

---

40. Procksch, *Sagenbuch*, 248–55.
41. Jenks, *The North Israelite Traditions*, 113–17.

part, for the fall of the kingdom, had to be purified for the future so that it could function as the religious center for those northern Israelites who have survived the disaster. This tension between affirmation of the shrine and yet condemnation of the calf cult is best explained after the destruction of the state of Israel. In similar fashion, Ezekiel condemned the temple cult in Ezekiel 8–11 as a primary reason for the destruction of Jerusalem in 586 BCE, but he envisioned a restored and purified temple cult in Ezekiel 40–48 that would be the center of Judahite life in the future. The shrine of Bethel for the Elohist, like the later temple for Ezekiel and others, remained a revered symbol for the believers of the north, despite its calf cult pollution. The same Elohist theologian most likely respected and recalled the comparable critique of Hosea against the calf cult.[42] Scholars have discussed for years the similarities between the two accounts of the golden calves (Exod 32:1–35; 1 Kgs 12:25–33), which may have influenced the other. The model that postulated an early Elohist tradition suggested that Exod 32:1–35 influenced 1 Kgs 12:25–33, but many commentators suspected that the Jeroboam narrative was the older account, or that there was an unrecoverable complex history of inter-relationships between the two passages. This new paradigm can accept the priority of some essential form of 1 Kgs 12:25–33, which then inspired the generation of Exod 32:1–35. The narrative with Aaron may then be seen as a direct critique of Jeroboam I, and all the later Israelite kings, because it was a post–722 BCE creation. The preservation of both narratives serves to condemn Israel's kings and their royal cult at Bethel, and thus implies yet again this behavior led to the destruction of the state.

In conclusion, a coherent argument can be construed to suggest a seventh- and sixth-century origin for Elohist traditions. Suggestive arguments posed by the Balaam traditions and dream reports point to the seventh century, as well as the priority of prophetic narratives to the Pentateuch Elohist. Viewing Elohist narratives as a response to the fall of Samaria appears to provide a good understanding for the nature of the texts, especially since the same phenomena occurred after the destruction of Jerusalem in 586 BCE. Several contemporary scholarly studies dovetail nicely with this hypothesis. Although the paradigm may appear tentative, nonetheless, a number of scholarly issues may make better sense in the light of this new theory.

42. Gnuse, "Calf, Cult, and King."

The Elohist

How does the Elohist relate to the fuller narrative in the Pentateuch? By Elohist we mean both the prophetic narratives (proto-Elohist, if you will) and the Pentateuchal narratives. They arose in the northern state of Israel and were related to each other literarily and theologically. The Elohist may never have been a unified oral or written epic; it may have been "pools of traditions," or at best cycles of separate accounts somewhat related to each other (as Yoreh suggested). Elohist narratives, both prophetic and pentateuchal, appear to have been used by the Deuteronomistic Historian in the seventh and sixth centuries and the Yahwist Historian in the late sixth century or early fifth. Elohist narratives were at best loosely connected so that they were absorbed into those southern cycles of literature and redacted by having additional narrative put into them and by having additional and parallel stories placed alongside Elohist accounts. That additional narrative was far more expansive than the original Elohist materials. Thus, Elohist stories were submerged into longer narratives that were predominately Yahwistic or Deuteronomistic in character and theological message. This is what makes recovery by modern scholars so difficult and subjective. The Elohist narrative or "pools" of Elohist tradition never became a truly overarching epic narrative (certainly lacking a Primeval History) until being absorbed in those more expansive histories. Ultimately, the Priestly Editors would create the final grand epic by reworking the Yahwist history and making Elohist accounts even more elusive to isolate.

The bulk of the Elohist traditions appear to have been drawn up into the Yahwist History. How might this have been done by the Yahwist Historian? In the mind of this author, that is still an undecided issue. There are two theories one might advocate. Perhaps, there was a fragmentary or loose Yahwistic oral tradition originating in Judah in the monarchic period similar to the "Elohist pools of tradition" in the north. The late sixth or early fifth-century Yahwist Historian then wove together both of these loose Elohistic and Yahwistic cycles of tradition. (This sounds like Carr's theory of the "proto-Genesis" author.) This would appear to be the old JE Redactor spoken of by scholars in years past. The other theory might suggest that the Yahwist Historian should be credited with the creation of much of the text. The Yahwist may have had some varied sources and crafted much of the narrative material to complement or critique Elohist texts, as Yoreh suggested. Or perhaps, the Yahwist had varied sources, which included a few Elohist accounts, in the generation of the creative new history, as Van Seters suggested.[43] Van Seters admitted the use of sources by the exilic Yahwist, and he admitted that those texts formerly called Elohistic might be some of the especially old sources used by the exilic Yahwist historian. Van Seters, however, demurred from discussing them as a truly significant theological entity, preferring to describe the historiographical skills of the exilic Yahwist author.

Either way, the supposition of a seventh- or sixth-century provenance of Elohistic tradition would not be incompatible with the evaluation of the Yahwist Historian, however you might wish to define that tradition. Ultimately, both the Yahwist and the Elohist received their final concrete literary formation at the hands of Priestly Editors during and after the Babylonian Exile. The northern prophetic narratives in Kings precipitated into written form in the hands of Deuteronomistic Historians in the seventh and sixth centuries. If I were to summarize this theory, it would be called the EDJP theory. In actuality, the process is probably far more complex than that. Perhaps, the full complexity of this oral and literary evolution of the Primary History (Genesis through 2 Kings) may never be recovered by us, for we only observe the final literary product.

---

43. Van Seters, *Abraham*, 130, 311 ; and Van Seters, *Prologue to History*, 5, 328.

6

Theology of the Elohist

The Message to Israelites

IF THE ELOHIST TRADITION is dated to the seventh or sixth century, then our evaluation of the theological message of these texts will change from what scholars have postulated in the past. Themes in the Pentateuchal Elohist would deal with foreign rule and the exile of the people. One of the significant critiques made to deny the existence of the Elohist is that there are insufficient texts from which to craft the Elohist's theological message.[1] Hopefully, with this new perspective, a significant theological message can be crafted. In what follows, I present an expanded exposition of the second half of one of my previously published articles, "The Elohist: A 7th Century BCE Theological Tradition," *BTB* 42 (2012) 59–69. Therefore, let us consider the themes that might be located in Elohist texts in the Pentateuch primarily and also the prophetic narratives.

Destruction of the Kingdom and Exile

If the Elohist fragments arose in the seventh century, then we should find hints of exile and national destruction. Schmitt suggested that certain Elohist texts reflect awareness of Israel's destruction (Genesis 22; Numbers 22) and foreign rule in the land (Gen 20:1; 21:23, 34).[2] Genesis 22 hints at the

---

1. Whybray, *Making of the Pentateuch*, 112.
2. Schmitt, *Alten Testament*, 228. See also Pleins, *Social Visions*, 126–34.

potential destruction of the kingdom by implying that the death of Isaac could occur. The death of the heir so early in patriarchal history would have destroyed the future of the kingdom. Numbers 22 hints that Israel's future might have been ended by the powerful seer Balaam were it not for divine intervention. Other passages also offer hints of an exiled audience. Abraham is described as an alien in Gen 20:1, he speaks of himself as an alien in the land according to Gen 21:23, and according to Gen 21:34 he is said to have been an alien for many days. The allusion to being an alien for "many days" may foreshadow the exile of the northern ten tribes. The underlying message is that God will be with the exiles who sojourn as aliens. I suspect that one of the significant agenda of the Elohist tales was to affirm that God was with the Israelites after the destruction of Samaria. Wherever they sojourned, they would not disappear, and as Isaac was spared and not sacrificed, so they also would be spared.

Justification for the Fall of Samaria

The Elohist may have addressed the fall of Samaria in a similar fashion to how the Deuteronomistic History addressed the fall of Jerusalem: the sins of the people brought about the destruction of their country. Elohist accounts criticize the actions of kings and the calf cult at Bethel, which kings sponsored. Perhaps, the Elohist highlighted these actions as the chief causes for the destruction of the kingdom. Perhaps, Hosea's critique of the calf cult was one of the precursors to Elohist thought. (He, too, saw Moses as a prophet, Hos 12:4.) The critique of the calf cult recalls Ezekiel 8–11 with its stern condemnation of the religious abuses at the temple in Jerusalem, thus justifying the Babylonian destruction the city and the temple. Both the Elohist and the Deuteronomistic History remind us of ancient Near Eastern laments that spoke of how destruction fell upon cities because of their religious sins. The biblical authors added that social sins, like the seizure of Naboth's vineyard by Ahab and Jezebel (1 Kgs 21:1–29), also brought divine wrath. People were warned. At the "mountain of God" they were told by God, "In the day when I visit, I will visit their sin upon them" (Exod 32:4). Perhaps the stern morality found in both of those traditions reflects the response by biblical authors after the destruction of the kingdom that called for an acceptance of the responsibility for that destruction, followed by a renewed commitment to God. Elohist texts allude to "great guilt" (Gen 20:9; Exod 32:30–31), perhaps an allusion to the sin of the people. Though the Elohist may hint at the notion of divine abandonment for the people's sins; nonetheless, God is still with the people in exile and has not forsaken them completely.

Divine Accompaniment

If the Elohist spoke to Israelites after they were dispersed, then a number of passages make much more sense to us. Often God speaks to the patriarchs and promises to be with them on their journey. Biblical commentators refer to this as the theme of divine accompaniment. This theme would take on deep existential importance, if the author implied that God would be with later Israelites wherever they might be scattered after the destruction of the kingdom. Burnett characterized this theme as an overarching theme in the Elohist narratives, and it possibly implies that the Elohist's accounts were part of a unified narrative.[3]

A number of passages allude to the landless situation of the biblical personage and the corresponding promise of divine presence. Many of these statements make reference to a "return to the land," which makes sense if the audience is either exiles or the remaining people in the land of Israel who anticipate the return of exiles. Abraham hears in Gen 21:22 that "God is with you in all that you do." Jacob affirms the divine presence for himself in Gen 31:5 when he declares, "the God of my father has been with me." In Gen 46:3, Jacob, whose name now is Israel, is told, "Do not be afraid to go down into Egypt." Is this a message that said to exiles from Israel that they should not fear to continue to take refuge in Egypt after the destruction of Samaria, for God will be with them in a foreign land? Interestingly, Hosea also recalls that there will be an exile of people to Egypt and ultimately a return to the land of Israel (Hos 11:5).

Graupner saw the message of divine accompaniment in the greater cycle of narratives. Thus, the movement in Jacob's life from his first encounter with God at Bethel in Genesis 28 to his return and commitment to God in Genesis 35 conveys to the listener the idea that God accompanied Jacob throughout his life and his journeys. The message of the entire Elohist tradition is that God will take care of the people and accompany them wherever they might be.[4]

---

3. Burnett, *Biblical Elohim*, 138–39.
4. Graupner, *Elohist.* 55–56, 308–11.

Theology of the Elohist

Promise of Return to the Land

Several biblical texts that speak of divine presence also make reference to a return to the land. In some instances the patriarch declares his intention to return to the land. In Gen 28:21 Jacob says, "I will return to the land of my fathers." In Gen 31:13 Jacob is characterized as an exile when he is told to "return to the land of your birth." Again, in Gen 35:1 Jacob is told, "arise go to Bethel, dwell there, and make an altar there." This passage would be poignant, if it were spoken to exiles after the shrine of Bethel was destroyed in the late eighth century. Later, Jacob is promised by God that he will return home in Gen 46:4, "I will surely bring you back up." In Gen 48:21 Jacob is again told, "God will be with you and will bring you back to the land of your fathers." Among commentators in the past these divine statements were seen to be hints of a message of divine presence for the patriarchs, which implied ownership of the land someday after Joshua's conquest of the land or David's unification of the country. But if we posit a date after the 722 BCE destruction of Israel and Samaria, they could refer to the hope of return for Israelites to the northern state, for Jacob is the eponym of the northern state. When God declares to Jacob that he will come back to his homeland, the listeners would certainly feel that the message was spoken also to them.

Graupner made an observation from a subtle reading of the text. The reference to bringing Joseph's bones back to Canaan (Exod 13:30) implies that the Israelites are returning home, not entering a new land.[5] This image might speak to exiles more clearly than an invasion account, for it tells them that they might have an exodus that brings them back home to Israel in peaceful fashion.

Balaam's vision for Israel's future appears to be dramatically hopeful, apparently not dampened by the harsh reality of defeat and exile of Israelites.[6] The rather extensive nature of the Balaam oracles in their original form, without those added allusions to Judah, indicate that a significant agenda for the Elohist was the proclamation of hope for the future.

---

5. Ibid., 74, 113.
6. Ibid., 398.

The Elohist

Restoration of Shrines and Worship

Scholars often have pointed out how Elohist texts allude to significant northern shrines, such as Beersheba (Gen 21:9–32), Bethel (Gen 31:2–16; 35:1–7), and Shechem (Gen 35:14). If we suppose a seventh- or sixth-century date for the Elohist, these allusions could be in the accounts in order to inspire the hope for the restoration of those shrines and the worship practices connected to them. The Elohist certainly does not advocate centralization in Jerusalem. The interest in northern shrines remains in the text even though our present narrative comes to us from later editors, like the Yahwist, who supported centralization in Jerusalem, and is clearly indicative of the use of earlier sources.[7]

Bethel seems to have been important for the Elohist. Even though the calf cult was established there and abrasively critiqued by the Elohist both in 1 Kgs 12:25–33 (perhaps an Elohist account lies behind this narrative) and Exod 32:1–24 (even more likely an Elohist account), Bethel was still the most premier shrine. In comparable fashion, the Deuteronomistic History could condemn religious abuses in the Jerusalem temple, but still proclaim the centrality of worship there.

Enhanced Ethical or Moral Awareness

Moralistic Elohist texts oft have been compared with the more earthy texts of the Yahwist by scholars for years, most recently by Joel Burnett.[8] In Genesis 20 the endangering of the ancestress theme contrasts with similar narratives in Genesis 12 and 26. In this narrative, Abraham is portrayed as truthful in declaring Sarah to be his sister (Gen 20:3, 12), we are told clearly that Abimelech did not touch Sarah (Gen 20:4a), Abimelech affirms that his people are "innocent" (Gen 20:4) (the "innocent people" reference in v. 4b may be Yahwist), God declares that Abimelech has "integrity" and was kept from sinning (Gen 20:6), Abimelech chides Abraham for his deception (Gen 20:9–10) but gives him generous gifts (Gen 20:14–15), and Abraham graciously intercedes in prayer for Abimelech's poor pregnant women whose delivery dates had been postponed (Gen 20:17–18). The story is sappy with examples of pious behavior and apologetic rhetoric, especially from Abimelech, the foreign king. Other examples of ethical

---

7. Pleins, *Social Visions*, 130.
8. Burnett, *Biblical Elohim*, 128.

and pious behavior include how Abraham has concern over Hagar's treatment by Sarah (Gen 21:11–12) and how Jacob's prosperity is attributed to divine providence, not his own cunning in sheep breeding (Gen 31:5–9, 16, 36–42). This increased piety and ethical sensitivity makes sense in the light of destruction and exile of Israelites. Biblical authors must encourage a people who have been conquered and exiled to preserve their religious identity, deep piety, and their moral integrity, as a way of surviving as a religious entity. As noted above, the Elohist and the Deuteronomistic History both share this same agenda, proclaiming a new stern morality after the destruction of the kingdom.

There is a passionate plea for moral behavior. People must commit themselves anew. As Jacob removed and buried the foreign gods (Gen 35:2), so people must do likewise in their new situation. Perhaps, they are now to totally reject the practice of infant sacrifice, following the lesson of how God told Abraham to sacrifice the ram instead of Isaac (Genesis 22). The image of the awesome transcendent deity may inspire the self-surrender of individuals and the community to the will of God. For leadership they should no longer look to the kings who failed them, but to God's appointed prophets. (After all, had not their prophets in the form of Elijah, defeated the prophets who represented the gods of foreign peoples?)

Transcendent Deity

When exiled people are scattered abroad in many lands, they need to be assured about the presence of their God. As mentioned above, Elohim accompanies believers. However, there is another aspect of the divine nature that must also receive increased theological attention. If God is a deity that can be present in all places, then God is a truly high and transcendent deity whose authority reigns over the entire world. Subsequently this high and distant God must also be able to communicate through the appropriate modes of revelation that preserve both the transcendence of the divine and the immediacy of divine presence required by revelation.

In Yahwist narratives God often is portrayed vividly in anthropomorphic and anthropopathic fashion so as to emphasize the nearness and the graciousness of God, but in Elohist narratives God is portrayed as more distant and this deity communicates through indirect modes of revelation. Elohim is high and distant because the biblical author wishes for the audience to perceive that their God can be worshipped anywhere in the world by the chosen people, who are now painfully scattered everywhere. The indirect modes of revelation by which that high and awesome deity communicates to the community of the faithful are the angel of God, dreams, fire, a voice from the heavens, and most important of all, the prophets.

The transcendence of God conveys a subtle psychological message. It implies that God is a high deity who is universal, the God of all people. But the high and majestic imagery connected to this deity also implies that people should have a fear of God that leads to obedience.[9] This is best demonstrated by the response of the people at Horeb where they exhibit fear in the presence of the awesome and majestic theophany up on the mountain. Furthermore, people are tested by this awesome deity to see whether they truly have a deep and sincere fear of God.[10] True obedience can lead to restoration and the avoidance of another disastrous experience like the 722 BCE destruction.

The Elohist affirms dreams as a mode of revelation for the divine, except for Moses, to whom God speaks clearly (Exod 19:12; 20:19; 33:7–11; Num 12:6–8). By contrast, Deuteronomy (Deut 12:2–6) and Jeremiah (Jer 23:25–32; 27:9–10; 29:8–9) condemn dreams. If, according to my model of development, these theological traditions were fairly contemporary, this difference of opinion may reflect regional pieties rather than theological evolution over the years. Dreams were not acceptable forms of revelation in the temple at the time of Jeremiah, while they may have been such at Bethel. After all, did not the eponym of the north, Jacob, receive a significant dream theophany at Bethel according to Gen 28:10–22? The Yahwist inserted vv. 13–14 so that Yahweh speaks directly to Jacob while standing beside him in order to lessen the imagery of a dream in Gen 28:10–22. But the dream imagery did not disappear completely, perhaps the Yahwist Historian did not totally share the critique of dreams found in the Deuteronomistic History, for the Yahwist ultimately preserved the elements of Elohist dream reports throughout Genesis.

Universal God of All People

Some critical scholars suggest that the Elohist's view of God portrays Elohim/Yahweh as the god of all people.[11] The dream revelations to Abimelech

---

9. Graupner, *Elohist*, 13–14.
10. Ibid., 152.
11. Ibid., 395; Pleins, *Social Visions*, 127–28; and Schmidt, *Alten Testament*, 230.

Theology of the Elohist

(Gen 20:3–7), Laban (Gen 31:24), and Balaam (Num 22:9; 23:4, 16), the divine address to Hagar (Gen 21:17–18), and the knowledge of God demonstrated by Jethro (Exod 18:12), all of whom are theoretically foreigners, imply that God can speak to and through all people, because God rules over all people in the world. Balaam, in particular, becomes a significant avenue for divine revelation, a very strong testimony to how Elohim/Yahweh is the God of all people. The divine affirmation of the trip into Egypt undertaken by Joseph and later by Jacob (Gen 46:1–4) may imply that God can work through these foreign rulers,[12] and this certainly speaks to Israelite exiles scattered across the ancient world. Some authors, such as McEvenue, go further and declare that the implications of such a concept of a universal deity include affirmation of universal friendship between all people, as epitomized by the working relationship between Abraham and Abimelech.[13]

The frequent use of both Elohim and Yahweh as divine names for God, even after the revelation of the special name Yahweh to Moses, may have special significance. The Elohist may wish to impress upon the audience that Elohim and Yahweh are the same deity because perhaps that was not the given understanding among all Israelites. The unification of these two names in the minds of people would have become increasingly important after the 722 BCE destruction.[14] If so, it may reflect a theological move in the direction of monotheism. One immediately is reminded of the challenge posed by Elijah to the people to worship Baal or Yahweh. The Elijah accounts may have been shaped after 722 BCE to reinforce this call to equate Elohim and Yahweh and to worship Yahweh more exclusively. Burnett suggested that the theophany to Moses in Exodus 3 and the contest on Mt. Carmel in 1 Kings 18 answer the same question: Who is God (Elohim)? The answer is that God is Yahweh, therefore we must worship Yahweh and no other.[15] This may not be an intolerant monotheism that radically denies the existence of other gods, as we find with Second Isaiah. But it is an exclusive monotheism that calls upon Israelites to make the equation of Elohim and Yahweh and then to worship only that one God.[16] Burnett suspected that the narrative movement that calls God Elohim until Exodus 3 and then

---

12. Pleins, *Social Visions*, 128.
13. McEvenue, *Pentateuch*, 102.
14. Burnett, *Biblical Elohim*, 150–51.
15. Ibid., 149.
16. Ibid., 148–49.

uses Yahweh and Elohim thereafter implies that the Elohist may have been a well-defined narrative tradition.

Fear of God and Obedience

Because God is transcendent, people should fear and obey God. The theme of "fear of God" occurs in several Pentateuchal texts and the notion of obedience to God emerges in several stories, even if the words are lacking. The near sacrifice of Isaac, whatever we might think of the barbaric implications of such a command, testifies to the staunch obedience of Abraham to God. The midwives, who refuse to kill the baby boys in Exod 1:15–21, do so because they piously fear God and not human rulers. The people stand in fear of God's presence on Sinai in Exod 20:18–21. Commentators have sensed that the Elohist texts contrast the obedience of the great leaders, Abraham, Jacob, Moses, and Joshua, with the disobedience displayed by the people when put to the test by God.[17] Prophetic narratives in the books of Kings highlight prophets who heed the word of God, and when they fail to do this, lions eat them. It would seem that the Elohist speaks to Israelites and calls upon them to demonstrate obedience to God; unlike the disobedience they displayed that led to the destruction of Samaria.

All the commentators on Elohist theology observe that the strong emphasis upon obedience indicates that the audience of the Elohist faced a social and religious crisis. It may have been the tenth-century creation of a new state, the ninth-century conflict between Elijah and the devotees of Baal, the ninth-century emergence of the new government under Jehu and its later weakened condition before the Arameans, the affluence of the eighth century under Jeroboam II which led to the oppression of the poor and the emergence of the classical prophets, or, as I suggest, the destruction of the state in 722 BCE and the need for Israelites in the land and in exile to create a new self-identity.

The strong emphasis upon fear of God and obedience betokens a call to repentance, to self-renewal, to action, and above all, a call to commitment to God as the starting point for a new identity. One would imagine that the highest agenda in this regard was the call for people to worship Yahweh exclusively, for he alone was the Elohim of all history. This exclusive worship was not necessarily absolute monotheism; rather, it was a

---

17. Jenks, "Elohist," 2:481.

radical commitment that called upon people simply to ignore the other gods, or elohim.

Civil Disobedience—Opposition to Kings and Tyrants

If we include the prophetic narratives in the books of Kings in our assessment of Elohistic theology, we can certainly find the theme of opposition to kings. According to the biblical narratives people should obey prophets, who are the spokespersons for God, and, if necessary, disobey their kings and rulers. The stories of Elijah and Elisha typify dramatic opposition to the king, especially if the king sets himself in opposition to God, as did the Omrides.

In the Pentateuch we can find the same message, especially in accounts concerning Moses, who dares to defy the mighty king of Egypt. Most dramatic is the narrative of the midwives who refuse to kill the baby boys in Exod 1:15–21 because they "feared God." Furthermore, they lie to him and he believes them, because the king is so removed from the real world, or stupid (a common theme throughout the Bible). Chung also saw this theme in Balaam's response to king Balak in Num 22:38 when Balaam states, "I have come to you now, but do I have power to say just anything? The word God puts in my mouth, that is what I must say." Balaam thus declares to the king that he cannot speak what the king demands, but he can only say what God directs him to speak.[18]

This theological theme especially merits our consideration so as to view the Elohist as a distinct theological tradition. The folly of kings was primarily responsible for Israel's destruction. The biblical author may recall indirectly those last few kings in the 730s and 720s BCE of Israel's existence, whose actions brought death and sorrow to so many Israelites as the Assyrian war machine rolled over them. Perhaps, the biblical author implies that in a future age, with some form of restoration, people should not turn to kings for leadership but turn to the prophets and seek their leadership. Perhaps this is why the Elohist seeks to portray Moses as a prophet. As Moses led the Israelite refugees in the wilderness, perhaps a new line of prophets, like Moses, or the seventy elders who prophesied, can lead the remnant of Israel in the future, and lead them authentically in the greater wilderness of the world in which they are dispersed. Maybe the promise of "one like

---

18. Chung, *Sin of the Calf*, 17.

Moses" who would come might have originally been an allusion to such a future figure in Elohist traditions.

Interest in Prophetic Identity

The old prophetic traditions in Samuel and Kings tell us much about prophets, as observed in the previous chapter. We noted particularly the many parallels to be found in the lives of Abraham, Moses, Samuel, Elijah, Elisha, and Joshua that demonstrate interesting patterns shared by the prophetic narratives and the Pentateuchal Elohist.

All of this interest in the prophets indicates that the Elohist believed it necessary for people to hearken to the voices of the prophets. The Elohistic Moses is a dramatic wonder worker as are the prophets Elijah and Elisha in the books of Kings; such representatives of God need to be heeded. The people should have listened to prophets before the destruction of Samaria, and perhaps they should heed the words of prophets in the future. Some biblical scholars suspect that the Elohist advocated charismatic, prophetic leadership for the people.[19] Such a message might be appropriate for people still remaining in the land of Israel after 722 BCE, for they had no state and were ruled by the Assyrians. The Elohist calls upon them to turn to the prophets, now that kings are gone. Perhaps, in light of this we might suggest that the disobedience of the midwives might be seen as some form of resistance to Assyrian rule over the province of Samarina in the seventh century. Such was the suggestion of Knauf, who saw the same message emanating from the stories of Jacob's dealings with Laban, narratives that advocate "resistance by collaboration."[20]

New Identity for the Israelites

If our biblical author hints that people should follow the lead of charismatic prophets, what might be the self-perception that Israelites in the land should have? It has been pointed out by Alan Jenks that the Elohistic texts focus upon prayer, sacrifice, pilgrimage, and prophets. Jenks believed the expression in Exod 19:6 that Israelites should be for God "a priestly kingdom and

---

19. Pleins, *Social Visions*, 130, believed this is a message given to people after the sixth-century Babylonian Exile.

20. Knauf, "Archaeology of the Hexateuch," 284.

a holy nation," is an important passage defining Israelite identity.[21] Jenks dated the Elohist early, but as I look at this passage, it appears to imply that the Elohist might be addressing exiles who lost their group identity. If Jenks is correct in assuming this passage (Exod 19:4–6) is Elohistic, this could be a cardinal testimony to the exilic context of the Elohist.

Thus, perhaps the Elohist called upon people to be a holy nation of priests throughout the world who heed the leadership of their inspired prophets. This would accord well with the Elohist portrayal of the Sinai/Horeb experience. For there the people are in the wilderness (a symbol for exile), they act with fear and reverence, and they are called "a priestly people and a holy nation," while they follow the leadership of Moses, the supreme prophet, who goes up on the mountain to speak "face to face" with God. It seems like the portrayal of the mountain experience in the wilderness provides hints to the audience as to how they should perceive themselves in the seventh century.

Revelation to the Prophets

If the narratives in the Elohist tradition were perhaps organized more than I have suggested, these accounts may have testified to some development in the prophetic tradition and the mode of revelation that occurred for the prophets. Graupner, for example, believed that the Elohist had two ages that were defined by the revelation of the name Yahweh to Moses in Exodus 3. Prior to that time God spoke to people in dreams, after that time revelation was more direct and through the prophets.[22] I would configure the evolutionary process somewhat differently. In the first age, God communicates to the patriarchs through dreams. Recall that Abraham is viewed as a prophet in Gen 20:7, 17. In the second age, God speaks directly to Moses and not through dreams (Num 12:5–8), a disavowal of the prior dream revelations. God speaks to Moses "face to face" (Exod 33:11; Num 14:14) and "mouth to mouth" (Num 12:8). In the third age, God speaks to the prophets in a still, small voice, which is first heard by Elijah (1 Kgs 19:13). Elijah's Horeb experience is the hallmark theophany for the later prophets of the north, for in his experience God no longer is present in wind, earthquake, and fire, perhaps a rejection of the revelatory modes by which God came to Moses. (This, of course, means that we must suggest that the creation of the

21. Jenks, "Elohist," 2:481.
22. Graupner, *Elohist*, 386–87.

Horeb theophany in 1 Kgs 19:9–18 is an Elohist redaction that is later than the other prophetic narratives, and yet not a Deuteronomistic redaction, as suggested by other critical scholars. This is very hypothetical.) I must admit that this interesting paradigm has a flaw, however. Samuel's combined prophetic call and auditory dream message experience in 1 Samuel 3 comes after Moses, not to mention Solomon's dream in 1 Kings 3, which conforms to the format of Elohist dream reports, but otherwise has no appearance of being an Elohist text. Furthermore, in the age of prophets, Elijah and Elisha, cultic functions are no longer performed by the prophets, as Moses and Samuel did when they offered sacrifice. This may reflect a prophetic disavowal of the cult projected into the past reflecting the disaster of 722 BCE. However, that is also rather tenuous to conclude. So perhaps, there was an overarching Elohist model for evolving revelation, but we have lost too many stories to adequately explain it.

I believe there are significant and valuable theological observations we can make, if we work with the model that the Elohist traditions arose in the seventh or sixth centuries as a response to the destruction of Samaria, and if we reflect upon the prophetic traditions in the books of Samuel and Kings along with the narratives in the Pentateuch to craft our theological observations. A meaningful new articulation of the theological message of these texts may provide us with resources for theology in general.

Theological Commentary on Select Elohist Stories

If the Elohist epic were recited orally or read aloud to exiles from the northern state of Israel in Assyria or to refugees remaining in the land, how would they have understood the message? Let us consider the possible meanings that some of these stories might have elicited for such depressed and defeated people.

Gen 15:12–21 (Abraham's vision). In the ancient Near East participants in a covenant making ritual walked between cut animals and called upon their deities to cut them in half, if they broke the stipulations of the covenant. God passes between cut animals and thus symbolically declares that God should be cut in half, if the promise to Abraham were broken. This is truly a powerful story with which to begin the Elohist epic. It would also be a powerful message of hope to exiles from the northern tribes in the seventh century that God would be forever faithful to them.

Gen 20:1–4a, 5–17 (Abimelech's court). As the pagan king Abimelech exhibits piety and has a conscience, so also other foreigners may exhibit such piety toward the true God. This universalism might be appropriate for an audience of seventh-century Israelites scattered among foreign lands.

Genesis 21:2–8 (Isaac's birth). The birth of a son to an old couple is truly a sign from God. Exiles would fear the loss of their family genealogies if they had no children, or if children were killed in the wars and the trials of exile. This account speaks a message of hope; God will give them children in exile to keep alive the promise.

Gen 21:9–21 (Hagar's flight). With ethical sensitivity the Elohist says that God provides for both Hagar and Ishmael, even though Hagar is an Egyptian, and they shall be blessed in their own way. Hagar and Ishmael find themselves in "exile," but they will be successful, and such is the promise this story gives to exiles who are in the "wilderness" like Hagar.

Gen 21:22–31 (covenant with Abimelech). Israelites may have peaceful relationships with foreigners, even formal legal relationships, just as mutual trust and loyalty existed between Abraham and Abimelech.[23] This might tell seventh-century Israelite exiles to accept their exile, work with those powers that rule, and thereby survive and maybe even prosper.

Gen 22:1–13, 19 (sacrifice of Isaac). To speak of testing and obedience is important for exiles to hear, for they probably asked why God let their kingdom be destroyed. Though the story sounds horrible to us, the Israelites had lived through brutal experiences and had seen many of their friends and family members slain. They are called upon to continue trusting in God, even though it seemed as if God had deserted them, as it seemed that God had deserted Abraham by making this request. The story ends with God preventing Abraham from sacrificing Isaac, so perhaps the story was meant to encourage Israelites no longer to offer up the first-born son as a burnt offering.

Gen 28:10–12, 16a, 17–21a, 22 (theophany at Bethel). This narrative is the founding legend for the shrine at Bethel, where Elohist traditions were generated. Bethel may have continued to be the place of worship for the remaining Israelites in the land, and the hope that it would continue to serve them was assured by the promise of its sacredness. Nor should we forget that Jacob receives a promise from God as he leaves his home to journey to Mesopotamia. He is like a seventh-century Israelite exile, leaving behind

---

23. McEvenue, *Pentateuch*, 102.

homeland and personal possessions, but who still receives the promise of divine presence and a hope to return someday.

Gen 29:1-30 (Jacob meeting Rachel). The existence of Jacob's two wives assure the genealogical line will continue and the promise to the ancestors will be fulfilled, a very necessary message of hope for seventh-century exiles.

Gen 31:4-42 (Jacob and Laban). Jacob's actions and his success are guided by God, for in a dream God directs Jacob to return home. The message to exiles is clear: when you are in a foreign land, you must follow the direction of God and be obedient to the will of God. Jacob leaves for home, a hope dear to all seventh-century exiles. Laban's reception of the dream is like Abimelech's dream experience, a dramatic message from God to a foreigner, which implies the Elohist's view that the God of Israel is the God of foreigners and all people in the world.[24]

Gen 31:43-49a, 50-55 (covenant with Laban). As with the covenant between Abimelech and Abraham, this story says to the exiles that they should cooperate with foreigners in foreign lands, for it will lead to security and perhaps success in life.

Gen 32:3-21 (journey to Esau). Perhaps the story offers to exiles the hope of return and tells them how they must turn to God in prayer and obedience for a peaceful restoration to their homes and homeland, especially when they encounter other people who are still in the land.

Gen 32:22-32 (Penuel). Exiles also would be called upon to grapple with God in prayer and the result could be the transformation of their lives, as God transformed Jacob.

Gen 33:1-17 (meeting Esau). This story speaks to exiles about the possibility of return to the land. It says that they should cooperate with foreigners in this process, but it also implies that they should act wisely, for Jacob chose to go a separate route so as to avoid any further confrontation with Esau.

Gen 35:1-7 (journey to Bethel). The calf cult at Bethel was viewed by the Elohist as a cause for the ultimate destruction of the state in 722 BCE. The calf cult needed to be stopped, and perhaps it was eradicated by reform-oriented priests after 722 BCE. If so, this story spoke directly of burying those idols, and it may have alluded to the termination of the calf cult. To exiles from Israel this story said they must reject all gods except Yahweh, and they must get rid of the idols and the gods represented by

---

24. Graupner, *Elohist*, 310-11.

them. They must worship only Yahweh, who is the true Elohim, and ignore the other gods.

Gen 46:1–4 (theophany at Beersheba). Exiles must trust in the presence of God throughout their journey, assuring them of divine protection, and offering hope of an ultimate return to the land. As Jacob's eyes were to be closed by Joseph, so the exiles were assured that their children after them would inherit the promise and the hope to continue the family and the nation.

Gen 48:8–22 (blessing of Ephraim and Manasseh). What stands out in this story is the hope of a future, and especially the future hope of Ephraim and Manasseh, the symbolic tribes of the Israelite heartland. Exiles would hear this promise and believe that once again the kingdom would be restored.

Gen 50:15–21 (Joseph's brothers). This passage speaks of forgiveness, perhaps the forgiveness of God for the entire people that might lead to restoration. The plan of God, in which the exile of Joseph into Egypt ultimately led to good, might lead exiles to believe that their exile was part of a divine plan. No matter how bad it might seem at first, events would work out for the good for them and for many other people in the world (the Egyptians symbolize all foreigners).

Exod 1:8–10, 15–21 (midwives). The story of the midwives clearly proclaims that people owe obedience to God over obedience to rulers. It is a text of civil disobedience. I believe it suggests that Israelites should have resisted their own Israelite kings who led them down the path to destruction in 722 BCE. The story may not be encouraging people to rebel against rulers in foreign lands, although it may encourage some form of resistance in the land of Israel to Assyrian rule in the province of Samarina, if the Assyrians forced the remaining Israelites to violate their Yahwistic customs and law. This is difficult to suggest, when other passages in the Elohist seem to encourage cooperation with foreigners. Certainly the text condemns the kings of Israel who led the kingdom into destruction. Calling pharaoh the "king of Egypt" seems to be an attempt to make people think of their own kings and their irresponsible behavior, especially in those late years before the fall. It implies that the people of Israel should have listened to the words of the prophets, instead of their kings, and the old prophets Elijah and Elisha set the standard for condemning such disobedience. This is an awesome message of civil disobedience for the first millennium BCE.

The Elohist

Exod 3:1, 2b, 3, 4b–6, 9–15, 18–22 (burning bush). Moses is the ultimate example of a leader for Israel, but he is not a king, he is a prophet. The story of Moses' call uses prophetic language, and perhaps the Elohist is saying that in the future Israelites should be led by charismatic prophets rather than kings.

Exod 14:5a, 7, 19–20, 24 (exodus). The images of pillar of fire and pillar of cloud speak of how God leads people in the wilderness, especially when the people are weak and vulnerable. Such an image would offer hope to seventh-century exiles from Israel living in Mesopotamia and those hoping to travel the arduous journey back home.

Exod 15:25b–26 (testing). Israelites in exile failed the tests that God had given them over the years, and that is why their kingdom was destroyed. Now as they live in exile, they must pass the test of obedience to Yahweh and faithfulness to the laws of Yahwism, as well as hearkening to the voices of the prophets in exile.

Exod 16:4–21 (manna and quail). God will provide food in the wilderness symbolically for seventh-century Israelite exiles by sustaining them through difficult times. The symbolic image of manna and quail could have been used as metaphors in many different ways by Israelites in exile.

Exod 17:1–7 (testing). This is another hopeful symbol for exiles, which implies that God still loves them despite their punishment of being in exile.

Exod 18:1–27 (Jethro). Perhaps the story says something about the need for seventh-century Israelite exiles to establish their own Yahwistic social structures, such as legal representatives, while they are in exile, in order to more effectively preserve their identity in their "wilderness."

Exod 19:16–19 (cloud on the mountain). This would tell exiles that they need to devote themselves exclusively to Yahweh and forget about Baal, the god of fertility who is symbolized by the storm, who may have received their veneration back in Palestine.

Exod 20:18–21 (people's response). For exiles this is a call to fear and reverence the majestic God of all creation and all people, who is their God in particular. The realization of the universality of God should be the source of true human fear and obedience.

Exod 24:1–2, 9–15 (elders and Joshua on the mount). The transcendence of God in this dramatic and artistic portrayal should lead to reverence, fear, and obedience among those exiles of Israel scattered all over the earth. Reference to the seventy elders might remind exiles of the need to have their own leaders, presumably prophetic types, to lead them in exile in Mesopotamia.

Exod 32:1–10, 15–24 (golden calf). This is a condemnation of both priests and Bethel for practices prior to 722 BCE, including the devotion to the calf, implying that in the future there should be no iconographic imagery for Yahweh. This story might be a cardinal message by the author to tell Israelites why they had to experience the judgment of God in their defeat for their sins.

Exod 33:7–11 (cloud). The reference to God speaking "face to face" to Moses may be a significant text in the Elohist narrative to compare Moses to earlier and later prophets, and perhaps even to delineate ages of prophecy. Certainly to exiles it spoke of the need for them to respect their prophetic leaders.

Lev 10:1–3 (Nadab and Abihu). If this originally was an Elohist account, it calls upon Israelite exiles in the seventh century to recognize the complicity of both kings and priests in the sins that brought upon them the destruction in 722 BCE.

Num 11:11–12, 14–17, 24b–30 (elders prophesy). This account may justify the rule of elders or charismatic prophets over the people rather than kings, especially after Israel lost its independence in 722 BCE. Some observe that Moses in this Elohist story is more generous about sharing power than in the rest of Numbers 11.[25] This might imply an exilic situation where the leadership needed to be exercised by prophets, perhaps of a charismatic nature, and people needed to cooperate in a power-sharing situation.

Num 12:1–15 (identity of Moses and Miriam). Israelites in exile are to see Moses as a positive symbol for prophets and Aaron as a negative symbol for priests. Apparently the Elohist wished not only to encourage the people to accept new charismatic prophetic leaders in exile, he wished to scapegoat the priests for the evils that befell the people.

Num 14:13–16 (cloud and Moses). If this is an Elohist text, even though it uses the name Yahweh, it reinforces themes about divine presence in exile and prophetic leadership.

Num 21:4–9 (bronze serpent). If this is an Elohist account, it says that Israelite exiles should look to God, symbolized by the bronze serpent, when they were faced with the problems of the exile.

Num 21:21–33, 35 (Sihon). This is another story about how Israel under Moses defeats enemies in battle, a concept that does not quite fit with

---

25. Sommer, "Reflecting on Moses," 601–24.

other Elohist themes. However, Sihon and the Amorites may have symbolized something for exiles, and their defeat symbolized the ability of exiles to prevail in challenging situations.

Num 22:1–7, 9–13a, 14–17, 20–21, 36–40; 23:1–2, 18–21a, 22–24, 27–30; 24:2–6a, 6c–11a, 14–25 (Balaam). Balaam's blessing of the Israelites in the wilderness, a blessing that promised a great political destiny, had to be a hopeful image for Israelites in seventh-century exile. It said to them that they would return to their land someday and have a glorious future. The Balaam story would have been a good ending to the Elohist narrative, or at least an ending to this particular Elohist cycle, if indeed there are other fairly independent cycles.

7

Commentary on Elohist Texts

The following texts are those that appear to be Elohist. In parentheses I indicate those scholars who attribute this text, either most or all of the passage, to the Elohist tradition. Some texts are questionable, and these are indicated with the word "perhaps." It is possible that these narratives contain portions or memory of a larger Elohist account, but they have been so reworked by the Yahwist or Priestly Editors that the Elohist characteristics are significantly muted. In addition, some narratives are so short as to be difficult to assign to the Elohist tradition with certitude.

With each text I list the critical scholars who have identified that passage as Elohist in order to respond to the criticism made by opponents of source criticism that source critics cannot agree on which texts belong to the Yahwist and the Elohist. It should be observed that there is often a great consensus, though not complete, on which passages are Elohist among more recent scholars.

Genesis

Perhaps Genesis 15:12–21
(Noth, Jenks, Fretheim, Campbell and O'Brien, Graupner)

A covenant-making ceremony made between God and Abram may provide the beginning of the Elohist narrative. This appears logical since a Yahwist covenant is located in Genesis 12 and a Priestly covenant in Genesis 17. However, studies focusing directly upon this passage have either found elements of all the sources in it, or have preferred not to identify the chapter with any tradition. It uses Yahweh for the divine name, suggesting the Yahwist tradition, but the manifestation of God with fire and the apparent imagery of a dream hint at Elohist origins. The mysterious transcendence of God also hints at Elohist themes. But the dream format is not like other Elohist texts, and the fire is associated with a pot and a torch, not directly with God. Maybe an Elohist account has been reworked by the Yahwist or Deuteronomist, or both, to produce this narrative. Leslie Brisman proposed that the bulk of the text is Elohist (especially vv. 1–6), and has been reworked by the Yahwist.[1]

This contains a divine promise to the ancestors and it has an aura of the mysterious and the numinous. God is somehow present in a strange fiery object, which by its awesome and bizarre nature preserves the transcendence of God. Yet at the same time there is a powerful image of divine presence as God passes between the cut animals. For in ancient Near Eastern understandings, when participants in a covenant making process passed between animals that had been cut in half, they effectively said, "May I be cut in half, if I break this promise." If it is the intent of the Elohist to have God take upon the divine nature such a heavy promise, this is truly a powerful story with which to begin the Elohist epic.

This promise to Abraham speaks of descendants (v. 5) and land (v. 18). The only other Elohist promise to a patriarch is the one given to Jacob in the Beersheba dream experience in Gen 46:2–5, which promises descendants (v. 3). A comparable promise to Isaac may have been lost. Both of the patriarchal promises come in the form of dreams, begin with the imperative, "do not fear" (Gen 15:1, 46:3), and speak of a return to the land from Egypt (Gen 15:13–14; 46:4), which are fairly distinctive characteristics, thus providing us with a very solid connecting link for the Elohist texts, even if there are only two examples of such promises in dreams.

Genesis 20:1–4a, 5–17
(Noth, Jenks, Fretheim, Friedman, McEvenue, Coote, Campbell and O'Brien, Schmidt, Graupner, Burnett, Yoreh)

Even authors who doubt the existence of the Elohist tradition admit that this narrative provides the best argument for the existence of a theoretic

---

1. Brisman, *The Voice of Jacob*, 37–41.

Commentary on Elohist Texts

Elohist source. It has a dream report, Abraham is called a prophet who prays for Abimelech's household, there is reference to the "fear of God" in v. 11, it is clearly noted that Abimelech did not touch Sarah (vv. 4–6), and both Abimelech and Abraham speak to each other with piety and respect. There is concern that "great guilt" could be brought upon Abimelech (v. 9), and this expression is used again in the Elohist version of the golden calf in Exod 32:30–31. Most importantly this is a doublet to Genesis 12, and Abraham is portrayed more positively in Genesis 20 than in Genesis 12 where he passed his wife off as a sister. He does not lie about her status (she was a half-sister), and he does not act out of sheer fear. Furthermore, he receives gifts generously bestowed by Abimelech, not loot from pharaoh in return for Sarah as in Genesis 12. Yoreh believed Genesis 12 knows Genesis 20 and thus indicates that the Yahwist Historian edited Elohist material by portraying Abraham as a more ambiguous personage.[2] Perhaps the Yahwist added the reference to the Lord in v. 4b. In addition, the reference to "innocent people" does not fit this story line wherein only Abimelech is threatened by God, so it may be a Yahwist addition also. Commentators have noted the high level of morality in this narrative, for it attempts to whitewash Abraham in light of other traditions about a patriarch almost losing his wife (Genesis 12, 26). The story is sappy with moralistic piety. The vocabulary reflects concern with such piety: righteous (v. 4), perfect (vv. 5, 6), sin (vv. 6, 9), and fear of God (v. 11). The last verse uses the sacred name Yahweh, but Baden suggested that in Elohist narratives the characters use the name Elohim, but the narrator may use Yahweh occasionally as he steps back from the narrative.[3] Or you might suggest, as do I, that the Yahwist added this last verse to explain the healing of the wombs mentioned in v. 17, for otherwise v. 17 could provide a satisfactory conclusion without this addition. McEvenue believes this verse provides "closure and climax" to the story, and it befits the Elohist's style in stressing God's control during the entire experience.[4]

Commentators frequently observe how Abraham's moral behavior in Genesis 20 is superior to his behavior in Genesis 12, so that obviously Genesis 20 is reacting against the portrayal in Genesis 12. But if we postulate that the Yahwist Historian emerged after the Elohist, how do we explain the dependence of Genesis 20 upon Genesis 12? The Yahwist Historian

2. Yoreh, *First Book of God*, 50–57.
3. Baden, *Redaction of the Pentateuch*, 228.
4. McEvenue, *Pentateuch*, 96.

gathered together sources, including the Elohist, and the two stories about the "endangering of the ancestress" in Genesis 12 and 26 must have been two old accounts that the Yahwist inherited. The Elohist may have reacted against an earlier version of the story prior to the work of the Yahwist. Perhaps the Yahwist added the imagery that made Genesis 12 appear to foreshadow the Exodus (vv. 16–17, the spoil and the plagues), but the basic plot of losing the wife was the original tale. The Yahwist may have portrayed the weak and sinful side of Abraham in Genesis 12 in order to stress the grace and mercy of God in contrast to human finitude.

In conjunction with this text some scholars have challenged the use of the dream motif as an indicator of the Elohist source. They maintain that since references to dreams also occur in some Yahwist texts, especially Gen 26:24, "and that very night the LORD appeared to him and said, 'I am the God of your father Abraham; do not be afraid, for I am with you and will bless you and make your offspring numerous for my servant Abraham.'" Therefore, dream reports cannot be used to indicate Elohist text.[5] However, closer inspection reveals that the language of this Yahwist text is form-critically different from the usual Elohist dream report formula, "and God/the Angel of God came to XX in a dream by night and said." Rather, what we have is further evidence for the distinct nature of the Elohist dream report formula by observation of the passage in Gen 26:24.

Theologically Genesis 20 speaks of the faithfulness of God in preserving the promise to Abraham, for God appears dramatically in a dream to a foreign king in order to save Sarah and preserve the promise. The story hints at universalism, for God speaks to foreigners, who thus can share in the self-revelation of this majestic God. These foreigners can be delivered from some divine punishment, like closed wombs, if the people of God intercede for them. As Abimelech exhibits piety and has a conscience, so also foreigners may exhibit such piety toward the true God. It also is a fitting story to follow the covenant made with Abraham in Genesis 15, if indeed the two accounts were connected directly, for the audience can hear how seriously God is committed to the promises made to Abraham.

---

5. Lichtenstein, "Dream Theophany"; and Wenham, *Genesis 16–50*, 69.

Commentary on Elohist Texts

Genesis 21:2–8
(Noth, Fretheim, Coote, Campbell and O'Brien, Burnett, Yoreh)

Many commentators agree that this is an Elohist narrative, at least partially, even though significant Elohist themes, other than the use of Elohim, are lacking. It does portray the birth of the new son, Isaac, in noble fashion. In Gen 18:13 Isaac's name results from Sarah's bitter laughter; however, in Yahwistic Gen 21:6 his name results from her more joyous laughter and this betokens the more serious nature of Elohistic narratives.

It is a clear sign of the divine promise to Abraham, for God's gift of Isaac to this couple is the divine action preserving the validity of the covenant promise. It would follow logically after Genesis 20, wherein Abraham almost lost Sarah, thus implying a logical plot connecting the Elohist tales. Keeping her meant the continuation of his genealogical line and movement toward the fulfillment of the promise.

Genesis 21:9–21
(Noth, Jenks, Fretheim, Friedman, Coote, Campbell and O'Brien, McEvenue, Schmidt, Graupner, Yoreh)

Most commentators view this second account of Hagar's flight as Elohist in contrast to the narrative in Genesis 16, which is deemed to be Yahwist.[6] In chapter 16 Hagar's scorn of Sarah causes her dismissal by Sarah, but in this chapter Ishmael's behavior toward Isaac leads Abraham to dismiss Hagar. In chapter 16 Hagar is a maid to Sarah, but in this chapter she is Abraham's concubine. In chapter 16 Hagar is proud and a rival to Sarah, but in this chapter she is weak and helpless. In chapter 16 Hagar flees from Sarah, but in this chapter she is expelled by Abraham. These differences cause readers to inquire as to the theological reasons for the different portrayals and assume that this chapter is Elohistic. In Genesis 21 Abraham is commended by Sarah to send Hagar away, and it is his decision. Though Abraham is distressed over this activity as harsh treatment, God reassures Abraham that Hagar and Ishmael will fare well. This is far more noble and moral than the apparent reason for Hagar's flight in Genesis 16, where she flees because of Sarah's harsh treatment. Furthermore, the mode of revelation to Hagar is Elohistic, the "angel of God" called to Hagar "from heaven" (v. 18) and tells

---

6. Nicholson, *The Pentateuch*, 232.

her not to fear, and some commentators assume that these are dreams.⁷ The language is somewhat similar to other Elohist revelations.

Genesis 21:22–31
(Noth, Jenks, Fretheim, Friedman, McEvenue, Coote, Campbell and O'Brien, Schmidt, Graupner, Burnett, Yoreh)

The covenant between Abraham and Abimelech is seen by most critics as Elohist (though Yoreh suspected that the actual verse alluding to the covenant is a Yahwist addition).⁸ Again, there is the moralistic and respectful dialogue between Abraham and Abimelech, interest in the city of Beersheba, and use of the divine name Elohim (vv. 22, 23). The aetiology of Beersheba's name is a natural ending to this little story. Though critics oft have divided this account between Yahwist and Elohist traditions, it is interesting to observe that the names Abraham and Abimelech each occur seven times in a narrative that plays with the imagery of seven (as in the seven lambs of vv. 28–30 and the words "swear" and "Sheba" that sound like the word for seven). Thus, one might suggest that the account is a unified Elohist account.

Genesis 22:1–13, 19
(Noth, Jenks, Fretheim, Friedman, McEvenue, Coote, Campbell and O'Brien, Schmidt, Graupner, Yoreh)

This chapter also is recognized as a classic Elohist text, even by those critical of the existence of the source. Leslie Brisman described the account as having the "essence of E with a purity nowhere else found."⁹ The Elohist theme of testing stands out foremost (v. 1, "God tested Abraham"), as well as the theme of obedience and piety demonstrated by Abraham in his willingness to sacrifice Isaac. Abraham is said to "fear" God (v. 12). His "fear" may foreshadow the "fear" of Israel at the mountain in Exod 20:18–21.¹⁰ God speaks to Abraham with the double vocative (v. 11), found elsewhere in Elohist texts, and a single vocative (v. 1). Abraham responds, "Here I am," twice

---

7. Burnett, *Biblical Elohim*, 129.
8. Yoreh, *First Book of God*, 63–64.
9. Brisman, *Voice of Jacob*, 55.
10. Graupner, *Elohist*, 355.

to God (vv. 1, 11) and once to Isaac (v. 7), as found elsewhere in Elohist texts. The divine being is the "angel of (the LORD) God" who speaks "from heaven" (v. 11). The Yahwist may have changed the expression "angel of God" into "angel of the LORD" in v. 11 according to some scholars.[11] Thus, Elohist themes and language abound. Finally, God speaks to Abraham (vv. 1–2), and Abraham "rose early in the morning" (v. 3), implying that the revelation might have come in a nighttime dream common to Elohist texts, but that format may have been lost in transmission by the Yahwist Historian. The Yahwist Historian probably added vv. 14–18 with the use of the sacred name for God and the special promise of many offspring.

As hideous as it may sound to us that Abraham even had the possibility of offering his son as a human sacrifice, we must acknowledge that their age was different from our own. In fact, if we omit v. 13 about the ram as a sacrifice, as some scholars do, then the story implies that Abraham actually sacrificed Isaac, and then v. 19 seems to imply likewise that Isaac did not return home with Abraham, for his name is not mentioned there. The Elohist lived in harsh times, after the destruction of a kingdom and the deaths of so many innocent people. Furthermore, human sacrifice was a phenomenon practiced in the ancient world, and probably undertaken by Israelites. Abraham is being tested, and his obedience must be proven, for these are important themes for the Elohist. We must also recognize the possibility that the story also said to the audience that sacrifice of newly born children should not occur, but that an animal sacrifice should be given instead. We do not know the extent to which infant sacrifice might have been practiced in eighth- and seventh-century Israel, but this story may have been a necessary admonition against such a practice. Ultimately, we cannot be sure if the Elohist tale concluded with the actual sacrifice of Isaac or if the story was designed to oppose the practice of infant sacrifice by having Isaac spared.

Perhaps Genesis 25:21–34
(Fretheim, Schmidt)

A few commentators have suggested that the birth narrative of Jacob and Esau is Elohist for the sake of maintaining a plot line in the Jacob narratives. Esau's disdain for the birthright, especially noted in v. 34, seems like a moralistic justification of Jacob's actions in "cheating" Esau, and this might

---

11. Brisman, *Voice of Jacob*, 59; and Yoreh, *First Book of God*, 67.

be Elohistic morality.[12] However, no Elohist language is apparent, and Yahweh is used as the divine name (vv. 21, 23). The theological significance would be that the birth of two children was a sign that God was faithful to the promises and kept the genealogical line of the patriarchal ancestors for another generation.

I suggest that "pools of Elohist" tradition existed, and perhaps there was no connecting link between Abraham and Isaac, simply separate Abraham and Jacob cycles. Similarly, Yoreh believed there were separate cycles about great heroes or ancestors (Abraham, Jacob, Joseph, Moses, Balaam) with no necessary connections. Furthermore, he believed that Abraham actually killed Isaac, whose real father was Abimelech (a fascinating suggestion), thus explaining the lack of Elohist references to Isaac.[13]

Genesis 28:10–12, 16a, 17–21a, 22
(Noth, Jenks, Fretheim, Friedman, McEvenue, Coote, Campbell and O'Brien, Schmidt, Graupner, Burnett, Yoreh)

Most critics agree that Yahwist and Elohist versions of the Bethel theophany have been woven together, though minor disagreement exists about some of the phrases. The Yahwist version has Yahweh stand beside Jacob (v. 13) and give the promise of offspring, future blessing, and divine accompaniment. In the Elohist version there is reference to a dream (v. 12) and awakening from the dream (vv. 16a, 18), which is part of the Elohist dream format. (Most commentators do not include v. 16a with the Elohist, but it is part of the dream format as I view it.) In the Elohist verses there is reference to "angels of God" (v. 12), and God (vv. 17, 20, 21, 22). Jacob experiences "fear of God" in v. 17. The expression, "place" (*maqom*), considered by many commentators to be an Elohist word, is found in vv. 11, 16, 17, 19, rather frequent usage in this narrative. The Elohist vow in vv. 20–21a, 22 unnecessarily parallels the Yahwist promise of vv. 13–15, implying two separate memories have been merged.

There is concern for the northern shrine of Bethel, otherwise not mentioned in the Yahwist versions. Jacob erects a *maṣṣebah*, a "sacred pillar (vv. 18, 22). The sacred name Yahweh is used in v. 21b, but since Jacob is especially identifying his particular god, the narrator had to step out of

---

12. Brisman, *Voice of Jacob*, 67.
13. Yoreh, *First Book of God*.

narrative consistency and use the sacred name here according to one scholar.[14] Or perhaps this is an editorial addition by the Yahwist Historian who used Elohist texts.

Graupner believed that the chapter contains both a well developed Yahwist and Elohist version of this experience of Jacob, and it indicated to him that both the Yahwist and the Elohist had significant, intact epic traditions.[15] However, to me the narrative appears to be an Elohist account with Yahwist material added to it, for the Elohist narrative can stand alone, but the Yahwist material cannot. Yahwist portions have the promise of the Lord and Jacob's response; the Elohist speaks of the journey to Bethel and the context of the revelatory experience. I suspect that a fairly intact Elohist tradition was augmented by Yahwist language, for so few verses appear to be Yahwist. The Yahwist narrative is not complete by itself, but the Elohist account is, and some commentators over the years have noted that.[16] Interestingly, the story begins with Jacob at Beersheba, while Genesis 22 ended with Abraham returning to Beersheba, and that was perhaps the last Elohist account of Abraham. This might indicate a certain connection between those two cycles, even if there is no plot continuity.

Opponents of the division into sources suggest that the supposed Yahwist expression, "Surely the LORD is in this place—and I did not know it!" (v. 16), flows naturally into the supposed Elohist expression "How awesome is this place! This is none other than the house of God, and this is the gate of heaven" (v. 17). They supposed that the awareness of the divine presence in the first expression leads to the fear of God in the second expression.[17] However, I sense that these two expressions articulate the same respect for the divine, but the first statement affirms divine presence all around Jacob (Yahwist theme) and the second stresses the divine presence originates from above, from the heavens (Elohist theme). Howsoever you may perceive these texts, it is a subjective interpretation to reject or affirm the two sources on the basis of these two phrases.

For the Elohist, this narrative is most important, for it is the founding legend for the shrine at Bethel, where Elohist traditions were generated. Blum believed this narrative speaks to an audience for whom the sanctuary was still is use, thus making it prior to its destruction by Josiah in 622

---

14. Baden, *Redaction of the Pentateuch*, 230–32.
15. Graupner, *Elohist*, 235.
16. Carr, *Fractures of Genesis*, 208.
17. Whybray, *Making of the Pentateuch*, 84.

BCE.[18] I would suggest this might be in the seventh century after the destruction of the kingdom of Israel.

The account appears to be the beginning of a cycle, which concludes with the account of Jacob's return to Bethel to bury the idols in Genesis 35. In Gen 35:1, 3, 7 God speaks to Jacob and refers to the revelation Jacob experienced here while fleeing Esau. This cycle elevates Bethel to be the most important of the shrines mentioned in Elohist tradition. The dream theophany portrays God in transcendent and dramatic fashion in accord with the importance of this shrine.[19] Jacob receives a promise from God as he runs from his home to Mesopotamia, like an Israelite exile, who has lost homeland and personal possessions, but still receives the promise of divine presence and a hope to return someday. Later Judahites could read the story in the same fashion, and thus the Yahwist Historian found it very meaningful to include these accounts of Jacob's exile and return home, for it spoke a similar message to the exiles of Judah.

Perhaps Genesis 29:1–30
(Fretheim, Schmidt, Yoreh)

A few commentators suspect that this chapter is Elohist in origin for the sake of the overall Jacob story line. No distinct Elohist language appears here, and there is no reference to divine being, either Elohim or Yahweh. Perhaps we could surmise the theological significance of these stories to be that existence of Jacob's two wives assures the genealogical line will continue and the promise to the ancestors will be fulfilled.

Genesis 29:31–35; 30:1–24a
(Noth, Fretheim, Friedman, Coote, Campbell and O'Brien, Schmidt, Graupner)

Most critics believe that all or part of this narrative is Elohist. The primary characteristic is use of Elohim for God, but also the concern with the all the tribes, including the northern tribes, points to northern agenda in the story. Also, Gen 30:1 uses the typical Elohist word for "maid" (*'amah*). The account culminates with the birth of Joseph, who will be the ancestor for

---

18. Blum, *Vätergeschichte*, 93–96, 175–76; and Carr, *Fractures of Genesis*, 265–66.
19. Graupner, *Elohist*, 241.

the major northern tribes of Ephraim and Manasseh. Yoreh proposed a radical theory with serious merit. He eliminated verses with the divine name Yahweh (Gen 29:32b, 33–35) and references to the tribes Simeon, Levi, Judah, Gad, and Asher, as well as the daughter Dinah (Gen 29:33–35; 30:9–13, 21). He believed that the Elohist knew of only six sons and seven tribes, and Yoreh edited the Joseph stories accordingly (Benjamin will receive a five-fold number of gifts equivalent to his "five" brothers later, Gen 43:34).[20] Though his theory has merit, I am reluctant to integrate it into my suggestions.

Genesis 31:4–42
(Noth, Jenks, Fretheim, Friedman, McEvenue, Coote, Campbell and O'Brien, Schmidt, Graupner, Propp, Burnett, Yoreh)

Most commentators assume that all or part of this chapter is Elohist. Jacob refers to his revelatory experience in Genesis 28 in his speech to his wives, for he identifies the deity as the "God of Bethel" to whom he anointed a pillar and swore an oath (v. 13). Jacob does not refer to a theophany in that experience, for the report of a theophany at Bethel may be a Yahwist addition (Gen 28:13–15) to the Elohist account.

Elohist moral sensitivity is evident; the text seeks to protect Jacob's character. Jacob's reason for returning home is nobler than the reason given in the previous chapter, for he is guided by divine providence, and his increased sheep are due to divine blessing, not his own cunning in creatively mating the sheep (Gen 30:25–43), a Yahwist narrative. Furthermore, in Genesis 30:25–26 Jacob simply wishes to leave, but in Gen 31:13 a divine imperative compels him to return home. In Gen 31:10–13 there is a classic Elohist dream report attributed to Jacob, while in v. 24 a short but well-defined dream report is attributed to Laban, and these are the most concrete signs of an Elohist origin for the narrative. Laban's reception of the dream is like Abimelech's dream, a dramatic message from God to a foreigner. Though he is angry, Laban's discourse with Jacob is restrained and respectful (vv. 26–30), similar to Abimelech's language in Genesis 20. Again, this is Elohist piety at work. Jacob's responses are spoken in anger, but they still appear to be somewhat respectful (vv. 31–32, 36–42). If this story attempts to clean up the mischievous version of the same events in

---

20. Yoreh, *First Book of God*, 88–93.

the previous chapter, then perhaps the Elohist knew the other story in some form before the Yahwist inherited it.

The divine name Elohim appears in vv. 5, 7, 9, 13, 16 (twice), 24, 29, 42 (twice), and "angel of God" appears in v. 11.ABraham responds to the divine address from God by saying, "here am I," in v. 11, a characteristic of other Elohist theophanies.

Genesis 31:43–49a, 50–55
(Noth, Jenks, Fretheim, Friedman, Coote, Campbell and O'Brien, Schmidt, Graupner, Burnett, Yoreh)

The covenant between Laban and Jacob appears Elohistic. It uses the name Elohim, and it refers to a "pillar" (vv. 45, 49a, 51, 52). The Elohist prefers the word "pillar" while the Yahwist likes the term "altar" for sacred sites. The covenant appears to reflect some form of political relations between Israel in the north (Jacob) and the country of Syria (Laban). It uses Elohim for the divine name (vv. 50, 53).

Genesis 32:1–2
(Noth, Fretheim, Friedman, Coote, Campbell and O'Brien, Schmidt, Graupner, Yoreh)

This small text provides the aetiology for Mahanaim, a northern shrine, and it speaks of the "angels of God" (v. 1), making it most likely Elohistic. It may be a parallel text to the encounter between Jacob and the divine being at Penuel in Genesis 34.

Perhaps Genesis 32:3–21
(Noth, Fretheim, Friedman, Campbell and O'Brien, Schmidt, Graupner)

A few commentators consider part or all of this passage to be Elohistic. It lacks clear Elohistic motifs other than a pious prayer by Jacob (vv. 9–12) to protect him when he encounters Esau. The sacred name Yahweh may be added in v. 9 by the Yahwist.

Perhaps Genesis 32:22–32 (Friedman, Schmidt, Yoreh)

Frequently commentators see the Penuel encounter as Elohistic, although it portrays God as very physically present in the wrestling match. Penuel is a northern shrine, built by Jeroboam (1 Kgs 12:25), hence of interest to the Elohist, and the name Elohim is used once (v. 30). The story fits with the Elohist's narrative plot line at this point.

This story impresses many as presenting God in a fashion too physical and earthy for Elohist sensitivities. I am impressed by that argument, but not completely persuaded. Maybe this account is meant to be especially dramatic, for Jacob is transformed into Israel, and his persona appears perhaps to become more moral, less mischievous after that point. Perhaps the portrayal of God is adjusted for the context of this dramatic account. The direct encounter with God gives birth to the nation. Or, maybe this is simply wild speculation on my part, and this account is really a Yahwist account.

Perhaps Genesis 33:1–17 (Noth, Jenks, Fretheim, Friedman, McEvenue, Campbell and O'Brien, Schmidt, Graupner)

Jacob's encounter with Esau is viewed as Elohist simply to maintain some plot line in the Jacob traditions. Gen 33:5–7 alludes back to the list of Jacob's children in Gen 29:31–30:24, and the plenitude of flocks mentioned in Gen 33:13–14 refers back to the flocks Jacob gained in Gen 31:8–9 (without an allusion to the humorous Yahwist story in Gen 30:31–43), implying that both accounts are part of a narrative sequence. Jacob's reference to how God has been good to him may allude back to the hope for material blessings uttered by Jacob in the experience at Bethel (Gen 28:20). Elohim is used in vv. 5, 10, 11. The story recounts the origin of the city of Succoth, and the aetiology of the name appears to properly end the account. The rather random allusions to Joseph along with Rachel in Gen 33:2, 7 may indicate that a northern audience is being addressed, since Israel was sometimes called the "house of Joseph."[21]

---

21. Carr, *Fractures of Genesis*, 265.

The Elohist

Perhaps Genesis 33:18–20
(Noth, Fretheim, Friedman, Coote, Campbell and O'Brien, Schmidt)

Commentators often view the reference to Shechem and Hamor, as well as the creation of an altar as an item of interest to the Elohist. If this text is Elohist, Jacob may build this shrine as part of keeping his oath made at Bethel in Gen 28:20.

Genesis 35:1–7
(Noth, Jenks, Fretheim, Friedman, McEvenue, Coote, Campbell and O'Brien, Graupner, Burnett, Yoreh)

Most critics view the pilgrimage by Jacob to Bethel as Elohist and an aetiology for the importance of the shrine of Bethel in the north, a place where Elohist traditions may have emerged. Elohim is used in vv. 1, 5, 7; El is used in vv. 1, 3, 7. The rejection of foreign gods, which is the focus of the story, may have been a significant theme in Elohist thought. Shechem, another northern shrine, is mentioned also in v. 4.

There are connections between Gen 28:10–22 and the larger text of Gen 35:1–15, which has led many commentators to speak of a Bethel narrative from Genesis 28 through 35. Throughout these chapters there are allusions to the eventual return of Jacob to Bethel and especially the building of an altar there (Gen 28:20; 31:13; 35:1, 3, 7).[22]

Since the rejection of the idols occurs at Bethel, we usually assume this is criticism of the old calf cult at Bethel. The notable reference to earrings that are disavowed in v. 4 may foreshadow the use of earrings by Aaron to make the golden calf in Exod 32:2–3, and this may be a deliberate attempt to connect Bethel with Aaron's golden calf so as to condemn Bethel's calf created by Jeroboam I. This is an important theme for the Elohist, for the calf cult at Bethel was viewed by the Elohist as a cause for the ultimate destruction of the state in 722 BCE. The calf cult needed to be stopped, and perhaps it was eradicated by reform-oriented priests after 722 BCE. If so, this story may have alluded to the termination of the calf cult.

---

22. Gomes, *Sanctuary of Bethel*, 64–76.

Genesis 35:8–15
(Schmidt)

The appearance of God to Jacob in Paddan-Aram and Jacob's erection of a pillar (v. 14) are mentioned in this story, both of are interest to the Elohist. The erection of the pillar parallels the Elohist pillar erected in Gen 28:18 and 31:45. The death of Deborah most likely is Elohist also (v. 8). The story takes interest in the shrine of Bethel, for Deborah is reputedly buried below Bethel. The name Elohim appears in vv. 9, 10, 11, 13, 15. In this account God again tells Jacob that his name is Israel (v. 10), as happened at Penuel (Gen 32:28). One might be tempted to separate these accounts into two separate traditions; these are texts that classically look like doublets. Joel Baden suspected that vv. 9–13 are Priestly because the story is a doublet.[23] But there are differences between the two accounts. In Gen 32:28 a mysterious man names Jacob and gives an aetiology for his name, whereas in Gen 35:10 God names him Israel and provides no aetiology. The name Elohim appears in both accounts, and both accounts are connected to shrines important in the north. Why would the Yahwist or the Priestly Editors be concerned with Penuel or Bethel? So by default we might assume this is an Elohist account. I suspect that the Elohist provides two complementary accounts of Jacob's names with these differences (though I could be wrong).

Baden also believed that vv. 16b–18, 20 are Elohist because in them Rachel dies in Bethel as Benjamin is born and Jacob sets up a pillar for her grave in Bethel, whereas in the Priestly version of vv. 16a, 19 she dies on the way to Bethlehem.[24] He made a very good argument, but I am not totally convinced.

Genesis 37, 39–50

Various scholars have seen Elohistic origins for much of the story of Joseph, especially because Joseph represents the northern tribes and because we read of six dream accounts in this narratives. However, the two dreams by Joseph (Genesis 37), dreams by the butler and the baker (Genesis 40), and the two dreams by pharaoh (Genesis 41) are all symbolic dreams. Elsewhere the Elohist uses auditory message dreams. I personally believe this is a significant difference and that the symbolic dream is not a motif of the

23. Baden, *The Composition of the Pentateuch*, 236–39.
24. Ibid.

The Elohist

Elohist. I believe the character and the narrative style of the Joseph story indicates that most of the text is a post-exilic novel to be dated after 500 BCE.[25] In a previous work I attempted to demonstrate that the narratives about Joseph interpreting the dreams of pharaoh are dependent upon a stock narrative about a poor prisoner appearing before a ruler and obtaining freedom and honor by providing wise insight to the ruler. I believe the biblical author may have been influenced by accounts in the writings of Herodotus. If so, our biblical narrative, in its present form, can date no earlier than 450 BCE.[26] It is not part of the Elohist tradition. However, the novel may have picked up a few Elohist stories and it may actually have displaced Elohist narratives about Joseph. Though he does not accept the notion of a Yahwist and Elohist source division, Carr likewise suggested that an early Joseph story in Genesis 39–41 had further extensive additions to create our present text.[27] In its present extended form the Joseph story should not be considered Elohistic. Its present form is a rather smooth narrative, with only a few duplications in the early chapters. This implies that there were two versions of the narrative at some early point, but there is too little textual evidence to sort out passages into two such theoretic narratives. Even though the Elohist is fragmentary in Genesis 12–36, there is far more evidence in those chapters to find some narrative than in the Joseph story.

Yoreh made a cogent argument for the Joseph material to be viewed as one of the independent cycles of Elohist narratives. He consistently reconstructed the narrative using the divine name Elohim and Jacob's name as "Israel" as indicators (the reverse of what we usually suspect). In addition, the notion that Jacob had only six sons leads to the elimination of any references to the other sons (including the symbolic dream of the sun, moon, and stars in Gen 37:9–11).[28] I am impressed by his argument, but not quite convinced. Problematic for his scenario is the use of Jacob as a name in Gen 46:1–4, a problem he acknowledges.

Baden has made a cogent argument for the Reuben narrative being Elohist in Gen 37:18–36, wherein Reuben convinces the brothers to put Joseph in a pit so he can save him later, but during their meal the Midianites

---

25. This argument was made initially by Redford, *Joseph*, more recently by Hyun Kim, "Reading the Joseph Story."
26. Gnuse, "From Prison to Prestige."
27. Carr, *Fractures of Genesis*, 289.
28. Yoreh, *First Book of God*, 119–61.

steal Joseph from the pit and sell him to Potiphar in Egypt, where Joseph will later interpret pharaoh's dreams (Gen 37:18, 21–22, 24, 28–30).[29] I can accept that the Reuben narrative might have been drawn from Elohist tales by the post-exilic author of the Joseph Novella, and perhaps other fragments likewise have been drawn into the composition.

Genesis 46:1–4
(Noth, Jenks, Fretheim, Friedman, McEvenue, Coote, Campbell and O'Brien, Schmidt, Graupner, Yoreh)

Critics who believe that Elohist fragments are too few to even merit discussing the Elohist as a significant theological tradition accept that this is an Elohist account.[30] This short patriarchal account, probably inserted into the Joseph Narrative, has the Elohist dream format. It also contains the double vocative by God (v. 2) and the response of Jacob, "Here am I" (v. 2), consistent with the language to Abraham in Gen 22:11 and to Samuel in 1 Sam 3:4–10, both of which I view as Elohist texts. The name for God is Elohim (vv. 1, 2, 3 [twice]). This little narrative combines themes from the patriarchal narratives, the Joseph Narrative, and the descent and exodus out of Egypt, which may imply that the Elohist had some organized account that included all three of these dramatic narratives.[31] The reference to Joseph closing Jacob's eyes alludes to a story that has been lost to us, evidence that probably some Elohist material was excised.[32] Theologically the story describes Jacob leaving the land promised to the ancestors, yet God promises to be with him and assures him that this is part of the plan. This reference to a return from Egypt is not found in other patriarchal promises and might be unique to the Elohist for a significant reason connected to events in the seventh century.

---

29. Baden, *Composition of the Pentateuch*, 38–40.
30. Coats, *Genesis*, 297.
31. Graupner, *Elohist*, 353.
32. Ibid., 9

Genesis 48:8–22
(Noth, Jenks, Fretheim, Friedman, McEvenue, Campbell and O'Brien, Graupner, Burnett, Yoreh)

Most commentators observe that the blessing of Joseph appears to be secondary to the narrative context.[33] Commentators also are convinced that Jacob's blessing of Ephraim and Manasseh reflects northern political agenda and tribal history, and hence the Elohist seeks to recall this. Elohim is the name for God in vv. 9, 11,15, 20, 21, there is a reference to the "angel" who is God in v. 16, and the word "Amorite" in v. 22 is believed by some scholars to be the Elohist term equivalent to the Yahwist term "Canaanite." The allusions in v. 21 refer both to the ancestors and the future exodus, an image that may connect the cycle of stories about the patriarchs and the exodus in such a way as to indicate that the Elohist was once a unified narrative.[34]

Perhaps Genesis 50:15–21
(Noth, Jenks, Fretheim, McEvenue, Coote, Campbell and O'Brien, Schmidt, Graupner, Yoreh)

Commentators often suggest that various parts of this chapter are Elohistic; some also include vv. 22–26 (the death of Joseph).[35] The importance of Joseph for northern traditions might make this account Elohistic. Joseph assures his brothers that their actions really followed God's plan (vv. 19–20), which sounds like Elohist moralizing again. Elohim appears in vv. 17, 19, 20, but otherwise no real Elohistic themes appear.

The brothers refer to Jacob's direction to them to plead with Joseph (vv. 16–17), an allusion to narrative material we seem to be lacking; yet another indication that Elohist narratives have been lost.

---

33. Carr, *Fractures of Genesis*, 210.
34. Graupner, *Elohist*, 29.
35. McEvenue, *Pentateuch*, 112–13.

Commentary on Elohist Texts

Exodus

Exodus 1:8–10, 15–21
(Noth, Jenks, Fretheim, Friedman, McEvenue, Coote, Campbell and O'Brien, Schmidt, Graupner, Propp, Yoreh)

I consider the story of the midwives to be one of the most important theological Elohist passages. It appears to be somewhat of a duplicate account to the story of throwing the babies into the river (Exodus 1:22), for in both stories the hero is endangered as a baby. The ruler of Egypt is called the "king" or the "king of Egypt" (vv. 8, 15, 17, 18), except in v. 19 where the word pharaoh may be a Yahwist addition.[36] The Elohist narrative refers to the people as the Hebrews (vv. 15, 16, 19), while the Yahwist versions prefers to call them the Israelites (v. 12), and the reference to "Israelite people" in v. 9 seems to be difficult to classify in this story. There is reference to the "fear of God" (vv. 17, 21), and elsewhere the "fear of God" appears in Elohist texts (Gen 20:11; 22:12; Exod 18:21). Elohim is the divine name (vv. 17, 20, 21). This Elohist version of the endangered child story implies that Israel's population in Egypt has not expanded, for they have only been in Egypt four generations, not long after the death of Joseph. Thus, it takes only two midwives to serve the community. The king of Egypt fears their potential might when they become numerous, implying that they are not numerous at the time of the story. His concern parallels that of king Balak in another Elohist narrative (Num 24:6). In this account all the babies are saved, but in the subsequent Yahwist account only Moses survives in his floating basket.[37]

Exodus 3:1, 2b, 3, 4b–6, 9–15, 18–22
(Noth, Jenks, Fretheim, Friedman, McEvenue, Coote, Campbell and O'Brien, Schmidt, Graupner, Propp, Yoreh)

In the Elohist narrative the first appearance of Moses is his call experience, which is an appropriate mode of introduction for such a great hero. The other early Moses stories appear to be Yahwist. Elohist presentations are terse and do not say much about heroes of the faith or their origins; rather,

---

36. Campbell and O'Brien, *Pentateuch*, 184.
37. Propp, *Exodus 1–18*, 138, 145.

they move directly into the narration of their actions, and hence the prophetic call experience is a logical initial narrative for Moses.

Commentators have often sensed that two call narratives for Moses have been placed together in Exodus 3–4, one Yahwist and the other Elohist. There has not been total agreement on how to separate them, however. Each scholar listed above divides the passages in slightly different fashion. The passages I selected above have several classic motifs: 1) fire as a medium of divine revelation (vv. 2–6); 2) the double vocative in addressing Moses (v. 4); 3) the response of Moses, saying "here am I" (v. 4); 4) two references to the "king of Egypt" (vv. 18–19); 5) Moses' fear of the awesome burning bush; 6) the mountain is called both "Horeb" and the "mountain of God" (v. 1); 7) the people will worship God at the mountain (v. 12), which sounds more like the Elohist description of the people's response at Horeb; 8) the theme of obedience on Moses' part in serving God; 9) Moses' leadership as a prophet on God's behalf (vv. 9–12), whereas the Yahwist has God lead the people; and 10) most importantly, I believe, is the use of Elohim for God (even though this is the point at which Yahweh is clearly revealed as the divine name in the Elohist tradition). The narrative moves smoothly and has a dramatic climax in Exod 3:15 with the revelation of the sacred name, Yahweh, which Moses must announce to the "Israelites." Since Exod 3:16 repeats the same idea that Moses should announce the sacred name to the "Elders of Israel" in Egypt, these two verses belong to different traditions, and Exod 3:15 is the Elohist version (contra Yoreh who considers both verses to be Yahwist). The sacred name will be used again twice in v. 18.

Overall, in this narrative there is the portrayal of the majesty of God in transcendent fashion through fire and an auditory mode of discourse without physical appearance, which betokens the Elohist style of portraying revelation. Moses' prophetic call experience contains the elements that we find in call experiences of classical prophets, like Isaiah, Jeremiah, and Ezekiel (theophany, commission by God, the prophet's reluctance, God's response, and a sign of the calling). If we date the Elohist as late as the seventh century, Moses' call is contemporary with the classical prophetic call format, which makes sense because the form of Moses' call appears well developed.

Commentary on Elohist Texts

Exodus 4:17–18, 20; 5:3–4
(Noth, Jenks, Fretheim, Friedman, Coote, Campbell and O'Brien, Schmidt, Graupner)

In this short story we have reference to: 1) Jethro (4:18), 2) the staff of Moses (4:17, 20), which will appear again in Exod 17:5–6; 18:1–5, 3) Elohim as the divine name (4:20; 5:3–4), and 4) reference to the "king of Egypt" (5:3–4).

This text may have been attached to the previous Elohist narrative in Exodus 3, for the initial reference to the staff in v. 17 logically connects to the end of the call narrative, and the staff is again mentioned in v. 20. In v. 19 the Lord tells Moses to return to Egypt, but Moses already decided to do so in v. 18. Thus, v. 19 may be a later Yahwist addition. These few verses (vv. 17–18) are connected back to the call of Moses by reference to the staff and the plagues. The reference to whether any people are still alive in v. 18 anticipates the king's arrogant response to Moses and Aaron (Exod 5:4). The reference to three days' journey into the wilderness in Exod 5:3 resonates with the reference in Exod 3:18, a further connection between these accounts.

Plagues

Some scholars attempt to isolate certain plagues as originating in the Elohist texts, but this is very challenging and critical assessments vary greatly. Friedman believed the Elohist had the plagues of blood, frogs, flies, cattle disease, hail, locusts, darkness, and death of the first-born.[38] Propp believed that the Elohist had seven or eight plagues, most probably eight (blood, frogs, *'arob*, murrain, hail, locusts, perhaps darkness, and death of first born). Yoreh made a very cogent argument that only three plagues belong to the Elohist (hail, locusts, darkness), which are brought upon Egypt by the power of Moses himself with the staff as an unexpected show of extreme power to effect the release of the Israelites.[39] Yoreh's arguments were consistent in his selection of texts (Exod 9:23a, 24–25; 10:13a, 13c, 14–15, 22–23a), but he isolated so few texts as to make the argument seem implausible to me, or perhaps he isolated the only few fragments that survived Yahwist and Priestly editing. At the other extreme, Propp suggested an

---

38. Friedman, *Disappearance of God*, 94.
39. Yoreh, *First Book of God*, 181–90.

The Elohist

Elohist formula wherein Moses is told to "take his stand to meet pharaoh," thus indicating the Elohist plagues that belong together. The expression occurs with all but the darkness plague, and that would imply a large number of plagues come from the Elohist.[40] Finally, some suggest that the Elohist had no plague narratives because Moses was the agent of divine deliverance and God would not act so directly as to bring plagues upon people.[41]

Baden suggested that there were no plague narratives; rather, the Israelites leave Egypt in less than the hostile fashion portrayed by the Yahwist, so that the Egyptians actually give them silver and gold ornaments willingly as they leave (Exod 12:35–36), which was foretold to Abraham (Gen 15:14) and Moses (Exod 3:22), and the ornaments will be used for the golden calf (Exod 32:2).[42]

I suspect that the plagues do not really portray God as acting too directly, and Moses appears to be a powerful personage (despite Yahwist reworking of the texts), so I suspect the Elohist tradition did recall the plagues, and some of this imagery was picked up in the Yahwist narratives. However, these texts have been reworked so much by the Yahwist Historian that all we might isolate are short phrases and key vocabulary. References to the "king of Egypt" (Exod 5:3–4), the staff of Moses or Aaron, and fire imagery could be Elohist snippets that the Yahwist Historian worked into the final narrative. I simply cannot isolate texts that seem specifically Elohist in the plague narratives.

Exodus 13:17–22
(Noth, Jenks, Fretheim, Friedman, McEvenue, Coote, Campbell and O'Brien, Graupner, Propp)

This passage appears to be Elohist, though most scholars believe that the Elohist material really is limited to vv. 17–19, and others reject it as Elohist altogether (Yoreh). The name Elohim is used in vv. 17–19, but Yahweh appears in v. 21, hence the caution for including vv. 20–22. The Yahwist may have rephrased the Elohist story a little with the reference to pharaoh in v. 17 and LORD in v. 20. Otherwise the mention of Joseph's bones in v. 20, the pillar of cloud and pillar of fire in v. 22, and the divine name Elohim in vv. 17–19 imply this is an Elohist passage.

---

40. Propp, *Exodus 1–18*, 315–16.
41. Graupner, *Elohist*, 70–77; and Baden, *Redaction of the Pentateuch*, 220–21.
42. Baden, *Composition of the Pentateuch*, 122–23.

The concern with the bones of Joseph in the panic process of fleeing Egypt also betokens a significant degree of piety. Graupner observed that the concern with Joseph's bones is a theme that unites patriarchal stories with the exodus account and implies that the Elohist was a unified narrative. It also portrays the exodus as a homeward flight rather than an invasion of a new land.[43]

Exodus 14:5a, 7, 19–20, 24
(Noth, Jenks, Fretheim, Yoreh)

Exodus 14 has always been viewed as a pastiche of the various traditions (J, E, P), so one should expect to find some Elohist language adapted by the Yahwist historian and later Priestly editors. Scholars listed above disagree on the exact division of verses. Yoreh especially stands out with his selection of vv. 5a, 7, 19–21a, c, 22–23a, 27a, 28a. The reference to the "king of Egypt" (v. 5a), the "angel of God" (v. 19), the "pillar of cloud" (vv. 19–20, 24), the "pillar of fire" (v. 24) are examples of such Elohist language. The reference to how the king heard that the Israelites had fled reminds us of how Laban heard that Jacob had fled in an earlier Elohist account (Gen 31:21–22). Perhaps, the allusion to "fear" in v. 13 and the staff of Moses in v. 16 might have been Elohist terms. The reference to six hundred chariots (v. 7) is a small force of Egyptians, but according to the Elohist the number of Israelites is also small.

Overall, this is a Yahwist narrative that used some Elohist language and was later edited by Priestly theologians, making it difficult for us to sort out the passages. One would expect heavy editing in a narrative that was so emotionally important to a later Jewish audience.

Exodus 15:20
(Jenks, Fretheim, Propp)

This chapter contains archaic poems that cannot be connected to traditional sources. However, the reference to Miriam as a prophet in v. 20 strongly suggests an Elohist origin. Miriam is called Aaron's sister, hinting

---

43. Graupner, *Elohist*, 74–76.

that perhaps in this tradition she is not directly Moses' sister. Miriam sings because Moses is not a good speaker in the Elohist tradition according to Propp.[44]

Perhaps Exodus 15:25b–26 (Fretheim, Friedman)

The reference to how the Lord tested people in v. 25b makes many scholars suggest that this story about Marah might be Elohist, even though the name, Yahweh, is used. The Elohist narratives speak of testing, and the demand for Abraham to sacrifice Isaac is the supreme narrative example. However, in regard to this story Yoreh saw the Elohist version in vv. 22–24, 27, in which the people complained until they came to the waters of Elim.[45] No testing of the people occurs in this reconstruction, so I am disinclined to follow this division.

Perhaps Exodus 16:4–21

The provision of manna and quail might be an Elohist account, even though the divine name is Yahweh throughout. It has the element of testing and human murmuring, but otherwise it lacks clear Elohistic indicators. Furthermore, the allusions to the "glory of the Lord" in vv. 7 and 10 usually are seen as Priestly terms.

Even though this text in its present form appears to be dubious in terms of its connection to the Elohist tradition, I would assume that some form of a manna and quail tradition circulated in Elohist circles.[46] The story has thematic continuity with other Elohist accounts, especially the provision of food provided by prophets in the prophetic narratives, most especially the feeding of Elijah by the ravens (1 Kgs 17:6).

---

44. Propp, *Exodus 1–18*, 214, 482.
45. Yoreh, *First Book of God*, 201.
46. Schwartz, "Visit of Jethro."

Commentary on Elohist Texts

Perhaps Exodus 17:1–7
(Jenks, Fretheim, Friedman)

Some scholars have identified all or part of this story of water from the rock as Elohist on the basis of the reference to testing the LORD (v. 2), and the location of the account is at Massah and Meribah. The narrative uses the sacred name Yahweh instead of Elohim, thus leading some scholars to be cautious about calling this story Elohist. Baden believed this is not an Elohist text because it implies that Horeb is a place name for somewhere prior to their arrival at the sacred mountain.[47]

Perhaps Exodus 17:8–16
(Jenks, Fretheim, Friedman, Propp, Baden, Yoreh)

The battle with Amalek has sometimes been identified as Elohist on the basis of the presence of Joshua and Hur in the story, as well as the reference to God in v. 9 and the "staff of God," already referred to in Exod 4:17. Hur is also found in the Elohist text of Exod 24:14. Yoreh limited the narrative to vv. 8–13, since the sacred name Yahweh appears in the final three verses, while Baden identified the narrative as vv. 8–15, believing the Elohist will use the name of Yahweh after Exodus 3. Baden also observed that in Elohist narratives the Israelites have weapons as they move quickly through the wilderness, but this is not the case in the Yahwist narratives where they wander in the wilderness for a prolonged time.[48] As a story it offers hope to Israelites or Judahites of any age, stating that God will protect them against their enemies.

Exodus 18:1–27
(Noth, Jenks, Fretheim, Friedman, Coote, Campbell and O'Brien, Schmidt, Graupner, Propp, Baden, Yoreh)

The story of Jethro has often been viewed as Elohist either completely or partially, for the name Jethro is seen as his Elohist name and Hobab as his Yahwist name. In this account Elohim is usually the name for God (vv. 1, 5, 12, 15, 16, 19, 21, 23) but Yahweh also occurs (vv. 8, 9, 10,11), so Yoreh

---

47. Baden, *Composition of the Pentateuch*, 122.
48. Ibid., 121–25.

excluded those verses. Also, the reference to "mountain of God" (v. 5) appears. The selected judges are to "fear" God (v. 21). Aaron and the elders appear (v. 12). Otherwise distinctive Elohist themes are missing. In terms of plot-line, however, Jethro brings Moses' family (Exod 18:5), whereas in the Yahwist narrative Moses took his family with him (Exod 4:20), so that we can at least observe a doublet in this story even without distinctive vocabulary.[49]

Baruch Schwartz noted that Jethro's visit to Moses implies that the Israelites are encamped at Sinai, for sacrifice is offered (v. 12), which presumably fulfills the mandate to sacrifice at the mountain according to an Elohist text in Exod 3:12. When Exod 19:1–2 describes their arrival at the mountain, we realize that we have two versions of the arrival at the sacred mountain that conflict with each other, the Elohist version in Exodus 18 and the Yawhist version in Exodus 19. Schwartz believed this indicates that the Elohist was once a unified and coherent source.[50]

This story betokens Elohist universalism, for God is speaking through a Midianite foreigner. Thus, it appears that indirect revelation occurs as God really speaks to Moses through Jethro.[51]

Perhaps Exodus 19:2b–6
(Jenks, Fretheim, Friedman)

Sometimes this short passage is seen as Elohist. Sinai is simply called the mountain, a characteristic of the Elohist. If the passage is Elohist, the truly significant imagery is the reference to how the people should be a "priestly kingdom and a holy nation," a very significant identity for people to assume in exile for the sake of preserving their culture and religion. Otherwise, the passage might be Priestly in origin and saying the same thing to Jews in the sixth and fifth centuries.

---

49. Ibid., 121.
50. Schwartz, "Visit of Jethro," 29–48.
51. Graupner, *Elohist*, 111.

COMMENTARY ON ELOHIST TEXTS

Exodus 19:16–19
(Jenks, Fretheim, Friedman, Coote, Campbell and O'Brien, Schmidt, Baden, Yoreh)

This passage describes the "mountain" in dramatic fashion with thunder and lightning, and the Lord descending in fire and smoke, themes characteristic of the Elohist. The people trembled (v. 16), a sign of appropriate Elohistic fear before God. The name Elohim is used in vv. 17 and 19, while Yahweh is used in v. 18 to describe the truly dramatic descent of the deity.

Perhaps Exodus 20:1–4a, 7–8, 12–17
(Noth, Fretheim, Schmidt, Baden)

The Ten Commandments in Exodus 20 oft have been described as Elohist, with later Priestly editing, while the corresponding Yahwist commandments are said to be in Exodus 34. Often the Book of the Covenant in Exod 20:23–23:33 is included with the Decalogue as Elohist.[52] Some have suggested that only certain of these commandments first appeared in the original form. Yoreh suggested seven commandments, omitting commandments on images, name, and Sabbath, because they are inflated with additional language and the sacred name Yahweh occurs with those commandments but not the others. (This is a good argument!)[53] Laws and law codes are difficult to connect to sources; I believe it is better to assume that they had a prior existence in some early form and were taken up by biblical historians, and thus cannot be clearly identified with sources. For theological reasons the Elohist might have included an early form of the Decalogue as a good example of the laws of Yahweh that people in exile ought to observe, especially to preserve their identity. (The final form of the Decalogue has clear Deuteronomistic and Priestly additions.) If the Elohist had these commandments, they might all have been short, two or three words long, and all stated in the negative. Perhaps the word blaspheme was used in commandments now stated in positive fashion (Sabbath and parents), and over the years pious transmitters did not wish to have the word "blaspheme" in the code with the sacred name for God, Yahweh. But this is pure conjecture on my part (in an article still unpublished).

---

52. Baden, *Composition of the Pentateuch*, 117 et passim, has most recently suggested this model.

53. Yoreh, *First Book of God*, 213–15.

The Elohist

Baden observed that one of the reasons for including the Decalogue in the Elohist narrative is that the image of people hearing the voice of God commanding them to obey this law really validates Moses as a true prophet and assures acceptance of the other laws that he will bring to them. For Baden, removal of the Decalogue from the Elohist narrative is incomprehensible; the plot line would be incomplete.[54] One could also note that such laws provide guidelines for the community's obedient response to an awesome God who inspires fear among believers. The general idea of a grand law, such as the Decalogue, fits rather well with the overall theology of the Elohist.

Exodus 20:18–21
(Noth, Jenks, Fretheim, Coote, Campbell and O'Brien, Schmidt, Graupner, Baden, Yoreh)

The response of the people at the foot of the mountain appears to be Elohistic, for they were afraid and trembled at the sight of thunder and lightning and smoke (v. 18). These theophanic phenomena, which include fire imagery, also reflect Elohist style (v. 18). In similar Yahwist narratives the people are bold and wish to come up the mountain, and in Priestly accounts they are reverent, like priests. There is reference to testing of the people (v. 20), and the eventual result of such testing should be the "fear of God" (v. 20). God is portrayed distantly as being enveloped in thick darkness (v. 21), and Elohim is the name for God (vv. 19, 20, 21).

Exodus 24:1–2, 9–15
(Noth, Jenks, Fretheim, Friedman, Campbell and O'Brien, Schmidt, Graupner, Propp, Baden)

Elohistic themes include the following: God is portrayed in majestic fashion, there is an interest in Nadab and Abihu (v. 1) which foreshadows their later demise, there is reference to the seventy elders who will later prophesy, the people stand far from the mountain (vv. 1–2), Joshua is Moses' aide or "minister" (v. 13, which he will be called also in Exod 33:11; Num 11:28; Jos 1:1, all potentially Elohist texts), Aaron is present (v. 14), the mountain is called the "mountain of God" (v. 13), and the name Elohim is used (vv. 10,

---

54. Baden, *Redaction of the Pentateuch*, 156–58.

11, 13). The beautiful imagery, perhaps of lapis lazuli in the heavenly realm, might remind us of the vision of Jacob's ladder in Genesis 28. Both images stress divine transcendence.[55]

Exodus 32:1–10, 15–24
(Noth, Jenks, Fretheim, Friedman, Campbell and O'Brien)

The account of the golden calf is seen as Elohist by some critics, as Yahwistic by others, and a mixture of both sources by most. Not all agree on the verses. Yoreh was a minimalist, counting only vv. 1–4, 6, 15–20, excising verses with the sacred name.[56] Elohist themes include: reference to the mountain as simply the "mountain" (vv. 1, 15), allusion to the burning wrath of the Lord (v. 10) and the burning wrath of Moses (vv. 19, 22), reference to the burning of the calf (v. 20), a critical portrayal of Aaron, who represents the later priesthood, a target of Elohistic critique, an allusion to Joshua as an aide to Moses (v. 17), Moses speaking directly to God and thus functioning as a prophet, and above all, the critique of the calf cult, which would also be a target of Elohist critique. The divine name Elohim appears in vv. 1, 4, 16, 23, and Yahweh appears in vv. 5, 7, 9, but after the revelation of the divine name in Exodus 3, this may not be a good distinguishing characteristic.

The golden calf is the ultimate symbol of the evil that got Israel in trouble with God and led to the destruction of the state in 722 BCE. The presence of Aaron in the story symbolizes the cooperation of priests with the kings in creating this royal cult that so offended God. The allusion to the earrings that went into the creation of the golden calf (Exod 32:2–3) reminds us of the earrings rejected and buried by Jacob as idolatrous (Gen 35:4). This motif connects the golden calf to Bethel in the ancient stories and would remind the Elohist's audience even more of Jeroboam's golden calf at Bethel. Moses' breaking of the tablets may symbolize the destruction of the covenant Israel had with God by venerating the calf statue in Bethel. Perhaps Moses' destruction of the calf may recall symbolically how the statue ultimately was destroyed, or, if not, it certainly describes what the Elohist felt should have been done with the statue. An alternative recent explanation suggests that the Deuteronomistic Historian added the image of the calf, which thereby made the readers think of Bethel in a negative light, but the original Elohist account merely condemned Aaron for idolatry,

---

55. Graupner, *Elohist*, 135.
56. Yoreh, *First Book of God*, 216–20.

thereby castigating the priesthood.⁵⁷ My explanation more simply accepts the text as is and views it as condemnation of both priests and Bethel for practices prior to 722 BCE, including the devotion to the calf.

Perhaps Exodus 33:7–11
(Jenks, Fretheim, Friedman, Propp, Baden)

The reference to the "pillar of cloud" (v. 9), the reverence of the people (v. 10), and the description of Joshua as "minister" (v. 11, found also in Exod 24:13; Num 11:28; Josh 1:1) imply Elohist origins. In this narrative the tent of meeting appears to be the site of prophetic revelation, if we view Moses as a prophet receiving the divine messages from God. Comparable passages about the tent of meeting include Num 11:16–17; 12:4–10; and Deut 31:14–15. The prophetic image of Moses in these texts may reflect Elohist nuances in the narrative portrayal. Also, the tent of meeting is located outside the camp, as it also the case with the Elohist account in Num 11:16–17, 24b–30.⁵⁸ This portrayal of the tent diverges from those priestly texts that place the tent inside the camp and emphasize the holiness of the tent (Lev 16:2; Num 3:7–10, 38). The prophetic portrayal views God as coming down from the heavenly realm to reveal a message, thus emphasizing the transcendence of God; while the priestly portrayal views God as present in the midst of Israel, as the temple was in the midst of Jerusalem, thus emphasizing the immanence of God.⁵⁹

However, the sacred name Yahweh is used in vv. 7, 9, 11. The people inquire of the Lord by coming to this Tent, but according to the Elohist in Exodus 18, Moses seems to have created judges for this reason, unless people seek the Lord at the tent for different reasons. Yoreh excluded this passage for these two reasons and because he believed that God is never in a cloud for the Elohist. He therefore suggested that neither Exod 33:7–11 nor Num 11:16–17, 24b–30 are Elohist.⁶⁰

---

57. White, "Elohist Depiction of Aaron."
58. Sommer, "Reflecting on Moses," 605.
59. Knohl, "Two Aspects of the 'Tent of Meeting,'" 73–79.
60. Yoreh, *First Book of God*, 255.

Commentary on Elohist Texts

Leviticus

Leviticus 10:1–3

This short account in its present form appears to be a Priestly text, but originally it might have been from Elohist circles. The image of fire as the agent of God's punishment stands out. The death of Nadab and Abihu, the sons of Aaron, for unholy behavior does not appear to be a story that Priestly editors would generate, but rather it is consistent with the Elohist critique of Aaron and priests in general.[61] One would not expect the Priestly tradition to generate a narrative that depicts priests and especially Aaron's sons so negatively. Also, since two sons of Jeroboam, Abijah, and Nadab (1 Kgs 15:25) have such similar names, one cannot avoid the suspicion that this is a veiled critique of northern kings. Abijah died as a child and Nadab as king was assassinated. Both Aaron and Jeroboam made golden calves. This cannot be a coincidence.[62] Propp believed that Nadab and Abihu were priests serving the calf cult in Bethel.[63]

Numbers

Numbers 11:1–3
(Jenks, Fretheim, Friedman)

The short story of Taberah is often viewed as Elohist because of the reference to fire as a tool of divine punishment, and the importance of Moses as an intercessor to stop the destruction of the people. Again, this is another story about punishment for sin, a story designed to lead Israelites to recognize that their sin led to the destruction of the state.[64]

---

61. Nicholson, *Pentateuch*, 211.
62. Aberback and Smolar, "Golden Calves"; and Sweeney, *I & II Kings*, 184.
63. Propp, *Exodus 19–40*, 578.
64. Snaith, *Leviticus and Numbers*, 139; and Baden, *Redaction of the Pentateuch*, 106–14.

The Elohist

Perhaps Numbers 11:11–12, 14–17, 24b–30
(Jenks, Fretheim, Friedman, Baden)

The common theme which unites these passages is that Moses must "bear the people" and this "burden is too much for him, so seventy elders must be appointed to assist Moses. The unity of this account has been established by Baden's careful analysis of it.[65] It appears that this complaint of Moses would have followed the incident with the golden calf, so one can understand Moses' frustration in this Elohist narrative.

Recalling the prophetic experience of the seventy elders in the wilderness would appear to be Elohist, considering the Elohist's interest in prophets. (However, this might stand in tension with the notion that Moses appoints judges over the people in Exodus 18 to provide directions from God.) Furthermore, when Moses hears that Eldad and Medad prophesied in the camp (v. 26), he responds, "Would that all the Lord's people were prophets" (v. 29), a rather strong affirmation of prophets in general. Also, the Lord comes down in the cloud (v. 25), as was the case in the Elohist text of Exod 33:9–10, Joshua appears as Moses' assistant or "minister" yet again (v. 28), as was the case in Exod 33:11, and the tent of meeting is outside the camp as it was according Exod 33:7–11. This is one of four texts in which the tent of meeting is connected to the image of prophetic revelation (the others are Exod 33:6–11; Num 12:4–10; Deut 31:14–15). However, Yahweh is the sacred name for God in vv. 16, 25, 29, and the image of God coming down in a cloud as an Elohist motif has been challenged by some. But in Elohist texts the cloud comes down and verifies Moses' authority (Exod 19:9; 20:16), and such is the case here. If you exclude this passage from Elohist texts, you also exclude Exod 33:7–11.[66]

It is possible in the Elohist narrative that this account belonged to the experiences at Horeb, since we lack any narratives that are connected to the departure of the people from the mountain. The election of the elders would fit with the other activities connected to the mountain, most obviously the laws, for both elders and the laws give shape to the community of people who fear God and respond in obedience. In the Yahwist narrative of Exod 24:1, 9 the elders simply accompany Moses up the mountain, but this narrative sees them as active in a leadership role over the people. In the Yahwist God leads the people directly, but in the Elohist God has Moses

---

65. Baden, *Composition of the Pentateuch*, 85–94.
66. Yoreh, *First Book of God*, 255; and Baden, *Composition of the Pentateuch*, 98–101.

and now the elders lead the people while the "messenger of God" actually leads them physically through the wilderness (Exod 32:34).[67]

Numbers 12:1–15
(Jenks, Fretheim, Friedman, Baden)

When Miriam and Aaron criticize Moses for his Cushite wife, the divine response to them is an affirmation of Moses' prophetic role. The LORD comes down in the pillar of cloud (v. 5) and declares the validity of visions and dreams, Elohist modes of divine revelation. The divine speech also declares that the LORD speaks "face to face" with Moses, thus affirming his role as the greatest of all prophets. There is an allusion to "fear" that Aaron and Miriam should have experienced (v. 8). Moses is an intercessor for Miriam (v. 13). Thus, a number of Elohist themes appear. Again the tent of meeting appears in a text connected to the imagery of prophetic revelation (Exod 33:6–11; Num 11:16–17; Deut 31:14–15). The use of Yahweh may imply Yahwist reworking of this passage or the use of the sacred name by the Elohist for a dramatically important account after the revelation of that name in Exodus 3.

Moses and his unique authority is emphasized in contrast to Miraim and Aaron, and although the account speaks only of Miriam's punishment, it has been suggested that traditions may have been excised about Aaron's corresponding punishment by later Priestly editors.

Perhaps Numbers 14:13–16
(Fretheim)

Some commentators suggest that Moses' prayer to the Lord is Elohist. He is a prophetic intercessor for the people, there is allusion to the "cloud" and the "pillar of cloud" by day and the "pillar of fire" by night (v. 14), there is another allusion to seeing the Lord "face to face" (obviously in reference to Moses), and in general there is the idea that fear of the Lord is being experienced.[68] If this is an Elohist text, even though it uses the name Yahweh, it reinforces some of the themes previously mentioned about divine presence in exile and prophetic leadership.

---

67. Baden, *Composition of the Pentateuch*, 98.
68. Snaith, *Leviticus and Numbers*, 145.

The Elohist

Perhaps Numbers 21:4–9
(Fretheim, Friedman, Coote, Baden, Yoreh)

Some believe the story of the Bronze serpent may have been Elohist. Yoreh accepted it as Elohist after omitting vv. 4a, 5b, 7b–8, all of which mention the sacred name.[69] Moses' authority is challenged (v. 5) and he performs the role of intercessor for the people (v. 7). As in other Elohist accounts he appears to be almost like a powerful magician. The bronze serpent, or *nehustan*, in later years was in the Jerusalem temple, and Hezekiah destroyed it. So it is strange why the Elohist would have been interested in this account about a Judahite relic.

Perhaps Numbers 21:21–33, 35
(Noth, Fretheim, Campbell and O'Brien, Baden, Yoreh)

A few suggest that this passage about Sihon of the Amorites may be Elohist. Fire as a destructive force, perhaps divine in origin, occurs in the ballad in vv. 28, 30. It uses the nomenclature "Amorite" to describe the people, an ethic identification used in Gen 15:16, which may have originally been Elohist in some form, and Gen 48:22, a text usually considered to be Elohist. In Yahwist texts the word "Canaanite" appears instead of "Amorite." The term may reflect the political experience of the northern kingdom of Israel, and it may have been used to identity a particular group of people.[70] Verse 25 records that the Israelites settled in those Tranjordanian Amorite cities, including Hesbon, and that reflects northern and Elohist concerns. In Yahwist texts, like Num 14:20–25 the Israelites simply wander in the wilderness, and that includes the Transjordan.[71]

In an extremely well argued presentation Baden proposed that the encounter with Sihon reflects an important component of the overall Elohist itinerary for the movement of the Israelites from Egypt to the land of Canaan. He believed the Elohist narrative portrays the angel or messenger of God leading the Israelites into the wilderness (Exod 23:20, 23; 32:34) instead of Yahweh directly, as in the Yahwist narrative. The Elohist recalls the stay in Egypt lasting four generations, instead of one generation, as in the Yahwist, and thus the Elohist law concerning the "stranger" (Exod

---

69. Yoreh, *First Book of God*, 224–25.
70. Graupner, *Elohist*, 152.
71. Yoreh, *First Book of God*, 227–29.

Commentary on Elohist Texts

22:21–24) reflects a concern for sojourners in an alien land. The Elohist knows nothing of a sea crossing nor a prolonged stay in the wilderness, for the generation that left Egypt went into Canaan. (Deut 4:9–13; 5:3–4; 29:1–7 recalls those old Elohist images.) This entry was accomplished by skirting Edom (Num 21:4a) and entering Canaan from the east. Baden believed that Num 20:22a and 21:4a were connected to each other and originally read, "They set out from Kadesh to skirt the land of Edom." Thus, in Num 21:12–15 the Israelites are beyond the Arnon River between Moab and the Amorites poised to enter the land and ready for battle with Sihon the Amorite. This conforms to the Elohist vision of the Israelite movement in the wilderness and entry into the land. Baden's analysis demonstrated how the Sihon narrative fits into the Elohist account, but he also included in this overall narrative the references to Miriam's death (Num 20:1) and Moses' dialogue with the king of Edom (Num 20:14–22), especially because of its reference to the divine messenger in Num 20:26. He also saw allusions to hardships during the wilderness journey (Num 20:14; cf. Exod 18:8; 20:17; 22:4; Num 16:14) and to a long stay in Egypt (Num 20:15) as Elohist motifs.[72] I have not included the Edom narrative in my listing, for I am not totally convinced that these passages are Elohist, but I am impressed with Baden's attempt to bring these texts together into a consistent narrative.

Complementary to Baden's argument is the evaluation of Numbers 32 by Liane Marquis, who discerned a Priestly and an Elohist version of the narrative about Gad and Reuben in the Transjordan. He observed an Elohist narrative in select fragmented verses of Numbers 32 wherein the two tribes approach Moses and offer to help in the conquest of the Transjordan after they have already settled in the Transjordan; the Priestly version promises them the land only after they have participated in the fighting. The Elohist motifs observed by him are the reference to Sihon and the lack of reference to God leading the people in battle, which are found in both Yahwist and Priestly narratives.[73]

---

72. Baden, "Narratives of Numbers 20–21," 644–51.
73. Marquis, "Composition of Numbers 32," 413, 422, 427–28.

The Elohist

Numbers 22:1–7, 9–13a, 14–17, 20–21, 36–40; 23:1–2, 18–21a, 22–24, 27–30; 24:2–6a, 6c–11a, 14–25
(Noth, Jenks, Fretheim, Friedman, Campbell and O'Brien, Schmidt, Graupner, Propp)

Most commentators believe the Balaam story to be Elohist, although some believe that parts of it, such as chapter 23 (Noth) or chapter 24 are not Elohist (Noth, Jenks, Schmidt). I omit selected verses in a fashion similar to Yoreh. Verses with the sacred name may be passages added by the Yahwist Historian. The dream reports in Num 22:9–13, 20–21 contain the Elohist pattern. As the "king of Egypt" fears the strength of Israel in Exod 1:9–10, so also Balak has the same concern in Num 24:6 with very similar language. Also, the allusion to "fear" in Num 22:3 implies Elohist influence. Balaam is obedient to God and he gives blessings upon Israel, not the curses demanded by Barak (who should have gotten his money back). So again, this is a story about obedience. The story has been reworked by the Yahwist Historian in parts of the text, such as Num 24:17–19 that may allude to the Davidic kingdom in a nostalgic sense.

Graupner believed that the Elohist epic ends with the Balaam narratives and this dramatic blessing of Israel, for it gives hope to Israelites in the political turmoil of the late ninth century after Jehu's revolt.[74] He likewise argued that Yahwist material appears to be inserted into the core of Elohist narrative.[75] This would make better sense if the Yahwist Historian took a fairly expansive Elohist narrative about Balaam and added materials to it in the late sixth century.

In the Elohist texts, Balaam is portrayed as magician with the power to bless or curse people. Elohim or God comes to Balaam dramatically in dreams and commands him to speak the blessings that ensue instead of the curses Balaam initially intended. In the Yahwist portrayal of Balaam, Balaam is a more faithful steward of Yahweh who faithfully speaks the words that Yahweh gives, and he can turn to Yahweh to learn what to say. He is less a powerful magician and more a faithful messenger of Yahweh.[76]

---

74. Graupner, *Elohist*, 174–76.
75. Ibid., 172.
76. Yoreh, *First Book of God*, 237–51.

Deuteronomy

Some accounts either cannibalized an Elohist source or quote from an Elohist document. As noted earlier, Baden has shown how the texts in Deuteronomy seem to quote Elohist traditions but are unaware of corresponding Yahwist traditions. The following passages appear to be good examples of texts used by Deuteronomy that have their own identity, that is, they do not refer back to stories in Exodus and Numbers. Thus, we consider them here as though they are perhaps independent Elohist passages.

Perhaps Deuteronomy 31:14–15
(Jenks, Fretheim, Friedman, Baden)

Some believe this little reference is Elohist due to the references to the "tent of meeting" (vv. 14–15), to the "pillar of cloud" (v. 15), and Joshua's role as Moses' aide (v. 14). This is one of four texts about the tent of meeting that appears to portray the tent as a place of prophetic revelation (cf. Exod 33:7–11; Num 11:16–17; 12:4–10). This imagery corresponds very closely to prior Elohist narratives.[77]

Perhaps Deuteronomy 34:5, 10–12

This might be a summary to the Elohist epic or at least the Moses cycle. The image of Moses going to pharaoh (v. 11) is comparable to the language of Exod 3:13–15. The overall praise for Moses as a great prophet makes the text appear Elohistic.[78]

These passages constitute those texts worthy of consideration when trying to articulate the theological perspective of the Elohist. Of course, we can never be sure about a host of texts that contain Elohist ideas that were radically rewritten by the Yahwist in terms of vocabulary, but some of the Elohist thought remained. Nonetheless, there are significant themes in many of these texts that stand forth and deserve our attention and exposition.

---

77. Baden, *Composition of the Pentateuch*, 120.

78. Yoo, "Moses Death Accounts," 436–40; and Baden, *Composition of the Pentateuch*, 120, 148.

8

The Modern Relevance of the Elohist

AFTER REFLECTING UPON THE message that the Elohist might have provided to an audience over two millennia ago, it may be worthwhile to ponder what kind of relevant message could be addressed to us. There are numerous speculative directions that we might take, but I am impressed with several themes—the distance of God, the plight of refugees, the courage to oppose corrupt authority, and food for the hungry masses.

A Distant Deity

The God proclaimed by the Elohist is a high and transcendent deity, a *deus absconditus*, as Graupner observes, a "hidden god," unlike the *deus revelatus*, "a revealed god," or a very present god, as we find in the Yahwist texts.[1] In the seventh century many Israelites probably felt that their God had deserted them and become "hidden" from them. After the destruction of the state, many deaths, and exile, the folk of Israel probably felt that their state deity had withdrawn and become "hidden." The Elohist spoke to this by portraying God as indeed distant, but also by portraying this distant deity as one who accompanied the exiles just as "exiled" Jacob and escaped slaves in the wilderness were guided, guarded, and led by God. The Elohist attempted to portray God as both "hidden" yet "present" in a mysterious, deep way.

As Rabbi Lou Silberman said once many years ago to my graduate class at Vanderbilt, "Every generation sees God as present for their spiritual ancestors in the past, but distant in their own present age." Probably those

---

1. Graupner, *Der Elohist*, 386.

texts that spoke so dramatically of divine presence, such as the narratives of the Yahwist, addressed people who felt that God was distant for them and sought to reassure them that God could be present for them in faith. The Elohist seemed to recognize that notion and attacked it head-on. The portrayal of deity is one of transcendence, an image that people could understand, but the Elohist then portrayed that distant deity as active in the lives of patriarchal ancestors and exiles in the wilderness, thereby implying that the deity could be present somehow for believers in their own age.

Contemporary biblical scholars have theologized on this imagery in the past generation. Terrien crafted a theology of the Old Testament around the concept of the "elusive God," explicating how all the Old Testament texts seek to show that God is present for people, but yet at the same time not easily encapsulated by human thought.[2] Friedman wrote a theology about the apparent gradual disappearance of God in the biblical text from the Primeval History in Genesis 1–11 onward.[3] His portrait may reflect the movement from the predominantly Yahwist texts of Genesis 1–11, which portray God anthropomorphically, through the Patriarchal narratives of Genesis 12–36, with their selections of Elohist passages that view God in more transcendent fashion, to the post-exilic novel of Joseph in Genesis 37–50, and post-exilic novels often portray God very much in the background with human emotions and decisions driving the plot. Nevertheless, his characterization does hit the nerve of this sensitive existential and religious question, "Where is God?"—a question voiced by many. It recognizes that in the canonical text there is the recognition of divine distance from human existence. Burnett reviewed a great number of personal names both in the Old Testament and the rest of the ancient Near East that asked the same question about God. So many names alluded to the distance of the deity or the divine. His point was that this human feeling about divine absence is a universal phenomenon in all cultures. He then sought to show that the Old Testament in all its discourse about God is really trying to tell people how God, Yahweh of Israel, may be found.[4] Ultimately it is a faith question in any age to find God.

Our modern age has been increasingly awed by the size and grandeur of the universe around us. This has been driven home to us most recently by images from the Hubble space telescope that enable us to peer into the vast

---

2. Terrien, *Elusive Presence*.
3. Friedman, *Disappearance of God*, 7–140.
4. Burnett, *Where is God?*, 12–42.

distances of space, as well as time, since the light has traveled thousands and millions of years before its observation by our telescopes. How insignificant we are in the vastness of space. For those who still believe in God, or a divine being in the universe, one can only wonder how insignificant we might be in the divine scheme of things. One can imagine such imagery dovetailing nicely with the biblical imagery of a distant God. Yet the Elohist envisioned this distant God communicating to people with indirect forms of revelation, and thus becoming present for them. As the Elohist spoke then of a distant God becoming near, so also people today can speak of the divine being present in the lives of people.

We today might speak of the presence of the divine most notably in human consciousness. As the Elohist described the divine presence in human dreams, the angel of God, fire, and a distant voice from the heavens, so we today might speak of the divine presence in our own human consciousness. It is our consciousness that makes our human species reflect upon the existence of God, and that same human consciousness that believers would confess to be the point of contact for divine revelation. It has been said that the evolution of consciousness in the human species is the universe's way of looking at itself. This observation sounds like a non-theistic way of confessing the existence of God, but it is still theologically profound.

I am reminded of the Hindu tradition, which speaks of Brahma as the divine ground of being, but speaks of Brahma in two ways. Nirguna Brahma or Para Brahma (the Brahma that is "above," which is the meaning of the Sanskrit word Para) is the distant Brahma that lies outside the universe and cannot be known, the Brahma that is beyond existence and can almost be said to "not exist." But Brahma "fleshes" itself or himself out as the universe to become Saguna Brahma or Apara Brahma (the Brahma that is "not above," which is the meaning of the Sanskrit word Apara). The world is thus sometimes described as "the foot of Brahma" in this process of total cosmic incarnation. Brahma becomes the entire physical world. The most significant manifestation of Apara Brahma, however, is human consciousness or the atman (soul), and human consciousness seeks to return to Brahma through successive reincarnations.[5] This dramatic tension between the transcendent Para Brahma and the immanent Apara Brahma reminds us of the Christian tension between the transcendent God who is *deus absconditus*, "totally other," and beyond human understanding and the complete immanence of God in the incarnation of Jesus Christ. I dare

---

5. Noss, *World's Religions*, 87–88; and Nigosian, *World Religions*, 148–51.

say that our Christian encounter with Hindu thought from India in the past two centuries has actually deepened the dramatic way we speak of the nature of God in Christian theology. Perhaps Hindu thought has made us more prone to speak of the divine as being present in human consciousness. Yet again we can appreciate the imagery of the Elohist who works with the vision of a high and transcendent God, who then becomes available for people through indirect forms of revelation.

I have often said that in the Christian tradition people have asked three questions over the years. In the ancient church the Philippian jailor asked the question, "What must I do to be saved?" This was the question of the first Christians—"How do I find salvation?" By that they meant, how do I find a community where I can experience the power of God or the Spirit in this life and have hope of an afterlife? By the time of the Reformation, after centuries of black plagues had left people with the image of God as a horrible judge punishing them with plague for their sins, people asked, "How can I find a gracious God?" Both Protestants and Roman Catholics alike answered with talk about grace mediated to people through the proclaimed word of the Gospel from the pulpit (Protestant) or through the sacraments administered by the church (Roman Catholic), with a strong emphasis on how the death of Jesus absorbed the wrath of the father. In the modern age the question seems to be, "Is there a God at all?" Perhaps the question is also, "Is there any meaning and purpose to life in general, and my life in particular, especially if there is no God?" This is really a question that has been asked by people all along throughout history, but it has truly come to the fore in the modern age.[6]

Perhaps the stories of the Elohist speak to this concern. The Elohist may have addressed Israelites, who experienced destruction and exile and consequently questioned the existence of God. The Elohist did not give them an answer, for religions can never give concrete answers to the great questions of life, only suggestions that faith might apprehend. The Elohist spoke of a distant God who was somehow present for people who could believe that this deity accompanied them in their lives and directed them toward a meaningful and hopeful future. Perhaps, such texts might still speak to people in dark existential despair, and such imagery can inspire them to craft new images of hope.

I myself cannot speak of a distant God, for such a *deus absconditus* is no God at all, for that is the point of saying God is hidden—that there

---

6. Gnuse, *Process Theology*, 1–12.

is no God. I am a process theologian and I prefer to speak of God and the divine being present in people and in the human process of development and evolution.[7] Of course, my theological discourse is not an answer either, nor is it rational. It is simply a message of hope to utter to people in order to give meaning to their lives. To say that God identifies with the human condition and suffers with people is a statement of faith as dramatic as the Elohist's confession of faith. Some Old Testament theologians have moved in this direction in their explications of the biblical text.[8] It is simply another way, somewhat different from that of the Elohist, which hopefully speaks to people.

Many people share the existential despair that perhaps we are alone in the universe on a piece of rock hurtling through space. To such despair the Elohist may speak. Elohist imagery of a distant God who can still be present for people in the darkness of the night, in the darkness of life, is a meaningful metaphor, if we can apply it correctly.

I have often said, "If there is a God, we need to treat each other with love and respect out of response to the divine imperatives; but if there is no God, we need to treat each other with love and respect, because we only have each other." If we seek to treat each other with love, dignity, and respect, then there are some social justice issues that can be raised by the consideration of the Elohist texts.

World Wide Refugees

We live in a world of refugees. Several years ago (October, 2010) I read on the BBC web site how the European Union was sending extra military support to Greece to stem the tide of Afghan refugees who were fleeing across the Middle East through Turkey in order to get into Greece. Here they hoped to have a better life, even though Greece itself was experiencing economic turmoil. Some would attempt to leave Greece at some later time in order to reach other European countries. This activity still continues today. This boggles my mind. The distance that these people have to travel from Afghanistan to Greece is unbelievable. The journey from Turkey to various parts of Greece by itself, much of it on foot, is arduous and difficult. But so great is their desire to flee a war-torn country, that they undertake

---

7. Ibid.

8. Heschel, *Prophets*, who spoke of the pathos of God; Fretheim, *Suffering of God*; and Gnuse, *Process Theology*, 65–83.

The Modern Relevance of the Elohist

this perilous journey. So great are their numbers that they create chaos in Greece and a crisis for Europe.

The world is awash with refugees, fleeing war, famine, or political oppression. Tremendous numbers of refugees are currently fleeing Syria (2013–15) from the horrid strife there, and they are creating a potential humanitarian refugee crisis in the neighboring countries of Turkey and Jordan. More recently people fleeing the worn torn country of Libya are fleeing to Italy in boats, many drowning at sea, and it has become a humanitarian crisis for Italy and European nations in general (2015). Refugees from Somalia and the province of Darfur in the Sudan flee war and starvation creating a humanitarian crisis in East Africa. Refugees from war torn Sri Lanka leave the country fearing political repression now that the civil war is over. Muslim tribal minorities in Myanmar (formerly known as Burma) flee persecution from the Buddhist tribal majority and take to the sea in boats desperately trying to sail to Indonesia. As in the Mediterranean, many of these refugees tragically drown at sea. Mexicans storm the borders of the United States hoping to find jobs and a better life for themselves and their families, too often becoming tragic victims of unscrupulous guides and sometimes becoming mules for drug cartels. For years Cubans and Haitians floated out into the waters hoping to find the promised land of Florida. The list could go on. It seems that we have a larger number of displaced human beings in our world today than was the case in Europe after World War II, which was an era of tremendous and horrible human displacement also. We have an overpopulated world and the limited resources of our world are possessed disproportionately by a small minority of rich people. This alone causes refugees to flee their homelands for a better life elsewhere. When you add to that the horrors of war, civil and tribal strife, again caused by the shortage of resources in many instances, the flood of refugees becomes staggering in our world.

Suddenly those Elohist passages speak again. They speak of a divine presence for human beings who have been cut adrift from their homelands. The passages speak of the hope for return to the homeland, or I suppose, it can speak of the hope of finding a new homeland.

Ancient Israelites and Judahites dragged into exile in the eighth and sixth centuries often found themselves used as slaves on building projects in the Assyrian and Babylonian empires. (They spun off tales about the fall of such oppressive empires in parables like the Tower of Babel in Genesis

11.)[9] They experienced the brutality that captives, exiles, slaves, and refugees encounter in any age. It is happening again in our own age on a worldwide basis.

Who reads the ancient texts in the Bible? We do. To be sure, many of these refugees, who are Christians, do so also, and perhaps they identify with Abraham, Isaac, and Jacob, who wandered without a land, and the slaves who fled Egypt for freedom in the wilderness. But ultimately we who read the text can do something. If we appreciate the message that is found in the Pentateuch, perhaps we might more deeply realize how God identifies with the homeless and the landless poor in the immortalized words of the sacred text. (How can television preachers prattle constantly about our devotion to the biblical text and then not really hear its deeper message?) Perhaps if we realize where divine commitment is placed according to those sacred words, perhaps we might try to place our commitment in the same direction and seek to help the refugees of the world.

We, who have the power, need to do whatever is possible to create political stability in our world, feed the hungry masses, and find homes for the displaced refugees. Yes, we have done that in the past; we have done that since World War II. But we need to continue and accelerate our efforts in that regard. To that end the biblical texts can be used to inspire our efforts. I believe, whether rightly or wrongly, the isolation of texts called the "Elohist" by critical scholars can enable us to focus even more clearly on that poignant biblical message, for therein we may discern yet again God's love of the poor, the refugees, and landless people of the world.

Civil Disobedience

Elohist narratives bespeak an attitude of resistance to kings. This is especially true when the prophetic narratives in the books of 1 and 2 Kings are taken into account, for herein we see the memories of prophetic critique and resistance by Elijah and Elisha to the kings of the northern state of Israel. But we also have some material in the Tetrateuch worth considering.

The tale of the midwives in Exod 1:15–21 is an incredible story of civil disobedience. Two midwives, who were either Hebrew or Egyptian, defied pharaoh. Midwives were among the lower classes of society, while pharaoh in Egypt was viewed as a god—the incarnate god Horus, son of Osiris. But

---

9. Gnuse, "The Tale of Babel," 229–44.

The Modern Relevance of the Elohist

the biblical text declares that the midwives "feared God" (v. 17), and this enabled them courageously to defy pharaoh. Would that Christians in the past two thousand years could have so feared God to refrain from genocide!

Their names are recalled by the Elohist; they were Shiphrah and Puah. Pharaoh, who is called the king of Egypt by the Elohist, has no name. He is a nameless and faceless tyrant. The powerless women have been immortalized; pharaoh has been forgotten. Powerful pharaoh has his will bent by two peasant women, who have prevailed over him.[10] Throughout the exodus traditions this nameless pharaoh symbolizes tyrants of every age, the nameless beasts who oppress and kill helpless people with all the power that organized states can muster. He tragically recalls the holocaust of the mid-twentieth century wherein a "Nazi pharaoh" sought to kill all the "babies" or to throw all the Jews into the river, or into the ovens. We still remain appalled by how a modern civilized state could marshal its scientific and technological resources in a cold and calculating fashion to thoroughly annihilate a helpless people. But in the distant past the sacred text speaks of a different symbolic story. The small and insignificant midwives, who were but flotsam in the machinery of a great imperial state, prevailed, and they can inspire us. Their protection of the Israelite babies created Israel, for without them and their rebellion, there would have been no Israelites for Moses to liberate.

As we read this story, these women become the individuals of any era who stand up and defy imperial states and powerful pharaohs. In their act of disobedience Israel was born. They are remembered forever by the Elohist, and the king of Egypt, with all his glorious splendor and might, remains nameless.[11] Perhaps pharaoh is called the king of Egypt in this story so that the Israelite audience and we might realize that this persona represents the later kings of Israel who led the kingdom to destruction, and moreover he represents the kings and politicians of any age who lead their people to ruin and destruction.

Not only did the midwives disobey the king of Egypt, they played him for a fool. They disparaged Egyptian women as weaker than Hebrew women, for they said that Hebrew women gave birth and were quickly out in the fields working, so that the midwives could not find them. (Their strong newborn babies were probably making bricks, too!) I think this statement on their lips implies that they were Egyptian; Hebrews would not

10. Fretheim, *Exodus*, 31–32.
11. Ibid., 34.

speak so boldly of their own race to pharaoh, nor would pharaoh have been deceived by them. For the Elohist to portray such arrogance in the women who should have trembled before the divine pharaoh was remarkable for any culture in that ancient age. The king of Egypt was portrayed by the biblical author as a fool, for he believed the women. Secure in the delusion of his Horus divinity, surrounded by fawning advisors, under-girded by an imperial state, he assumed that no mortal, much less a woman and a midwife, would dare lie to him. Such is the nature of tyrants and kings in any age, according to the biblical text, they are fools who wallow in the chimera of their pretentious power and are shielded from reality by the self-serving "yes-men" who surround them.

A conquering or ruling race, upon subjugating a less fortunate people, might commit genocide against them. To effectively commit genocide one should kill the females, who reproduce, not the males, who can be a slave labor source until they die.[12] Tragically, this has been the form of genocide our world too often has seen. Sometimes, however, the women are not killed, but a different strategy is used. In Yugoslavian wars of the 1990s women were the targets of methodical group rape. The oppressors attempted to destroy the Bosnians by impregnating the women with babies holding a different ethnic identity, relying on the Bosnian condemnation of abortion to insure that the babies would be born. Such rapes were organized by political leaders. This was an organized political procedure, not the result of the random insanity of war.

In seminary I attended some courses in Old Testament under a visiting professor from Germany. When he was a young professor in Germany he studied this story of the women who rebelled against pharaoh. He realized that Israel was born in an act of rebellion when these two women defied the state and refused to kill the baby boys. He argued that the women were Egyptian, so that they sided with the helpless foreigners against their own mighty ruler and fellow countrymen. As a German he was raised to obey his political leaders unconditionally with fear and obedience. But this story inspired him to engage in resistance against his own government. He ultimately became one of the Lutheran clergy who conspired with German generals in the failed bomb plot against Adolph Hitler's life. He was not caught, but Dietrich Bonhoeffer, his friend, was caught and executed. We seminary students knew about Bonhoeffer's participation, but we had no idea that this professor was also involved. Apparently he only spoke of

---

12. Childs, *Exodus*, 11.

this to American students when he taught in this country. He told us that Americans could understand this story because our nation was born in an act of revolution two centuries ago. The tale of the midwives, as well as other biblical stories, led a quiet little university professor to go up against one of the greatest tyrants of all time. Imagine if people read this story today and realized the depth of meaning in this narrative. In my opinion this short story by itself justifies the affirmation of the existence of theological tradition called the Elohist in my scholarly research.

The Elohist tradition had a strong sense of obedience to God rather than kings and those in power. This would make the Elohist tradition an ethic of civil disobedience, a remarkable intellectual tradition to locate in the first millennium BCE. It is a theological tradition that can still inspire us today.

When we include the prophetic narratives from the book of Kings into this theological reflection, we find stories that dynamically resonate the theme of civil disobedience. Both Elijah and Elisha opposed the royal politics of their age. The story of Naboth's vineyard in 1 Kgs 21:1–29 immediately comes to mind, as it recalls Elijah's condemnation of Ahab's seizure of a citizen's private property as well as his execution. The defeat of the prophets of Baal by Elijah in 1 Kgs 18:20–40 appears to be an attack upon religious functionaries supported by the royal court. In 2 Kgs 2:1–16 Elijah acts defiantly by killing two companies of royal soldiers and finally condemning king Ahaziah. Granted, the Elijah narratives probably were reworked in two editions by the Deuteronomistic Historian in the seventh and sixth centuries, but we assume that in some form, the memories of Elijah, recalled in Elohist circles, placed him in opposition to kings so as to justify the later theological elaboration upon that theme.

If we turn to the Elisha traditions, we see opposition to royal prerogatives. Elisha committed the ultimate act of civil disobedience by inspiring a revolution that overthrew two kings. In 2 Kgs 9:1–12 he commissioned a prophet to anoint general Jehu king and inspire him to overthrow the Omride dynasts of both Israel and Judah (2 Kgs 9:13–37; 10:1–28).

It has been suggested that the anti-royal polemic in both the Elijah and Elisha traditions was crafted as an anti-Omride polemic during the reign of Jehu in the ninth century to legitimate the regicide committed by Jehu as he ascended the throne of Israel.[13] If this is true, then by the seventh century the Elohist inherited traditions with an anti-royal polemic in them,

---

13. White, *The Elijah Legends*, 1–78.

which would reinforce the Elohist demand to obey God rather than kings. This theory would assume that the Elijah traditions were fairly developed by the beginning of the seventh century and not a complete Deuteronomistic creation.

With or without the Elijah traditions in their final form, the Elohist would have organized prophetic accounts, especially the Elisha traditions, with sufficient anti-royal rhetoric within them to reinforce his theological and ethical stance to obey God rather than kings. If we take the Pentateuchal account of the midwives together with the prophetic stories and attribute them to north prophetic or Elohist circles, we can sense that there is a strong imperative to oppose kings, if it is necessary. In other writings I have maintained that these texts have inspired democratic thought in the western tradition, especially among American political authors in the eighteenth century.[14] The biblical message is still meaningful for us today. It proclaims the rights and the responsibilities of believers to stand up for their convictions and oppose actions by their government, if they believe such actions oppress their fellow humanity.

Sufficient Food

In the Pentateuchal narratives we hear how God provided food for escaped slaves in the wilderness. This theme would speak to exiles in the seventh century for whom survival often was a difficult task. The story said to them not to fear, but that somehow God would take care of them. When we turn to the prophetic narratives there are many accounts that speak of prophets providing food for people, when kings could not.

The role of kings in any society was to guarantee security for people and to protect their property. In the ancient world the king was responsible for fertility by interceding with the divine realm to bring good crop yields. This was an integral part of royal ceremonies, such as the *Sed* Festival in Egypt, which renewed kingship and the fertility of the land, and the *Akitu* New Year's ceremony in Mesopotamia, which brought protection to the land from flooding and chaos, as well as assuring fertility of the land. Our editor of the books of Kings placed prophetic stories into the greater

---

14. Gnuse, *No Tolerance*.

narrative that reflected how kings failed to protect property and provide food, while the prophets fulfilled these functions.[15]

At the beginning Elijah narratives, we learn that a drought and a famine have struck the land of Israel, and this drought was announced to the king by the word of the prophet (1 Kgs 17:1). The king was helpless to end the drought until finally the word of the Lord came through the prophet once more (1 Kgs 18:41–46).

Elijah or Elisha provided food on several occasions. In 1 Kgs 17:8–16 Elijah resided with a widow of Zarephath, who was a foreigner, and he insured that her jar of meal and jug of oil did not become empty during the famine. In similar fashion, Elisha helped a widow by preventing a creditor from seizing her land by multiplying oil in jars so that she could pay her debt (2 Kgs 4:1–7). Whereas the king failed to provide food during a drought and later failed to protect a widow's land, a prophet intervened to bring a boundless supply of food in both instances. In both Mesopotamia and Egypt, kings bragged about how they protected poor widows. Elijah and Elisha both usurped the function of the king because Israel's kings were remiss in this honorable task.

During a famine caused by a siege of Samaria (2 Kgs 6:24–30) the king again failed to provide food for his people. When called upon by a woman for help (we do not know if she was a widow), he said, "How can I help you?" (v. 27). She remonstrated that she had made a deal with another woman that both would kill and eat their small children. The woman who complained had given her child to be eaten, but the other woman had reneged on her promise, so the first woman appealed to the king to force the other woman to surrender her child. The king was appalled by the nature of these actions, but the deeper implication was that the king, the perceived source of fertility, failed completely in his royal function. It is incredible that the biblical narratives included this heart-rending account in such blunt fashion to so humiliate the king.[16] In contrast to the helpless king, however, stood the prophet, ready to bring fertility and food to the people. In other narratives Elisha provided food for a hundred people by multiplying twenty loaves of barley and fresh ears of grain brought by a man from Baal-shalishah (2 Kgs 4:42–44), foreshadowing Jesus feeding the masses with a few loaves and fish. Not only did the prophet provide food, the prophet elevated the quality of food to be consumed. In 2 Kgs 4:38–41

15. Grottanelli, "Religious Ideals," 38.
16. Sweeney, *I & II Kings*, 311.

Elisha made unfit stew edible. We can sense a bit of sarcasm by the biblical editors as they inserted these stories into our text to comment upon royal incompetence.

The king was seen as the source of life. But it was Elijah who raised the widow of Zarephath's son (1 Kgs 17:17–24) and Elisha who raised the Shunammite woman's son (2 Kgs 4:8–37). Again, we observe paired stories about both Elijah and Elisha in these crucial activities. Raising someone from the dead was a dramatic action, for in the ancient world this was the prerogative of the gods, and perhaps some would attribute this power of resuscitation only to a fertility god who brought the world back to life in the spring. Since the patron god associated with the king in the accounts of Elijah and Elisha was the god of vegetation and fertility, Baal, it appears that Elijah and Elisha usurped the authority of the fertility god sponsored by the royal cult. Apparently the king could not even choose the correct deity.

This poor choice of deity by the king was most evident in the contest on Mount Carmel where Elijah defeated the prophets of Baal in a contest to bring fire down from the heavens to ignite a sacrifice (1 Kgs 18:20–40). The story was one about the defeat of the god Baal by Yahweh, and although Baal was the god of fertility, he was shown to be powerless. After the contest the drought ended (1 Kgs 18:41–46), which added insult to injury upon Baal's inability to provide fertility and food. Behind the story, of course, was the implication that Ahab, the king, chose the wrong deity for fertility, another stunning critique of the king and his devoted supporters.

In the ancient world the king, as the source of life, was responsible for providing water through irrigation, as in Egypt and Mesopotamia. The king should have had at his disposal diviners who could inform when the famine would begin or end, but instead he was forced to heed the prophetic word. Elijah predicted for Ahab that there would be a drought (1 Kgs 17:1–7) and when the drought would end (1 Kgs 18:41–46). The prophet brought water, while the king waited for the word of the prophet to discern what was happening.

As we in the western world read these stories today, most of us realize that we are not in the same condition as the people who first heard these narratives. Most of us are well fed; certainly the people likely to read this book are probably in good economic conditions. The message for us is to become the prophets in the narratives and become the ones who provide food for others. We live in a world where increasingly a larger number of people are starving, a world in which population increases in poor areas force more people onto the cusp of slow death by malnutrition and outright starvation. We need to act.

Increasingly, social scientists point out that water resources worldwide are being stretched to their limits, and very likely local wars in the future may arise over the possession of water and right of access to water. One such war has already been fought between central Asian countries that were formerly part of the Soviet Union. Just recently I attended a conference on ecological issues and how the church needs to respond to such problems. I was shocked to see the estimates of how little fresh water would be left in the world's water systems in ten years; even more was I shocked to see how badly the fresh water in America would likewise decline in that same period of time.[17] We must begin to immediately engage in wise stewardship of our underground aquifers in this country. We must engage in what the speaker called "watershed discipleship."

We must be the prophets who seek to provide adequate food and water for the masses in our world both through our benevolent actions and through the efforts of agencies such as the United Nations and various church world relief programs. It is our responsibility to provide food for the hungry masses of our world. But even more importantly, it is our responsibility to use technology wisely so as to produce more bountiful harvests for the world. It is our responsibility to encourage a more sensible and environmentally sound use of the world's resources. It is our responsibility, perhaps, to encourage wiser population growth, so that the world's population will not strain the planet to the point that no technological breakthroughs can produce sufficient food for an overwhelming number of people. We must be the prophets. But we do not engage in wondrous acts, such as the increase of food caused by Elisha. Our wondrous acts must be accomplished through the use of technology and common sense in worldwide social and economic planning.

Conclusions

There are probably other theological ideas that could be derived from Elohist texts. I simply offer these suggestions up as testimony to the enduring relevance of these ancient texts. The Elohist narratives lie embedded in the greater Pentateuch, which, of course, has significant meaning and value as a

---

17. Myers, "From the Wilderness."

corpus of literature. But I believe that the isolation of these Elohist texts and relating them to their social context brings their message into clearer focus for us. These texts have specific value for us in providing provocative and inspirational thought, which if we listen closely, can be of great value to us.

9

Conclusion

THE ELOHIST TRADITION HAS been a shadow in the history of critical biblical scholarship. At times in the minds of some scholars it appears to be present, at other times it retreats into the dark and is hidden in the Yahwist traditions according to the vision of other scholars. It would seem that the Elohist is as elusive as our nighttime dreams, a fitting metaphor for a theological tradition that envisions dreams as a mode of revelation for a high, transcendent, and distant deity.

The Elohist's existence has been denied by critical scholars since the 1930s, yet often they admitted that certain stories bore an unmistakable mark of supposed Elohist characteristics (Genesis 20; 22). Thus, they were deemed to be either supplements to the Yahwist narrative or sources used by the Yahwist. I prefer the latter option. But I would strongly affirm that such sources, fragmentary though they might appear to some scholars, are nevertheless worthy of consideration and theological articulation. I believe these texts may be used to craft a theological message. We could hypothetically reconstruct what they might have said to that bygone age, but we can certainly use these texts with their Elohistic personality to craft a meaningful message for the modern age. It has been the primary focus of this volume to accomplish that mission. Though the Elohist texts are fragmentary, either because much has been lost or perhaps they originally were separate "pools of oral tradition," we still may discern religious themes and idioms that reflect a coherent religious message.

My approach has been to accomplish several goals: 1) There are a number of terms and expression that tend to occur together in the same texts. Though critics maintain that using vocabulary to gather texts into a source is a circular argument, they overlook that these terms do occur together with frequency and do not occur regularly in other texts deemed to be Yahwist or Priestly. In this study I sought to demonstrate how key vocabulary, unique to what have always been deemed Elohist texts, do indeed occur together. Furthermore, these words are not random, but together share a common theological identity. Critics of the Elohist have never sought to show that this Elohistic vocabulary is incongruent or that the words are at least unrelated to each other in a theological sense. It is the theological unity of this language that leads me to suspect that there is indeed a source worthy of being called the Elohist.

2) My previous consideration of the prophetic narratives in the books of Samuel and Kings led me to see similarity with Pentateuchal texts usually associated with the Elohist. These prophetic texts appear to be prior to the Pentateuchal narratives in terms of theological expression. Combining the prophetic narratives with the Pentateuchal texts provides greater opportunity for theological reflection. If prophetic narratives precede the Pentateuchal texts, this implies a date for the Pentateuchal traditions at least after the ninth century, and more likely after the eighth century.

3) My study of dreams in the ancient Near East implies that biblical dream reports appear to have been inspired by seventh- and sixth-century Assyrian and Chaldean Babylonian dream reports. Biblical dream reports appear primarily in texts associated with Elohist or prophetic narratives (Samuel's dream). This suggests that the Elohist should be dated to the seventh or sixth centuries.

4) If we assume that the Elohist Pentateuchal narratives came together after the destruction of Samaria in 722 BCE, we can make sense out of many of the accounts. They spoke to the needs of exiles in Mesopotamia and war-ravaged refugees remaining in the land of Israel. The texts can be seen as speaking words of hope, encouragement, and the promise of eventual return. Though one might be tempted to say these texts are Yahwistic messages to sixth century BCE folk from Judah, I would respond that there seem to be hints of an earlier date and a northern provenance. The positive attitude toward Esau points to a date earlier than the sixth century, and the concern with the shrine at Bethel points to theological concern of the northern state.

5) Placing the Elohist traditions prior to the Yahwist and assuming that the Yahwist used Elohist traditions for his history solves many problems. It dispenses with the JE redactor, whose existence has been criticized.

Conclusion

It explains the abbreviated nature of the Elohist source. It explains why some passages appear to be a blurred compromise of Yahwist and Elohist thought and vocabulary, for the Yahwist may have rewritten some of the Elohist texts. It would explain, in particular, why the theophany at Bethel appears coherent as an Elohistic text but has only Yahwistic additions.

6) A coherent argument can be made for the provenance of the Elohist traditions in Bethel after 722 BCE. Our contemporary perspective on ancient deportations permits us to suggest that a substantial population remained in the lands of Israel and Judah, and that these folk could have been responsible for the emergence of theological traditions. It also makes sense that a theological tradition generated after the collapse of a nation (Elohist for Israel, Deuteronomist for Judah) would speak in terms of defending the justice of God, accepting the judgment of defeat, and then offering hope for exiles and proposing alternative structures for leadership in society (such as prophets for the Elohist or priests for the Priestly Tradition). A seventh century BCE paradigm for Elohist narratives makes more sense than our previous scholarly proposals.

7) A final subjective argument can be the consideration of Elohist theological themes. The view of a transcendent God, who is available for foreigners (Abimelech, Laban, and Balaam), betokens assumptions that began to emerge in the seventh and sixth centuries BCE with a monotheistic perspective of God. This may or may not be a compelling argument by itself, but with the other arguments it strengthens the overall thesis.

The proto-Elohistic prophetic narratives and the Elohistic Pentateuchal narratives arose in the northern state of Israel and were related to each other literarily and theologically. These "pools of traditions," or cycles of separate related accounts were used by the Deuteronomistic Historian in the seventh and sixth centuries BCE and the Yahwist Historian in the late sixth or early fifth centuries BCE. (Remember Baden's arguments that the Deuteronomistic Historian appears to use Elohist texts and is unaware of the Yahwist parallels.) Absorbed into those expansive southern cycles of literature and redacted extensively, Elohist themes were submerged and difficult to isolate. The Elohist never produced an overarching epic narrative; that work would be accomplished by the later historians, Deuteronomistic, Yahwist, and Priestly. Whether the Yahwist, in particular, absorbed the Elohist material even-handedly with other sources or sought to critically and creatively respond to Elohist texts and ideas may be debated. It is possible that the Yahwist may have done a little of both in crafting the grand narrative.

Regardless of the submersion of the Elohist narratives into those later histories, enough texts were preserved faithfully by the later historians (DJP), that scholars throughout the ages have been able to glimpse the distinctive language of theological themes of these texts. Though some scholars might not consider them to be significant enough to call a source or to theologize upon, I believe they are sufficient to merit our attention. I believe that a theological assessment can bear fruit for us. Hopefully, this monograph has done theological justice to the Elohist texts by endeavoring to recreate the message they once had for a people in exile. Even more, I hope this monograph has discovered the message that can be proclaimed to a modern age, especially to people in the modern era, who feel the distance of God, who also languish in exile, who suffer for want of food and water, and for those empowered people who need to heed the call to stand up courageously for human rights and dignity when the powers that be try to crush the weak and the powerless.

Bibliography

Aberback, Moses, and Leivy Smolar. "Aaron, Jeroboam and the Golden Calves." *JBL* 86 (1967) 129–40.
Ahlström, Gösta. "Another Moses Tradition." *JNES* 39 (1980) 65–69.
Amit, Yairah. "Epoch and Genre: The Sixth Century and the Growth of Hidden Polemics." In *Judah and Judeans in the Neo-Babylonian Period*, edited by Oded Lipschits and Joseph Blenkinsopp, 135–51. Winona Lake, IN: Eisenbrauns, 2006.
Anderson, Bernhard. *Understanding the Old Testament*. 3rd ed. Englewood Cliffs, NJ: Prentice Hall, 1975.
Auld, Graeme. *Kings Without Privilege: David and Moses in the Story of the Bible's Kings*. Edinburgh: T. & T. Clark, 1994.
Baden, Joel. *The Composition of the Pentateuch: Renewing the Documentary Hypothesis*. New Haven: Yale University Press, 2012.
———. "From Joseph to Moses: The Narratives of Exodus 1–2." *VT* 62 (2012) 133–58.
———. *J, E, and the Reaction of the Pentateuch*. FAT. Tübingen: Mohr/Siebeck, 2009.
———. "The Narratives of Numbers 20–13." *CBQ* 76 (2014) 634–52.
Bergmann, J., et al. "ḥalam." In *TDOT* 4:421–32.
Blenkinsopp, Joseph. "Bethel in the Neo-Babylonian Period." In *Judah and the Judeans in the Neo-Babylonian Period*, edited by Oded Lipschits and Joseph Blenkinsopp, 93–107. Winona Lake, IN: Eisenbrauns, 2006.
———. "The Judean Priesthood during the Neo-Babylonian and Achaemenid Periods: A Hypothetical Reconstruction." *CBQ* 60 (1998) 25–43.
———. *The Pentateuch: An Introduction to the First Five Books of the Bible*. New York: Doubleday, 1992.
Blum, Erhard. *Die Komposition der Vätergeschichte*. WMANT 57. Neukirchen-Vluyn: Neukirchener, 1984.
———. *Studien zur Komposition des Pentateuch*. BZAW 189. Berlin: de Gruyter, 1990.
Brisman, Leslie. *The Voice of Jacob: On the Composition of Genesis*. Indiana Studies in Biblical Literature. Bloomington: Indiana University Press, 1990.
Burnett, Joel. *A Reassessment of Biblical Elohim*. SBLDS 183. Atlanta, GA: Society of Biblical Literature, 2001.
———. *Where Is God? Divine Absence in the Hebrew Bible*. Minneapolis: Fortress, 2010.
Campbell, Antony F., and Mark A. O'Brien. *Sources of the Pentateuch: Texts, Introductions, Annotations*. Minneapolis: Fortress, 1993.
Carr, David M. *Reading the Fractures of Genesis: Historical and Literary Approaches*. Louisville: Westminster John Knox, 1996.

Bibliography

Carroll, Robert P. "The Elijah–Elisha Sagas: Some Remarks on Prophetic Succession in Ancient Israel." *Vetus Testamentum* 19 (1969) 400–415.

Childs, Brevard S. *The Book of Exodus*. OTL. Philadelphia: Westminster, 1974.

Chung, Youn Ho. *The Sin of the Calf: The Rise of the Bible's Negative Attitude toward the Golden Calf.* LHBOTS 523. New York: T. & T. Clark, 2010.

Clements, Ronald. *One Hundred Years of Old Testament Interpretation*. Philadelphia: Westminster, 1976.

Coats, George W. *Genesis, with an Introduction to Narrative Literature*. FOTL 1. Grand Rapids: Eerdmans, 1983.

Coogan, Michael D. "Canaanite Origins and Lineage: Reflections on the Religion of Ancient Israel." In *Ancient Israelite Religion: Essays in Honor of Frank Moore Cross*, edited by Patrick Miller et al., 115–24. Philadelphia: Fortress, 1987.

Coote, Robert B. *In Defense of Revolution: The Elohist History*. Minneapolis: Fortress, 1991.

Cross, Frank M. "Ammonite Ostraca from Heshbon: Heshbon Ostraca IV–VIII." *AUSS* 13 (1975) 1–20.

———. *Canaanite Myth and Hebrew Epic: Essays in the History of the Religion of Israel*. Cambridge: Harvard University Press, 1973.

———. "Notes on the Ammonite Inscription from Tell Siran." *BASOR* 212 (1973) 12–15.

Davies, Philip R. *The Origins of Biblical Israel*. LHBOTS 485. London: T. & T. Clark, 2007.

Dozeman, Thomas. "Geography and Ideology in the Wilderness Journey from Kadesh through the Transjordan." In *Abschied von Jahwisten: Die Komposition des Hexateuch in der jüngsten Diskussion*, edited by Christian Gertz et al., 173–89. BZAW 315. New York: de Gruyter, 2002.

———, and Konrad Schmidt, eds. *A Farewell to the Yahwist? The Composition of the Pentateuch in Recent European Interpretation*. SBL Symposium Series 34. Atlanta: Society of Biblical Literature, 2006.

Engnell, Ivan. *A Rigid Scrutiny: Critical Essays on the Old Testament*. Translated by John T. Willis. Nashville: Vanderbilt University Press, 1969.

Fretheim, Terence E. "Elohist." In *IDBS* 259–63.

———. *Exodus*. Interpretation. Louisville: John Knox, 1991.

———. *The Suffering of God*. OBT. Philadelphia: Fortress, 1984.

Friedman, Richard Elliott. *The Disappearance of God: A Divine Mystery*. New York: Little, Brown, 1995.

———. *The Hidden Book in the Bible: The Discovery of the First Prose Masterpiece*. San Francisco: HarperSanFrancisco, 1998.

———. "The Recession of Biblical Source Criticism." In *The Future of Biblical Studies: The Hebrew Scriptures*, edited by Richard Elliott Friedman and H. G. M. Williamson, 81–101. SBLSS. Atlanta: Scholars, 1987.

———. *Who Wrote the Bible?* Englewood Cliffs, NJ: Prentice Hall, 1987.

Gnuse, Robert Karl. "Calf, Cult, and King: The Unity of Hosea 8:1–13 on the Basis of Structural and Thematic Evidence." *BZ* 26 (1982) 83–92.

———. *The Dream Theophany of Samuel: Its Structure in Relation to Ancient Near Eastern Dreams and Its Theological Significance*. Lanham, MD: University Press of America, 1984.

———. *Dreams and Dream Reports in the Writings of Josephus*. AGJU 36. Leiden: Brill, 1996.

BIBLIOGRAPHY

———. "Dreams and Their Theological Significance in the Biblical Tradition." *CurrTM* 8 (1981) 166–71.

———. "Dreams in the Night—Scholarly Mirage or Theophanic Formula?: The Dream Report as a Motif of the So-Called Elohist Tradition." *BZ* 39 (1995) 28–53.

———. "The Elohist: A 7th Century BCE Theological Tradition." *BTB* 42 (2012) 59–69.

———. "From Prison to Prestige: The Hero Who Helps a King in Jewish and Greek Literature." *CBQ* 72 (2010) 31–45.

———. *No Other Gods: Emergent Monotheism in Israel.* JSOTSup 241. Sheffield: Sheffield Academic, 1997.

———. *No Tolerance for Tyrants: The Biblical Assault upon Kings and Kingship.* Collegeville, MN: Liturgical, 2011.

———. "Northern Prophetic Traditions in the Books of Samuel and Kings as Precursor to the Elohist." *ZAW* 122 (2010) 374–86.

———. *The Old Testament and Process Theology.* St. Louis: Chalice, 2000.

———. "A Reconsideration of the Form–Critical Structure in 1 Samuel 3: An Ancient Near Eastern Dream Theophany." *ZAW* 94 (1982) 379–90.

———. "Redefining the Elohist: 'Pools of Oral Tradition.'" *JBL* 119 (2000) 201–20.

———. "The Tower of Babel: Parable of Divine Judgment or Human Cultural Diversification?" *BZ* 54 (2010) 229–44.

Gomes, Jules. *The Sanctuary of Bethel and the Configuration of Israelite Identity.* BZAW 368. Berlin: de Gruyter, 2006.

Gottwald, Norman K. *The Hebrew Bible: A Socio-Literary Introduction.* Philadelphia: Fortress, 1985.

Goulder, Michael D. "Asaph's History of Israel (Elohist Press, Bethel, 725 BCE)." *JSOT* 65 (1995) 71–81.

———. *The Psalms of Asaph and the Pentateuch: Studies in the Psalter III.* JSOTSup 233. Sheffield: Sheffield Academic, 1996.

Graupner, Alex. *Der Elohist: Gegenwart und Wirksamkeit des Transzendenten Gottes in der Geschichte.* WMANT 97. Neukirchen-Vluyn: Neukirchener, 2002.

———. "Der Erzahlkunst des Elohisten: Zur Makrostructur und Intention der elohistischen Darstellung der Gründungsgeschichte Israels." In *Das Alte Testament und die Kunst*, edited by John Barton et al., 67–90. Altes Testament und Moderne 15. Münster: Lit, 2005.

Gray, John. *I & II Kings.* 2nd ed. OTL. Philadelphia: Westminster, 1984.

Grottanelli, Christiano. "Religious Ideals and the Distribution of Cereal Grains in the Hebrew Bible." In *Kings and Prophets: Monarchic Power, Inspired Leadership, and Sacred Text in Biblical Narrative*, 31–45. New York: Oxford University Press, 1999.

Guillaume, Philippe. *Waiting for Josiah: The Judges.* JSPSup 385. New York: T. & T. Clark, 2004.

Hacket, Jo Ann. *The Balaam Text from Deir 'Alla.* HSM 31. Chico, CA: Scholars, 1984.

Hahn, Herbert. *The Old Testament in Modern Research.* Philadelphia: Fortress, 1966.

Hayes, John H. *An Introduction to Old Testament Study.* Nashville: Abingdon, 1979.

Heschel, Abraham Joshua. *The Prophets.* 2 vols. New York: Harper & Row, 1962.

Hoftijzer, Jacob, and G. van der Kooij. *Aramaic Texts from Deir 'Alla.* Documenta et Monumenta Orientis Antiqui 19. Leiden: Brill, 1976.

Hölscher, Gustav. *Geschichtsschreibung in Israel. Untersuchung zum Jahwisten und Elohisten.* Skrifter utg. av Kungl. Humanistiska vetenskapssamfundet i Lund 50. Lund: Gleerup, 1952.

BIBLIOGRAPHY

Hurowitz, Victor. "Babylon in Bethel—New Light on Jacob's Dream." In *Orientalism, Assyriology and the Bible*, edited by Steven W. Holloway, 436–48. Hebrew Bible Monographs 10. Sheffield: Sheffield Phoenix, 2007.

Jaroš, Karl. *Die Stellung des Elohisten zur Kanaanäischen Religion*. OBO 4. Göttingen: Vandenhoeck & Ruprecht, 1982.

Jenks, Alan W. "Elohist." In *ABD* 2:478–82.

———. "The Elohist and North Israelite Traditions." Th.D. dissertation. Harvard University, 1965.

———. *The Elohist and North Israelite Traditions*. SBLMS 22. Missoula, MT: Scholars Press, 1977.

Jones, Gwilym. *1 and 2 Kings*, vol. 2. NCB. Grand Rapids: Eerdmans, 1984,

Kaiser, Otto. *Grundriss der Einleitung in die kanonischen und deuterokanonischen Schriften des Alten Testaments*. Vol. 1: *Die erzählenden Werke*. Gütersloh: Gütersloher, 1992.

———. *Introduction to the Old Testament: A Presentation of Its Results and Problems*. Translated by John Study. Minneapolis: Augsburg, 1975.

Kammenhuber, Annalies. *Orakelpraxis, Träume und Vorzeichenschau bei den Hethitern*. Texte der Hethiter 7. Heidelberg: Winter, 1976.

Kim, Hyun Chul Paul. "Reading the Joseph Story (Genesis 37–50) as a Diaspora Narrative." *CBQ* 75 (2013) 219–38.

Klein, Hans. "Ort und Zeit des Elohisten." *EvT* 37 (1977) 247–60.

Knauf, Ernst. "Bethel: The Israelite Impact on Judean Language and Literature." In *Judah and Judeans in the Persian Period*, edited by Oded Lipschits and Manfred Oeming, 291–350. Winona Lake, IN: Eisenbrauns, 2006.

———. "Towards an Archaeology of the Hexateuch." In *Abschied von Jahwisten: Die Komposition des Hexateuch in der jüngsten Diskussion*, edited by Jan Gertz et al., 275–94. BZAW 315. New York: de Gruyter, 2002.

Knight, Douglas A. "The Pentateuch." In *The Hebrew Bible and Its Modern Interpreters*, edited by Douglas A. Knight and Gene M. Tucker, 263–96. Philadelphia: Fortress, 1985.

Knohl, Israel. "Two Aspects of the 'Tent of Meeting.'" In *Tehillah le-Moshe: Biblical and Judaic Studies in Honor of Moshe Greenberg*, edited by Mordecai Cogan et al., 73–79. Winona Lake, IN: Eisenbrauns, 1997.

Knoppers, Gary N. "In Search of Post-Exilic Israel and Samaria After the Fall of the Northern Kingdom." In *In Search of Pre-exilic Israel: Proceedings of the Oxford Old Testament Seminar*, edited by John Day, 150–80. JSOTSup 406. London: T. & T. Clark, 2004.

Kraus, Hans-Joachim. *Geschichte der Historisch-kritischen Erforschung des Alten Testaments*. Neukirchen-Vluyn: Neukirchener, 1969.

Lang, Bernhard. "The Yahweh-Alone Movement and Making of Jewish Monotheism." In *Monotheism and the Prophetic Minority*, 13–59. SWBA 1. Sheffield: Almond, 1983.

Lehnart, Bernhard. *Prophet und König im Nordreich Israel: Studien zur sogenannten vorklassischen Prophetie im Nordreich Israel anhand der Samuel-, Elija- und Elischa-Überlieferungen*. VTSup 96. Leiden: Brill, 2003.

Levin, Christoph. *Der Jahwist*. FRLANT 157. Göttingen: Vandenhoeck & Ruprecht, 1993.

———. "The Yahwist and the Redactional Link between Genesis and Exodus." In *A Farewell to the Yahwist? The Composition of the Pentateuch in Recent European Interpretation*, edited by Thomas B. Dozeman and Konrad Schmidt, 131–41. SBLSymS 34. Atlanta: Society of Biblical Literature, 2006.

Bibliography

———. "The Yahwist: The Earliest Editor in the Pentateuch." *JBL* 126 (2007) 209–30.

Levine, Baruch A. "The Balaam Inscription from Deir 'Alla: Historical Aspects." In *Biblical Archaeology Today*, edited by Janet Amitai, 326–39. Jerusalem: IES, 1985.

———. *Numbers 21–36*. AB 4A. New York: Doubleday, 2000.

Lichtenstein, Murray. "Dream Theophany and the E Document." *JANES(CU)* 1–2 (1968–69) 45–54.

Lohfink, Norbert. "Das Alte Testament und sein Monotheismus." In *Der eine Gott und der dreieine Gott*, edited by Karl Rahner, 28–47. Munich: Schnell & Steiner, 1983.

———. "The Cult Reform of Josiah of Judah." In *Ancient Israelite Religion: Essays in Honor of Frank Moore Cross*, edited by Patrick D. Miller Jr. et al, 459–75. Philadelphia: Fortress, 1987.

———. "Zur Geschichte der Diskussion über den Monotheismus im Alten Israel." In *Gott, der Einzige: Zur Entstehung des Monotheismus in Israel*, edited by Ernst Haag, 9–25. QD 104. Freiburg: Herder, 1985.

Marquis, Liane. "The Composition of Numbers 32: A New Proposal." *VT* 63 (2013) 408–32.

Mayes, A. D. H. *The Story of Israel between Settlement and Exile: A Redactional Study of the Deuteronomistic History*. London: SCM, 1983.

McCarter, P. Kyle. "The Balaam Texts from Deir 'Alla: The First Combination." *BASOR* 239 (1980) 49–60.

———. "The Origins of Israelite Religion." In *Rise of Ancient Israel*, edited by Hershel Shanks, 118–41. Washington, DC: BAS, 1992.

McEvenue, Sean. *Interpreting the Pentateuch*. Collegeville, MN: Liturgical, 1990.

———. "A Return to Sources in Genesis 28:10–22?" *ZAW* 106 (1994) 375–89.

McKenzie, Steven L. *The Trouble with Kings: The Composition of the Book of Kings in the Deuteronomistic History*. VTSup 42. Leiden: Brill, 1991.

Moore, Meagan Bishop, and Brad E. Kelle. *Biblical History and Israel's Past: The Changing Study of the Bible and History*. Grand Rapids: Eerdmans, 2011.

Moore, Michael. *The Balaam Traditions*. SBLDS 113. Atlanta: Scholars, 1990.

Müller, Hans-Peter. "Die aramäische Inschrift von Deir 'Alla und die älteren Bileamsprüche." *ZAW* 94 (1982) 214–44.

Myers, Ched. "From the Wilderness Prophetic Tradition to Watershed Discipleship." The Tenth International Whitehead Conference, Claremont, CA, June 6, 2015.

Nelson, Richard. *The Double Redaction of the Deuteronomistic History*. JSOTSup 18. Sheffield: University of Sheffield Press, 1981.

Nicholson, Ernst. *The Pentateuch in the Twentieth Century: The Legacy of Julius Wellhausen*. Oxford: Oxford University Press, 1998.

Nigosian, S. A. *World Religions: A Historical Approach*. New York: St. Martins, 2008.

Noss, David. *A History of the World's Religions*. Upper Saddle, NY: Prentice Hall, 2003.

Noth, Martin. *A History of Pentateuchal Traditions*. Translated by Bernhard Anderson. Englewood Cliffs, NJ: Prentice Hall, 1972.

Oberman, Julian. "How Daniel Was Blessed with a Son: An Incubation Scene in Ugaritic." JAOSSup 6 (1946) 1–30.

Oppenheim, A. Leo. *The Interpretation of Dreams in the Ancient Near East*. APS, NS 46. Philadelphia: American Philosophical Society, 1956.

———. "Mantic Dreams in the Ancient Near East." In *The Dream and Human Societies*, edited by Gustave von Grunebaum and Roger Callois, 341–50. Berkeley: University of California Press, 1966.

Bibliography

———. "New Fragments of the Assyrian Dream-Book." *Iraq* 31 (1969) 153–65.
Pfeiffer, Henrik. *Das Heiligtum von Bethel im Spiegel des Hoseabuches*. Göttingen: Vandenhoeck & Ruprecht, 1999.
Pleins, J. David. *The Social Visions of the Hebrew Bible: A Theological Introduction*. Louisville: Westminster John Knox, 1996.
Procksch, Otto. *Das nordhebräische Sagenbuch: Die Elohimquelle*. Leipzig: Hinrichs, 1906.
Propp, William H. C. *Exodus 1–18*. AB 2. New York: Doubleday, 1999.
———. *Exodus 19–40*. AB 2A. New York: Doubleday, 2006.
Puech, Emile. "L'inscription súr plâtre de Tell Deir 'Alla." In *Biblical Archaeology Today*, edited by Janet Amitai, 354–65. Jerusalem: IES, 1985.
Rad, Gerhard von. *Old Testament Theology*. Vol 1. Translated by D. M. G. Stalker. New York: Harper & Row, 1962.
———. *The Problem of the Hexateuch and Other Essays*. Translated by E. W. Trueman Dicken. New York: McGraw-Hill, 1966. Reprinted as From Genesis to Chronicles: Explorations in Old Testament Theology. Edited by K. C. Hanson. Fortress Classics in Biblical Studies. Minneapolis: Fortress, 2005.
Redford, Donald B. *A Study of the Biblical Story of Joseph (Genesis 37–50)*. VTSup 20. Leiden: Brill, 1970.
Rendtorff, Rolf. *Das Uberlieferungsgeschichtliche Problem des Pentateuch*. BZAW 147. Berlin: de Gruyter, 1977.
———. "The 'Yahwist' as Theologian? The Dilemma of Pentateuchal Criticism." *JSOT* 3 (1977) 2–10.
Roberts, Kathryn. "God, Prophet, and King: Eating and Drinking on the Mountain in First Kings 18:41." *CBQ* 62 (2000) 632–44.
Rofé. Alexander. "Ephraimite versus Deuteronomistic History." In *Reconsidering Israel and Judah: Recent Studies in Deuteronomistic History*, edited by Gary Knoppers and Gordon McConville, 462–74. Winona Lake, IN: Eisenbrauns, 2000.
Rose, Martin. *Deuteronomist und Jahwist*. ATANT 67. Zürich: Theologisches Verlag, 1981.
Rouillard, Hedwige. *Le péricope de Balaam (Nombres 22–24): La prose et les "oracles."* EBib 4. Paris: Gabalda, 1985.
Rudolph, Wilhelm. *Elohist von Exodus bis Josua*. BZAW 68. Giessen: Töpelmann, 1938.
Ruppert, Lothar. "Der Elohist—Sprecher für Gottes Volk." In *Wort und Botschaft: Eine theologische und kritische Einführung in die Probleme de Alten Testaments*, edited by Josef Schreiner, 108–17. Würzburg: Echter, 1969.
Sasson, Jack M. "Mari Dreams." *JAOS* 103 (1983) 283–93.
Schmid, Hans Heinrich. *Der sogenannte Jahwist*. Zürich: Theologisches Verlag, 1976.
Schmidt, Ludwig, "Die Befurung des Mose in Exodus 3 als Beispiel für Jahwist (J) und Elohist (E)." *ZAW* 126 (2014) 339–57.
Schmitt, Hans-Christoph. *Arbeitsbuch zum Alten Testament: Grundzüge der Geschichte Israels und der alttestamentlichen Schriften*. UTB 2146. Göttingen: Vandenhoeck & Ruprecht, 2005.
———. *Die Nichtpriestlicher Josephsgeschichte: Ein Beitrag zur neuesten Pentateuchkritik*. BZAW 154. New York: de Gruyter, 1980.
Schüpphaus, Joachim. "Volk Gottes und Gesetz beim Elohisten." *TZ* 31 (1975) 193–201.
Schwartz, Baruch. "The Visit of Jethro: A Case of Chronological Displacement? The Source–Critical Solution." In *Mishneh Todah: Studies in Deuteronomy and Its Cultural Environment in Honor of Jeffrey H. Tigay*, edited by Neil Fox et al, 29–48. Winona Lake, IN: Eisenbrauns, 2009.

BIBLIOGRAPHY

Sherman, Phillip Michael. *Babel's Tower Translated: Genesis 11 and Ancient Jewish Interpretation.* BIS 117. Leiden: Brill, 2013.

Smend, Rudolph. *Die Erzählung des Hexateuchs auf ihre Quellen untersucht.* Berlin: Reimer, 1912.

Smith, Mark S. *Early History of God.* San Francisco, CA: Harper & Row, 1990.

———. "Yahweh and the Other Deities in Ancient Israel." In *Ein Gott allein?: JHWH-Verehrung und biblischer Monotheismus im Kontext der israelitischen und altorientalischen Religionsgeschichte,* edited by Werner Dietrich and Martin Klopfenstein, 197–234. OBO 139. Göttingen: Vandenhoeck & Ruprecht, 1994.

Snaith, Norman. *Leviticus and Numbers.* NCB. London: Oliphants, 1969.

Sommer, Benjamin. "Reflecting on Moses: The Redaction of Numbers 11." *JBL* 118 (1999) 601–24.

Stackert, Jeffrey. *A Prophet Like Moses: Prophecy, Law, and Israelite Religion.* New York: Oxford University Press, 2014.

Sweeney, Marvin A. *I & II Kings.* OTL. Louisville: Westminster John Knox, 2007.

Tappy, Ron E. *The Archaeology of Israelite Samaria.* Vol. 2, *The Eighth Century BCE.* HSS 50. Winona Lake, IN: Eisenbrauns, 2001.

Terrien, Samuel. *The Elusive Presence: Toward a New Biblical Theology.* 1978. Reprinted, Eugene, OR: Wipf & Stock, 2000.

Van Seters, John. *Abraham in History and Tradition.* New Haven: Yale University Press, 1975.

———. *In Search of History: Historiography in the Ancient World and the Origins of Biblical History.* New Haven: Yale University Press, 1983.

———. *The Life of Moses: The Yahwist as Historian in Exodus–Numbers.* Louisville: Westminster John Knox, 1994.

———. "The Pentateuch." In *The Hebrew Bible Today,* edited by Steven L. McKenzie and M. Patrick Graham, 3–49. Louisville: Westminster John Knox, 1998.

———. *The Pentateuch: A Social-Science Commentary.* Sheffield: Sheffield Academic, 1999.

———. *Prologue to History: The Yahwist as Historian in Genesis.* Louisville: Westminster John Knox, 1992.

———. *The Yahwist: A Historian of Israelite Origins.* Winona Lake, IN: Eisenbrauns, 2013.

Volz, Paul, and Wilhelm Rudolph. *Der Elohist als Erzähler.* BZAW 63. Giessen: Töpelmann, 1933.

Vörlander, Hermann. "Der Monotheism Israels als Antwort auf die Krise des Exils." In *Der einzige Gott: Die Geburt des biblischen Monotheismus,* edited by Bernhard Lang, 84–113. Munich: Kösel, 1981.

Walsh, Jerome T. *1 Kings.* Berit Olam. Collegeville, MN: Liturgical, 1996.

Wenham, Gordon. *Genesis 16–50.* WBC. Nashville: Nelson, 1994.

Weisman, Z. "National Consciousness in the Patriarchal Promises." *JSOT* 31 (1985) 55–73.

White, Marsha. *The Elijah Legends and Jehu's Coup.* BJS 311. Atlanta: Scholars, 1997.

———. "The Elohist Depiction of Aaron: A Study in the Levite–Zadokite Controversy." In *Studies in the Pentateuch,* edited by J. A. Emerton, 149–59. VTSup 41. Leiden: Brill, 1990.

Whybray, R. N. *The Making of the Pentateuch: A Methodological Study.* JSOTSup 53. Sheffield: Sheffield Academic, 1987.

Winnet, Frederick. "Re-Examining the Foundations." *JBL* 84 (1965) 1–19.

Bibliography

Wolff, Hans Walter. "The Elohistic Fragments in the Pentateuch." Translated by Keith Crim. *Int* 26 (1972) 158–72.

Yoo, Philip. "The Four Moses Death Accounts." *JBL* 131 (2012) 423–41.

Yoreh, Tzemah, *The First Book of God*. BZAW 402. Berlin: de Gruyter, 2010.

Zertal, Adam. "The Province of Samaria (Assyrian *Samarina*) in the Late Bronze Age (Iron III)." In *Judah and the Judeans in the Neo-Babylonian Period*, edited by Oded Lipschits and Joseph Blenkinsopp, 377–412. Winona Lake, IN: Eisenbrauns, 2003.

Zimmer, Frank. *Der Elohist als weisheitlich-prophetische Redaktionsschicht: Eine literarische und theologiegeschichtliche Untersuchung der sogenannten elohistischen Texte im Pentateuch*. European University Studies, series XXIII 656. Frankfort: Lang, 1999.

Zobel, Hans-Jürgen, and Karl-Martin Beyse. *Das Alte Testament und seine Botschaft: Geschichte-Literatur-Theologie*. 2nd ed. Berlin: Evangelische Verlagsanstalt, 1984.

———. "Das Selbstverständnis Israels nach dem Alten Testament." *ZAW* 85 (1973) 281–94.

Scripture Index

Genesis

1–11	69, 137
11	5, 68, 141–42
12–36	114, 137
12	18, 84, 99, 101–2
12:6	18, 55
12:14–16	20
13	18
13:18	55
15	16, 102
15:1	19, 37, 100
15:5–6	37
15:12–21	7, 64, 65, 92, 99–100
15:13–14	37, 100
15:14	35, 40
15:16	38, 132
15:17	19, 48
15:21	19
16	103
16:5–6	20
16:7	17
17	99
18:13	103
19	7, 52
20–22	36
20	1, 16, 67, 84, 101–2
20:1–17	7
20:1–8	64, 65
20:1–4a	7, 36, 93, 100–102
20:1–2	36
20:1	23, 70, 80, 81
20:2	36
20:3–7	87
20:3	9, 65, 66, 84
20:4–5	66
20:4	20, 84
20:4a	84
20:5–17	36, 93
20:5–7	100–102
20:6–7	36
20:6	9, 16, 20, 65, 84
20:7	17, 55, 91
20:8	65
20:9–16	18
20:9–10	84
20:9	18, 81
20:11	18, 19, 59, 117
20:12	20, 84
20:13	36
20:14–15	84
20:17–18	20, 55, 58, 84
20:17	18, 36, 91
20:18	36
21	103
21:2–21	36
21:2–8	7, 35, 93, 103
21:6	103
21:9–32	84
21:9–21	7, 18, 36, 93, 103–4
21:9–11	20
21:10	18
21:11–14	20
21:11–12	85
21:12	36
21:14	36
21:16	36
21:17–19	36

Scripture Index

21:17–18	36, 87	28:16	65
21:17	9, 17, 36	28:16a	8, 36, 93, 106–8
21:18	36	28:17–21a	7, 8, 36, 93, 106–8
21:19–20	36	28:17–18	17
21:19	36	28:18	9, 19, 37, 65
21:22–32	7	28:20–22	17
21:22–31	7, 93, 104	28:20–21	37
21:22	82	28:20	36, 111, 112
21:23	23, 70, 80, 81	28:21	83
21:24	23	28:22	8, 9, 19, 36, 93, 106–8
21:33	55		
21:34	70, 80, 81	29:1–30	8, 94, 108
22	1, 7, 16, 19, 67, 70, 80, 85, 107	29:31—30:24	31, 111
		29:31–35	108–9
22:1–19	31	29:31–32	8
22:1–13	7, 36, 52, 93, 104–5	29:32b	109
22:1	18, 56	29:33–35	109
22:2	36	30:1	108
22:3	18, 36	30:1–24a	8
22:4–8	36	30:1–23	7
22:9–10	36	30:1–2a	108–9
22:10	36	30:3	18
22:11–12	36	30:9–13	109
22:11	17, 50, 115	30:21	109
22:12–13	36	30:25–42	20
22:12	19, 36, 117	30:31–43	111
22:13	36	31:1–54	18
22:15	17	31:1–42	7
22:17	36	31:2–16	84
22:19	36, 93, 104–5	31:4–42	8, 37, 94, 109–10
23:21–34	69	31:5–9	85
24	18	31:5	82
25–33	30	31:6–12	20
25:21–34	7, 31, 105–6	31:8–9	111
26	84, 101	31:10–24	64
26:2–6	66	31:10	9, 16, 65
26:24–25	66	31:11–13	23
26:24	102	31:11	9, 16, 17, 18, 65, 66
28	62, 67, 68, 82	31:12	18, 65, 66
28:3	38	31:13	9, 18, 19, 36, 37, 65, 83, 112
28:10–22	23, 64, 76, 86, 112		
28:10–17	65	31:16	85
28:10–12	7, 8, 17, 36, 93, 106–8, 127	31:17	65
		31:21–22	121
28:12	9, 17	31:24	9, 16, 65, 66, 87
28:13–15	66	31:25–42	67
28:13	17, 18, 65	31:36–42	85

Scripture Index

Reference	Pages
31:42	37
31:43–54	7
31:43–49a	8, 94, 110
31:45	9, 19, 37
31:50–55	8, 94, 110
31:51	9, 19, 37
31:52	9, 19, 37
31:54	37
32:1–2	8, 110
32:1	9, 17
32:3–21	8, 69, 94, 110
32:9–12	110
32:22–32	8, 23, 37, 94, 111
33:1–17	8, 69, 94
33:1–7	111
33:2	111
33:5–7	111
33:7	111
33:13–14	111
33:18–20	8, 112
34	110
35	82
35:1–15	76, 112
35:1–7	7, 8, 37, 84, 94, 112
35:1	34, 36, 83, 108, 112
35:1–4	67
35:1–3	37
35:2	85
35:3	34, 36, 108, 112
35:4	127
35:7	34, 36, 37, 108, 112
35:8–15	8, 113
35:8	55
35:10	37
35:11	38
35:14	9, 19, 84
35:20	9, 19
37	9, 113
37:5–9	23
37:5	9
37:6	9
37:8	9
37:9	9
37:10	9
37:18–36	114
37:18	115
37:20	9
37:21–22	115
37:24	115
37:28–30	115
37:40–41	23
37–50	65
39–50	113
39–42	9
39–41	114
39:9–11	114
40:5	9
40:8	9
40:9	9
40:16	9
41:1	9
41:5	9
41:7	9
41:8	9
41:11	9
41:12	9
41:15	9
41:17	9
41:22	9
41:25	9
41:26	9
41:32	9
42	16
42:9	9
42:21	35
42:22	18
43:34	109
46:1–7	7, 64
46:1–5	31
46:1–4	8, 37, 65, 87, 94, 114, 115
46:2–5	100
46:2–3	18, 38, 66
46:2	65, 66
46:3	37, 65, 66, 82, 100
46:4	35, 38, 83, 100
48:4	38
48:8–22	7, 8, 31, 95
48:21	83
48:22	18, 132
50:15–21	8, 95
50:16–17	35
50:23	38
50:25–26	38

Scripture Index

50:25	35	4:18	18, 38, 119
		4:20	38, 119, 124
Exodus		5:3	119
1	16	5:3–4	8, 119, 120
1:8–10	8, 38, 95, 117	5:4	9, 119
1:8	9, 18	6:11	9
1:9–10	134	6:13	9
1:15–21	8, 18, 38, 88, 89, 95, 117, 142	6:27	9
		6:29	9
1:15	9, 18, 38	7:8–13	56
1:17	9, 18, 19, 59	7:14–19	19
1:18	9, 18	7:17–20	53
1:21	19, 59	7:20–22	56
1:22	117	8:5–6	53
2:15	56	8:16–17	53
2:16–22	56	9:23	48, 53
2:16	18	9:23a	119
2:23	9	9:24–25	119
3	16, 17, 119	10:1–3	8
3:1	8, 18, 38, 47, 52, 96, 117	10:12–14	19
		10:13	53
3:1—4:17	57	10:13a	119
3:2	9, 18	10:13c	119
3:2b	8, 38, 47, 96, 117	10:14–15	119
3:3	8, 96, 117	10:22–23a	119
3:4	18, 56, 118	12	18
3:4b–6	8, 38, 47, 96, 117	12:35–36	120
3:4b	38	13:17–22	8, 38, 120–21
3:5–6	18	13:19	35
3:6	17, 18	13:21–22	48
3:6b	38	13:21	9, 18, 19
3:9–15	8, 38, 96, 117	13:22	9, 18, 19
3:9–12	38	13:30	83
3:10	18, 38, 40	14:5	9, 18
3:12	40, 124	14:5a	8, 38, 96, 121
3:12b	38	14:6	53
3:13–15	19, 135	14:7	8, 96, 121
3:15	19, 118	14–15	53
3:16	118	14:16	19, 53, 57
3:18–22	8, 38, 96, 117	14:19–20	8, 96, 121
3:18	9, 18, 119	14:19	9, 17, 19, 50
3:19	9, 18	14:21	53
3:21–22	40	14:24	9, 18, 19, 48, 96, 121
3:22	35, 120	14:26–27	53
4:17	119, 123	15:14	120
4:17–18	8, 38, 119	15:20	8, 17, 55, 121–22

166

Scripture Index

15:25b–26	8, 96, 122	20:7–8	8, 125
16:4–21	8, 96, 122	20:12–17	8, 125
16:8	56	20:15	19, 39
16:12	56	20:16	41, 130
17	39	20:17	55, 133
17:1–7	8, 96, 123	20:18–22	39
17:3	119	20:18–21	8, 17, 88, 96, 104, 126
17:5–6	119	20:19	19, 40, 86
17:8–16	8, 19, 31, 42, 56, 57, 123	20:20	18, 19, 59
18	124, 128	20:21	40
18:1–27	8, 31, 96, 123–24	20:23—23:33	39, 125
18:1–5	119	22:4	133
18:1–2	38	22:20	38
18:1	18	22:21–24	132–33
18:5	18, 124	23:9	38
18:8	133	23:20–23a	17
18:12	38, 87	23:20–22	39
18:13–16	19	23:20	132
18:16	42	23:23	132
18:21	19, 59, 117	24	39
19	39, 124	24:1–2	8, 17, 21, 96, 126–27
19:1–2	124	24:1	130
19:2–9	19	24:3–8	39
19:2b–6	8, 124	24:4	9, 19
19:2b–9a	39	24:9–15	8, 96, 126–27
19:4–6	91	24:9–11	21
19:5	40	24:9–10	17
19:6	90	24:11b–15a	39
19:9	19, 39, 41, 130	24:11b	39
19:12	86	24:12–15a	19–20, 39
19:12–13	17	24:12–14	40
19:16–19	8, 39, 96, 125	24:13	9, 18, 20, 39, 40, 128
19:16–17	19, 42	24:14–25	123
19:16	48	24:18b	19–20, 39, 42
19:16b–17	19, 39	24:24	57
19:17	17, 18	31–34	39
19:18	9, 18	31:18	19–20, 39, 42
19:19	19, 42	31:18a	39
19:21–24	17	32–33	19
20–23	16, 75	32:1–35	77
20	16, 39	32:1–29	76
20:1	39	32:1–25	25, 39
20:1–4a	8, 125	32:1–24	84
20:2	18	32:1–10	8, 40, 97, 127–28
20:2–17	42		
20:7	55		

167

Scripture Index

32:1	18, 19, 39, 41	**Leviticus**	
32:2–3	37, 112, 127	10:1–3	97, 129
32:2	35, 40, 120	10:1–2	72
32:4	18, 81	10:2	20, 48, 58
32:7–14	40	16:2	40, 128
32:7–13	42	21:5	54
32:7–10	42		
32:7	18	**Numbers**	
32:8	18	3:7–10	40, 128
32:10	18	3:38	40
32:11–14	19	9:15–23	48
32:11–13	42	9:15–16	48
32:11	18	11:1–3	8, 9, 49, 129–134
32:15–24	8, 40, 97, 127–28	11:1	18
32:15–16	40	11:2	18
32:15	40, 42	11:3	18
32:16	42	11:11–12	8, 19, 31, 39, 41, 42, 97, 130–31
32:17	20, 39	11:12	39, 41
32:19	40, 42	11:14–17	8, 31, 39, 41, 97, 130–31
32:19b–20	42	11:14–15	19, 39, 41, 42
32:22–32	40	11:16–17	17, 39, 40, 128, 131, 135
32:22	18	11:17	39, 42
32:23	18	11:24b–30	8, 17, 31, 39, 40, 41, 97, 128, 130–31
32:24	20	11:25	39, 55
32:30–35	25, 39	11:26–29	17
32:30–34	19, 40	11:28–29	20, 39
32:30–31	81, 101	11:28	9, 40, 126, 128
32:32	19	11:29	17
32:34	17, 39, 132	12:1–15	8, 39, 97, 131
33:4	39	12:1–5	31
33:6–11	39, 41, 130, 131	12:1–2	19, 39, 41
33:6	18, 39	12:4–10	40, 41, 128, 130, 135
33:7–11	8, 17, 39, 40–41, 86, 97, 128, 130, 135	12:4–9	17, 39
33:9–10	41, 130	12:5–8	91
33:9	9, 19	12:5	9, 19, 39
33:10	9, 19	12:6–8	17, 19, 55, 86
33:11	9, 20, 39, 41, 91, 126, 130	12:6	9, 16
34	125	12:8	91
34:1	19–20, 39, 42	12:9	39
34:1–5	42	12:10–15	42
34:4	19–20, 39	12:16	20
34:5a	39		
34:5b	19–20		
34:27–29a	42		
34:28	19–20, 39, 42		

Scripture Index

14:13–16	8, 97, 131	22:19–21	65
14:14	9, 18, 19, 48, 91	22:20–21	8, 98, 134
14:20–25	132	22:20	65, 66
15	8	22:36–40	8, 98, 134
16	39	22:38	89
16:1–35	72	23:1–2	8, 98, 134
16:1–2	19, 39, 41	23:4	87
16:1b–2a	39	23:16	87
16:12–15	39	23:18–21a	8, 98, 134
16:12–14	19, 39, 41	23:22–24	8, 98, 134
16:14	133	23:27–30	8, 98, 134
16:25	39	24:2–6a	8, 98, 134
16:27b–34	39	24:2	64
16:28–30	19, 39, 41	24:6	117, 134
16:30	42	24:6c–11a	8, 98, 134
16:35	9, 18	24:14–25	98, 134
20:1	133	24:16	56
20:14	133	24:17–19	134
20:14–20	18	32	133
20:14–21	42, 68	32:1–2	42
20:14–22	133	32:4–5a	42
20:15	133	32:5b	42
20:22–24	42	32:6a	42
20:22a	133	32:6b	42
20:26	133	32:16a	42
21:4–9	8, 97, 132	32:17a	42
21:4a	133	32:18–19	42
21:12–31	42	32:20a	42
21:12–15	133	32:20aβ	42
21:12–13	42	32:20b	42
21:21–33	8, 31, 97, 132	32:24b–27	42
21:27–30	49	32:32–33	42
21:33–35	42	32:39–42	42
21:35	8, 31, 97, 132	38	128
22–24	63, 64		
22	70, 80, 81	**Deuteronomy**	
22:1–7	8, 98, 134	1–9	41, 75
22:3	134	1:1–4	42
22:8–21	64	1:9–12	42
22:8–13	65	2:2–6	42
22:8	65	2:13	42
22:9–21	63	2:14	42
22:9–13	134	2:26–27	42
22:9–13a	8, 98, 134	3:1–7	42
22:9	65, 87	3:12–20	42
22:10–11	66	4:9–13	133
22:14–17	8, 98, 134		

4:10–14	42	7:3–14	56
4:11	42	9:1—10:16	45
5:2–5	42	9:6	55
5:3–4	133	10:5–7	54
5:6–21	42	10:5–6	54
5:19–28	42	10:9–14	54
9:8–21	42	10:10–13	54
9:9	42	15:1–35	45
9:10	42	16:1–13	45
9:12–14	42	19:18–24	45
9:17	42	19:20–24	54
9:25–29	42	25:1	45
9:26–27	42		
10:1–5	42	**1 Kings**	
11:6	42	2:8	53
12:2–6	86	2:14	53
13:2–6	75	3	92
14:1	54	3:4–15	64
18:15–22	42	11:29–40	45
23:4–5	42	12:25	111
24:8–9	42	12:25–33	77, 84
25:17–19	42	12:26–32	76
29:1–7	133	13	59
31:14–15	8, 40, 41, 128, 130, 131, 135	13:1–32	45, 55
31:14	57	13:4	58
31:15	9, 19	13:6	58
34:1–8	57	13:14	54
34:5	8, 135	13:18	49
34:9	57	13:24	58
34:10–12	8, 135	14:1–18	45, 54
		14:6	55
Joshua		15:25	8n11, 49, 129
1:1	18, 40, 126, 128	17	45, 51
3:1–17	57	17:1–24	45
8:8–9	57	17:1–7	148
		17:1	59, 147
1 Samuel		17:2–6	56
1:1–28	45	17:6	54, 56, 57, 122
2:11–36	45	17:8–24	56
3	52–53, 92	17:8–16	147
3:1–21	45	17:13–16	54
3:1–18	64	17:14–16	54, 57
3:4–10	115	17:17–24	54, 148
3:4–6	56	18	87
3:4	56	18:1–46	45
		18:13	46

Scripture Index

18:17	59	2:15–18	54
18:19–40	51, 59	2:18–22	54, 57
18:20–40	56, 145, 148	2:23–24	54, 58
18:28	54	3:4–27	45
18:32	57	3:9–27	57
18:38	48	3:11–27	60
18:41–46	148	3:23–24	60
18:41	39	3:27	60
18:43	55	4:1–44	45
19	51	4:1–7	54, 58, 147
19:1–21	45, 51	4:1	54
19:1–18	57	4:8–37	148
19:4–5	54	4:16	55
19:5–6	54, 57	4:17	54
19:5	49	4:18–37	54
19:7	49	4:25	51
19:9–18	92	4:27	51
19:12	47, 51	4:38–41	54, 57, 147–48
19:13	91	4:38	54
19:16–21	57	4:42–44	54, 57, 147
19:18	46	5:1–27	45
20:13–22	45	5:1–19	54
20:13	55	5:22	54
20:22–24	55	6:1–7	45
20:28	55	6:1	54
20:35–43	45, 54, 55	6:7–15	45
20:36	58	6:8–23	45
21:1–29	45, 81, 145	6:16–17	55
22	59	6:17	47
22:1–40	45	6:18–20	58
22:17	55, 58	6:18–19	47
		6:24–33	45
2 Kings		6:24–30	147
		7:1–20	45
1–2	59	7:1	55
1:1–18	45	7:2	58
1:1–17	51, 54	7:17	58
1:3	50	8:1–6	45
1:9–14	48, 58	8:7–15	54
1:15	50	9:1–13	45, 55
2:1–25	45, 57	9:1–12	145
2:1–16	145	9:1	54
2:1–12	57	9:7–13	57
2:3–7	54	9:13–37	145
2:8	57	10	45
2:11–12	47, 48	10:1–28	145
2:14	57	12:17–19	55

171

Scripture Index

13:4	47
13:14–21	45
13:18–19	53
17	71
17:24–41	70
23	14
23:15–20	71
25	14

Nehemiah
8:8–9	41
8:14–15	41

Psalms
42	54
44–49	54
50	4
73–83	4
84–85	54
87–88	54

Isaiah
15:2	54

Jeremiah
16:6	54
23:25–32	75, 86
27:9–10	75, 86
29:8–9	75, 86
41:4	74

Ezekiel
7:18	54
8–11	77, 81
27:31	54
40–48	77

Hosea
11:5	82
12:4	81
12:14	76

Amos
7:10–13	58
8:10	54

Micah
1:16	54

Zechariah
7:2–3	74

Subject Index

Aaron
    earrings, for golden calf, 37, 40, 112, 127
    golden calf and (*See* golden calf)
    Miriam and, 20, 121–22, 131
    portrayal of, 20
    sons of, 20, 48–49, 58, 72, 129
    striking with special objects, 53
Abihu, 8, 48, 58, 72, 97, 126, 129
Abijah, 8, 48–49, 54, 129
Abimelech
    Abraham and, 55, 101–2, 104, 106, 109
    court of, 7, 93
    covenant with, 7, 93
    retribution, 58
    Sarah and, 20
Abiram, 42
Abraham
    Abimelech and, 55, 101–2, 104, 106, 109
    covenants, 92, 102, 103, 104
    fear of God, 16
    Hagar's flight, 103–4
    Isaac's near sacrifice, 7, 31, 36, 50, 52, 93, 104–5, 122
    promise to, 40, 100, 103
    as prophet, 17, 55
    return to Beersheba, 107
    Sarah's relationship, 20, 101–2
    visions, 7, 92
Abraham-Lot cycle, 30
Ahab, 45, 58
Ahaziah, 46–47, 50, 51, 54, 145
Ahijah, 45, 55

Akitu New Year's ceremony (Mesopotamia), 146
alien sojourners, 81, 132–33
altar
    at Bethel, 112
    Jacob building of, 37
    at Shechem, 112
    Yahwist terminology, 19, 110
Amalek, 8, 31, 42, 123
Amalekites, 56
Amaziah, 58
Ammon, 42
Amorite, Elohist term, 18, 116, 132
Amorite/Canaanite parallel, 31
Amorites, Sihon and, 98, 132, 133
Amos, 58
"angel of God"
    as circumlocution for God, 17, 50
    in dreams, 106
    as Elohist language, 121
    frequency of use, 9, 110
    intermediary figure from the divine, 36, 49–50
    speaks to Hager, 17, 103
angels, revelation through, 7
"anger burns hot," 18
animal sacrifices, 100, 105
anonymous prophets, 55
anti-royal polemic, 145–46
Apara Brahma, 138
Ar of Moab, 49
Arameans, 45
Ark of the Covenant, 17
Arnon River, 42, 133
Asaph Psalms, 4–5, 74
Ashurbanipal, 64

Subject Index

Assyrian deportations,, 70–71
Assyrian Dream Book, 65
auditory message dreams, 7, 16–17, 52, 56, 65, 113

Baal
    as fertility god, 21, 57, 148
    fire imagery, 46
    on Mt Carmel, 51
Baal-Peor, cult at, 21
Babylonian Exile, 23
Balaam, 8, 16, 56, 63–64, 98, 134
Balaam Oracles, 28
baldness, 54
Barak, 134
Beersheba
    Abraham/Abimelech dialogue, 104
    Abraham's return to, 107
    Jacob and, 107
    shrine at, 7, 69, 84
    theophany at, 7, 8, 95
Ben-Hadad, 54, 58
Bethel
    altar, 112
    calf cult (*See* calf cult)
    Deborah, buried below, 113
    Elohist traditions in, 153
    Jacob's reference to God of, 37, 109–10
    journey to, 7, 8, 67, 94–95
    ladder imagery, 17, 67–68, 127
    origin and significance of, 21
    pillar erected at, 37, 106, 109
    return to, 36, 112
    shrine, 3, 7, 69, 84
    theophany at, 7, 8, 93–94, 106–8, 153
    where Elohist was created, 70
biblical figures portrayed in positive fashion, 7
Book of the Covenant, 16, 40, 73, 125
Brahma (in Hinduism), 138
bronze serpent, 8, 21, 97, 132
burning bush, 8, 17, 38, 56, 96, 118

calf cult
    at Bethel, 71–73, 94–95
    critique of, 19, 37, 81, 112, 127
    at Dan, 76
    destruction of Israel and, 77
    Elohist rejection of, 21
    Nadab and Abihu serving, 129
    theme of, 7
calf shrines, 76
call experiences, 56, 117–18
Canaanite
    parallel word usage, 31
    religious beliefs, 21–22
    Yahwist term, 18, 116, 132
Chaldean Babylonian dream accounts, 63, 64
chariot and horses of fire, 47
civil disobedience, 89–90, 95, 142–46
clairvoyance, 55
cloud theme or imagery, 8, 17, 96, 97, 130
commentary on Elohist texts
    Deuteronomy, 135
    Exodus, 117–128
    Genesis, 99–116
    Leviticus, 129
    Numbers, 129–134
companies of the prophets, 54
consciousness of the state, 68
core vocabulary, 8–9
covenants
    Abimelech, 7, 93
    Abraham, 92, 102, 103, 104
    broken by golden calf, 40
    ceremonies and rituals, 39, 56, 99, 100
    concept of, 21
    Jacob, 100, 110
    Laban, 7, 8, 94, 110
    mediator of, 19, 56
    at Mount Horeb, 39
    Priestly covenant, 99
    tablets of, 39, 40
    Yahwist covenant, 99
    (*See also* Ark of the Covenant; Book of the Covenant)
criticism of sources, method of, 33–34

Subject Index

critics of the Elohist
   challenges to existence, 29–30
   continuity in texts, 35–41
      Exodus, 38–41
      Genesis, 36–37
      Numbers, 41
   Deuteronomy and, 41–42
   response to, 31–35

Dathan, 42
David, 55
Davidic Judah, 27
Deborah, death of, 55, 113
Decalogue, 8, 16, 40, 73, 125–26
Deir 'Alla inscription, 63
deity
   remoteness of, 7
   transcendence (*See* transcendent deity)
democratic thought, in western traditions, 146
deportations, 70–71
descendants, promise to, 37–38, 100, 103
destruction of the kingdom and exile, 80–81
Deuteronomic Reform, 27
Deuteronomistic Historians, 4–5, 46, 50, 57, 60, 72, 75, 78–79, 153
Deuteronomistic tradition, 30, 41, 145
dialogue
   double vocative (*See* double vocative dialogue)
   God with people, 18
disappearance of God, 137–40
distant deity, 136–40
divine accompaniment, 82
divine retribution, 58–59
divine revelation, 16–17, 26, 118
divine will, 3
"do not fear" or "fear not," 37, 65, 82, 100, 102
double vocative dialogue, 18, 38, 56, 104, 115, 118, 124
doublet story accounts, 20, 113
dream book, 65

dream report formula, 102
dreams
   Abraham and Abimelech, 101–2, 109
   Abraham and Isaac, 105
   Assyrian dream accounts, 65
   auditory messages, 7, 16–17, 52, 56, 65, 113
   Balaam story, 134
   Bethel theophany, 106, 108
   Chaldean Babylonian dream accounts, 63, 64, 65
   Deuteronomic traditions, 75
   elements of, 53
   Elohist traditions, 75, 152
   Jacob, 31, 37, 109
   in Joseph narrative, 6, 113–15
   Laban, 109
   Mesopotamian formulas, 65–66
   Neo-Assyrian, 63, 64
   of pharaoh, 114, 115
   promises, 100
   psychological status, 65
   revelation through, 7, 16, 21, 91–92
   revelatory, 64–65
   Samuel, 52–53
   symbolic messages, 65
   theological traditions regarding, 86
   visual messages, 65
   (*See also* "pillar of cloud")
droughts, 146–49

eagle's wings, 8
earrings, for Aaron's golden calf and, 37, 40, 112, 127
ecstasy, prophets and, 54, 56
Edom, 68–69
Egypt
   Israelites' mistreatment, 38
   Jacob sent by God to, 115
   king of, 7, 117, 118, 119, 120, 121, 134
   length of stay in, 132–33
   Sed Festival, 115
Eisaacic narrative, 22

Subject Index

Eldad, 17, 130
elders and Joshua on mount, 8
elders prophesy, 8, 31
  (*See also* seventy elders)
Elijah
  angel of God, 49–50
  civil disobedience, 142–46
  Elisha, parallel narratives, 56–57
  fire imagery, 46–47
  on Mt. Carmel, 52, 59–60
  on Mt. Horeb, 51, 52, 59–60
  Omrides prediction, 55, 89
  providing food, 57
  providing for widows, 56, 147–49
  retribution, 58–59
  striking with special objects, 53–54
  traditions, 45–46
  as "troubler of Israel," 59
Elisha
  boys and bears, 60
  chariot and horses of fire, 42
  civil disobedience, 142–46
  Elijah, parallel narratives, 56–57
  invasion of Moab, 60
  Jehu's revolution, 55
  providing food, 57
  providing for widows, 57, 147–49
  retribution, 58–59
  striking with special objects, 53–54
  traditions, 145–46
Elohim
  accompanies patriarchs in their travels, 7
  as name of God, 7, 12, 17, 23–24, 87, 118
  special title for God, 17
  use of after Yahweh revealed, 33
Elohist cycles, 25
Elohist text
  Abimelech, 93
  Abraham's vision, 92
  Bethel theophany, 93–94
  challenges to existence of, 29–30
  continuity in, 35–41
  cycles of, 5
  date ranges for, 6, 27–28, 77–79
  Deuteronomy and, 41–42
  God's faithfulness theme, 16
  Hagar's flight, 93
  historical research on, 11–16
  as independent theological tradition, 21
  Isaac, birth and sacrifice, 93
  narrative technique, 18–19
  placing prior to Yahwist, 152–53
  prophetic tradition, 44–61
  references to other Elohist accounts, 34–35
  as school of thought, 21
  settings for, 62, 70–79
  social and theological message, 22
  social ethics, 7, 23, 84–85
  strands of, 12
  as supplement to Yahwist, 1, 12, 22–23, 29
  themes, 6–7, 16–20, 153
  theological significance, 1–2
  theoretical model, 22
  traditions, 24
  vocabulary usage (*See* vocabulary usage)
"elusive God," 137
environmental stewardship, 149
Ephraim, blessing of, 7, 8, 31, 95, 116
Esarhaddon, 64
Esau
  birth narrative, 105–6
  Jacob and, 31, 37, 69, 111
  journey to, 8, 94
  meeting, 8, 94
ethical sensitivity theme, 7, 23, 84–85
exile, 23, 80–81, 108, 109
existential despair, 139–140
exodus, as homeward flight, 121
Ezekiel, 77, 118

famines, 146–49
"fear not" or "do not fear," 37, 65, 82, 100, 102
"fear of God"
  Abimelech and, 101
  awareness of God leading to, 107

Subject Index

Elohist defining concept, 7,
    15–16, 19
  Jacob and, 106
  judges and, 124
  at the mountain, 17
  obedience and, 3, 59, 86, 88–89,
    96, 104–5, 144
  prophetic tradition, 59
  testing and, 126
  in wisdom literature, 20
fertility god, 21, 148
fertility image, 57–58
fire imagery
  form of divine punishment, 7
  as mode of revelation, 7, 118
  as presence of God, 18, 100
  Sihon of the Amorites, 98, 132,
    133
  Taberah and, 129
  theme of, 46–49, 120
  theophanic phenomena, 126
flood narrative, 33
food
  meal eaten by king Ahab and
    Elijah, 39
  providing for, 54, 96, 122, 146–49
  as sign of Divine fertility, 57–58
foreign gods, rejection of, 112
foreigners, 38, 102, 124
forgiveness, 58
fragmentary accounts and theory, 12,
    14–15, 59–60, 151

"gate of heaven," 68
"glory of the Lord," 122
God
  of all people, 86–88
  dialogue with people, 18
  as a distant deity, 136–140
  existence of, 139–140
  "glory of the Lord," 122
  "man of God," 45, 49, 58, 59
  (*See also* "angel of God"; "fear of
    God"; transcendent deity)
"God brought you up out of the land
    of Egypt" expression, 18
"God of Bethel," 37, 109–10

golden calf
  Aaron and, 20, 72, 112, 129
  attitudes changed over time, 25
  at Bethel, 19, 97, 112
  condemnation of both priests and
    Bethel, 97
  covenant, breaking of, 40
  at Dan, 19
  as Elohist theme, 8, 127
  God's anger with, 42
  golden rings (earrings) and, 37,
    40, 112, 120
  great guilt and, 101
  idols, rejection of, 37, 112
  Jeroboam I and, 49, 72, 127, 129
  legitimacy of an Elohist tradition,
    35
  two accounts of, 77
golden rings from Egyptians, 34–35

Hagar
  angel of God speaks to, 17, 50
  flight of, 7, 20, 36, 93, 103–4
  Sarah and, 20
Hasael, 45
"Here am I" or "here I am," 56, 110,
    115, 118
Heshbon, 49
"hidden god," 136–140
Hindu tradition, 138–39
Hitler, Adolph, 144
holocaust, 143
Horeb. (*See* Mt. Horeb)
Hosea, 76, 77
house of Joseph, 111
human consciousness, 138–39
human heroes, 25
human sacrifices, 21, 105
Hur, in Amalek battle, 123

illness, prophets and, 54
imagery
  of fire, 46–49, 100, 118
  of seven, 104
infant sacrifices, 22, 105
innocent people, 101, 105

Subject Index

Isaac
    birth of, 7, 35, 93
    death of, 81
    name, meaning of, 103
    near sacrifice of, 7, 31, 36, 50, 52, 104–5, 122
Isaiah, call experiences, 118
Israel
    destruction of, 80–81
    fear of God, 16
Israelites
    avoiding Seir, 42
    Balaam's blessing of, 98
    crossing Zered and Arnon, 42
    deterioration of the state, 74
    Elohim/Yahweh worshiped by, 3
    mistreatment in Egypt, 38
    at Mt. Horeb, 19, 39, 42
    new identity for, 90–91
    religious identity, 21
    in the Transjordan, 64

Jacob
    Beersheba at, 107
    Bethel theophany, 106–8
    birth narrative, 105–6
    blessing of Ephraim and Manasseh, 7, 8, 31, 95, 116
    building an altar, 37
    children of, 7, 8, 35, 108–9
    covenants, 100, 110
    death of, 116
    dream theophanies, 31, 37, 109
    Esau and, 31, 37, 69, 111
    exile and return, 108, 109
    family genealogy, 31
    fear of God, 106
    "God of Bethel," 37, 109–10
    God's appearance at Paddan-Aram, 113
    Joseph closing eyes of, 35, 115
    journey to Bethel, 7, 8, 67, 94–95
    Laban and, 7, 8, 20, 37, 94
    ladder imagery, 17, 67–68, 127
    named Israel, 37, 111, 113, 114
    pillar erected at Bethel, 37, 106, 109
    pious prayer for protection, 110
    promise to, 37, 83, 100, 106, 108
    return to Bethel, 36, 112
    sent by God to Egypt, 115
    vision of God, 62
    wives of, 94, 108
    wrestling match at Penuel, 37, 76, 111
Jacob cycle, 30
Jacobic author, 22
JE Epic, 75
JE redactor, 5, 15, 24, 32–33, 62, 78, 152
Jehovist, 13, 14
Jehu, 24, 27, 45, 55
Jeremiah, 75, 118
Jeroboam I
    Ahijah and, 45
    Bethel's calf, 112
    calf shrines, 76
    calves of, 19
    court of, 22
    dating Elohist tradition, 27
    golden calf, 49, 72, 127, 129
    Jacob cycle, 30
    Penuel shrine, 111
    retribution, 58
    sons of, 8n11, 48, 72, 129
Jeroboam II, 27, 88
Jerusalem, 3, 74, 81, 84
Jethro
    as Elohist story, 123–24
    establishment of social structure, 96
    as Moses' father-in-law, 18
    Moses return to Egypt, 8, 119
    source of account, 31
Jethro/Reuel parallel, 31
Jordan River, 53–54
Joseph
    assures his brothers, 116
    bones of, 8, 35, 38, 83, 120, 121
    brothers of, 8, 95
    date of, 6
    fear of God, 16
    interpreting dreams of pharaoh, 113–14

Subject Index

Jacob blesses sons of, 7, 8, 31, 95, 116
   pleading with brothers, 35
   representing northern tribes, 113
Joshua
   in Amalek battle, 123
   as minister to Moses, 7, 9, 18, 20, 40–41, 126–28, 130, 135
   Moses, parallel narratives, 56–57
Josiah, 71–72, 73
Judah, 27, 67
judges, appointment of, 42

"king of Egypt"
   double references of, 118
   as Elohist language, 121
   frequency of use, 9
   idiom use instead of pharaoh, 7
   on Moses and Arron, 119
   on plagues, 120
   as ruler of Egypt, 18, 117
kingdom, destruction of, 80–81
kings, role of, 146–49
"King's Highway," 69
Korah, 54, 72–73

Laban
   covenant, 7, 8, 94, 110
   Jacob and, 7, 8, 20, 37, 94
   sheep of, 20
ladder imagery, 17, 67–68, 127
land, promise of return to, 83, 100
laws and law codes, 16, 26, 125–26
life, meaning and purpose of, 139–140
literary repetition, 33

magical striking with special objects, 53–54
Mahanaim, 8, 110
maid, Elohist word, 108
maidservant, 18, 20
"man of God," 45, 49, 58, 59
Manasseh, blessing of, 7, 8, 31, 95, 116
manna and quail, 8
Marah, 122

Medad, 17, 130
Medeba, 49
Mesopotamia
   Akitu New Year's ceremony, 146
   dream formulas, 65–66
   ziggurats, 67
Micaiah ben-Imlah, 45, 55, 58
midwives, 8, 16, 95, 142–46
Miriam
   Aaron and, 20, 121–22, 131
   death of, 133
   Moses and, 31, 97
   as prophet, 8, 17, 55, 121
   punishment for sin, 131
   skin disease, 42
Moab, 42, 45, 49, 60
modern relevance
   civil disobedience, 142–46
   distant deity, 136–140
   sufficient food, 146–49
   worldwide refugees, 140–42
monotheism, 66, 87, 88, 153
monotheistic values, 66–67
moralistic piety, 20, 101
morality, 7, 19, 75, 84–85
Moses
   authority of, 19, 130–31, 132
   breaking the tablets, 39, 42, 127
   burning bush, 8, 17, 38, 56, 96, 118
   call experience, 117–18
   fear of God, 16
   going to pharaoh, 135
   as human hero, 25
   identity of, 8
   as intercessor, 40, 42, 129, 131–32
   Israelites to despoil Egyptians, 40
   Jethro and, 8, 18
   Joshua, parallel narratives, 56–57
   leadership as a prophet, 7, 19–20, 39, 41, 118
   Miriam and, 31, 97
   mountain top experience, 52
   before pharaoh, 8, 19
   plagues, 19, 60, 119–120
   praise of, 8
   prayer to the Lord, 131

Subject Index

Moses (*continued*)
    as prophet, 17, 55
    seventy elders, 17, 39, 41, 55, 97–98, 126, 130
    staff or rod of, 19, 119, 120, 121
    striking with special objects, 53–54
mountain of God, 18, 39, 47, 52
mountain theme, 17, 42, 48, 51–52, 96, 118, 124–27, 130
Mt. Carmel, 51–52, 59–60, 87
Mt. Horeb
    Elijah on, 51, 52, 59–60
    Israelites at, 19, 39, 42
    as mountain of God, 18, 39, 52
    theophany phenomena, 47–48, 91–92
Mt. Sinai, mountain of God, 18, 47, 51, 60

Naaman, 45
Naboth's vineyard, 45, 81, 145
Nadab, 8, 48–49, 58, 72, 97, 126, 129
narrative technique, 18–19
Nathan, 46, 55
national leaders, 142–46
Nazi Germany, 143, 144
Neo-Assyrian dream accounts, 63, 64
Nile River, 54
Nirguna Brahma, 138
non-Priestly narrative, 23
northern cult sites, 7
northern tribes, 108–9

Obadiah, 46
obedience theme
    fear of God and, 3, 59, 86, 88–89, 96, 104–5, 144
    moral behavior and, 75
    Moses and, 118
    testing and, 7, 104–5
    (*See also* civil disobedience)
odd behaviors, 55
Og, defeat of, 42
older priestly texts, 12
Omrides' prediction, 54–55, 89
oral traditions, 13–14, 16

Paddan-Aram, God's appearance to Jacob, 113
Palestine, 18
Para Brahma, 138
parallel narratives, 31, 33, 56–57
Pentateuchal Elohist, 80–81
Pentateuchal narratives, 78, 152
Penuel
    exiles, 94
    Jacob named Israel, 113
    Jacob's wrestling match, 37, 76, 111
    shrine, 8, 30
people's response, 8
Philistines, 56
piety, 20, 84–85, 101–2, 104–5
pillar imagery
    at Bethel, 37, 106, 109
    Elohist word, 110
    erected at Paddan-Aram, 113
    ritual pillars, 7, 9
    as sacred object, 19
"pillar of cloud"
    continuity in Elohist text, 40
    as Elohist language, 120, 121
    as Elohist theme, 7, 8, 18–19, 128, 135
    frequency of use, 9
    God leading people in the wilderness, 96
    Moses' prayer to the Lord, 131
"pillar of fire"
    as Elohist language, 120, 121
    as Elohist theme, 7, 18
    frequency of use, 9
    God leading people in the wilderness, 48, 96
    Moses' prayer to the Lord, 131
place, as Elohist expression, 106, 107
plagues, 19, 48, 60, 119–120
pools of Elohist tradition, 2–3, 4, 25, 35, 45, 70, 78, 106
precursor texts, 23
Priestly Editors, 12, 16, 78, 79
"priestly kingdom and a holy nation," 124

Subject Index

Priestly tradition
    covenant, 99
    literary sources, 12
    sources for, 41–42
    terms, 122
promises
    to Abraham, 40, 100, 103
    descendants to, 37–38, 100, 103
    to Israelites, 38
    to Jacob, 37, 83, 100, 106, 108
    of return to the land, 83
    (*See also* covenants)
prophetic identity, 54–57, 90
prophetic narratives in Samuel and Kings
    Pentateuchal narratives and, 152
    prophetic traditions, 44–61
        angel of God, 49–50
        dreams, 52–53
        fear of God and obedience, 59
        fire imagery, 46–49
        food as sign of Divine fertility, 57–58
        fragmentary nature of many accounts, 59–60
        immediate Divine retribution, 58–59
        magical striking with special objects, 53–54
        mountains, 51–52
        strangeness in narratives, 60–61
        themes of prophetic identity, 54–57
prophetic strand (Elohist), 12
prophets
    all Lord's people, 17, 130
    call experiences, 56, 117–18
    fulfilling role of kings, 146–49
    importance of, 7
    as representatives of God, 17
    retribution, 58–59
    revelation to, 91–92
    vocabulary usage, 26
Protestant tradition, on salvation, 139
proto-Elohist, 45, 46, 49, 78, 153

proto-Genesis, 23, 30, 78
Psalms of Asaph, 4–5, 74
psychological status dreams,, 65
punishment for sin
    Miriam, 131
    Taberah, 129

Rachael, 8, 67, 94
refugees, 140–42
retribution, 58–59
Reuben narrative, 114
Reuel/Jethro parallel, 31
"revealed god," 136–140
revelation, divine, 16–17, 26, 91–92, 118
revelatory dreams, 64–65
ritual pillars, 7, 9
rod or staff of Moses, 19, 119, 120, 121
Roman Catholic tradition, on salvation, 139

sacred sites, names for, 110
sacrifices
    animals, 100, 105
    humans, 21, 105
    infants, 22, 105
    at the mountain, 124
Saguna Brahma, 138
salvation, questions of, 139
Samaria, 6, 81–82
Samuel, 45, 52–53, 55, 56
Sarah
    abduction of, 36
    Abimelech and, 20
    Abraham and, 20
    Hagar's flight, 20, 103–4
    relationship to Abraham, 101–2
Sargon, 67
Saul, 45, 55
scholarly research
    contemporary defenders, 21–26
    critical biblical scholarship, 151, 154
    history of research, 11–16
    range of dates suggested for, 27–28

Subject Index

scholarly research (*continued*)
    themes and theology as hypothesized by scholars, 16–20
Sed Festival (Egypt), 146
Sennacherib, 64
seven, imagery of, 104
seventy elders, 17, 39, 41, 55, 97–98, 126, 130
Shechem shrine, 7, 8, 84, 112
shrines
    Beersheba (*See* Beersheba)
    Bethel (*See* Bethel)
    Mahanaim, 8, 110
    Penuel (*See* Penuel)
    restoration of, 84
    Shechem, 7, 8, 84, 112
Shunammite woman, 45, 52, 148
Sihon, 8, 31, 42, 98, 132–33
sin
    punishment for, 81–82, 97, 129, 131
    verb used for, 18
Sinai, mountain of God, 18, 47, 51, 60
social and theological message, 22
social and theological setting
    additional observations, 67–70
    dream reports, 63–66
    monotheistic values, 66–67
    settings for Elohist, 70–79
social ethics, 23
sojourners, 132–33
sons of the prophets, 54
source criticism, methodology of, 33–34
staff or rod of Moses, 19, 119, 120, 121
stewardship, environmental, 149
strangeness in narratives, 60–61
strangers, 132–33
striking with special objects, 53–54
Succoth, city of, 111
supplemental theory, 1, 12, 22–23, 29
supplementary method, 34
symbolic dreams, 113, 114
symbolic message dreams, 65
syncretism, 21, 72

Taberah, 129
Taberah fire, 8
Ten Commandments, 125–26
tent of meeting, 7, 17, 26, 39, 40, 41, 128, 130, 131, 135
testing
    as Elohist theme, 8, 104–5
    fear of God, 126
    Israelites in exile, 96
    at Marah, 122
    obedience and, 7, 104–5
    purpose of, 19
    response of obedience, 7
    word use for, 18
theology of Elohist
    message to Israelites, 80–92
        civil disobedience, 89–90
        destruction of the kingdom and exile, 80–81
        Divine accompaniment, 82
        enhanced ethical or moral awareness, 84–85
        fear of God and obedience, 88–89
        justification for Samaria fall, 81–82
        new identity for Israelites, 90–91
        promise of return to the land, 83
        prophetic identity, 90
        restoration of shrines and worship, 84
        revelation to the prophets, 91–92
        transcendent deity, 85–86
        universal God of all people, 86–88
    theological commentary, 92–98
three days' journey into wilderness, 119
"to go out," meaning of, 18
Tower of Babel, 68
transcendent deity
    dream revelations, 21
    dualistic characteristic of, 138
    fire imagery as, 47

Subject Index

Jacob's ladder and, 127
meaningful presence of, 24
modes of revelation, 85–86
portrayal of, 41, 118, 128, 137
presence revealed, 3, 18, 100
Transjordan conquest, 7, 42
Transjordanian traditions, 54, 63, 64
trees, connections to, 54, 55
twins, birth of, 7
two, use and meaning of, 18
tyrants, 142–46

universalism, 93, 102, 124

values, monotheistic, 66–67
visual message dreams, 65
vocabulary usage, 8–9, 18–20, 26, 32, 43, 110, 151–53
vocal dreams. (*See* auditory message dreams)

water resources, 148–49
watershed discipleship, 149
widows, providing for, 45, 56, 57, 147–49
wisdom literature, 20
wisdom tradition, 24
wives, 101–2
women
    midwives, 8, 16, 95, 142–46
    prophets helping, 54, 55
    widows, 45, 56, 57, 147–49
    as wives, 101–2
written sources, 14, 16

Yahweh, as name of God, 12, 17, 87, 118, 123
Yahwist Historian, 1, 5, 23, 31, 34, 60, 62, 72, 78–79, 153
Yahwist tradition
    covenant, 99
    denial of, 30
    Elohist as supplement to, 1, 12, 22–23, 29
    literary sources, 12
    use of Elohist material, 32–33
younger priestly texts, 12

Yugoslavian wars (1990s), 144

Zered River, 42
ziggurats, 67–68

Name Index

Aberback, Moses, 8n11, 49n6, 129n62
Ahlström, Gösta, 63n4
Amit, Yairah, 73n31
Anderson, Bernhard W., 15, 27n36
Astruc, Jean, 11–12
Auld, A. Graeme, 45

Baden, Joel, 2n2, 13n3, 14n4, 14n5, 25–26, 29n1, 31, 35n18, 37n22, 38, 39, 41, 42, 75, 101, 107n14, 113, 114, 115n29, 120, 123, 125–26, 128, 129n64, 130–33, 131n67, 133, 135, 153
Benzinger, Immanuel, 13
Bergmann, J., 64n8
Beyse, Karl-Martin, 27
Blenkinsopp, Joseph, 11n1, 29n2, 30, 73n31
Blum, Erhard, 30, 107, 108n18
Bonhoeffer, Dietrich, 144
Brisman, Leslie, 22, 100, 104, 105n11, 106n12
Burnett, Joel, 6, 7, 23–24, 33, 82, 84, 87, 100–102, 103, 104, 106–11, 116, 137

Campbell, Antony F., 23, 99–111, 115–121, 123–28, 132–34
Carpenter, Joseph, 13
Carr, David M., 23, 30, 36n19, 78, 107n16, 108n18, 111n21, 114, 116n33
Carroll, Robert P., 57n16
Childs, Brevard S., 144n12

Chung, Youn Ho, 25, 40, 89
Clements, Ronald, 11n1
Coats, George W., 115n30
Coogan, Michael, 63n4
Coote, Robert B., 22, 27, 75n39, 100–111, 115–126, 132
Cross, Frank Moore, 63n3

Davies, Philip, 73n31
Dillmann, August, 13
Dozeman, Thomas, 30n6, 68, 69
Driver, Samuel R., 13

Eichhorn, Johann Gottfried, 11n2
Eissfeldt, Otto, 13
Engnell, Ivan, 14
Ewald, Heinrich, 12

Fretheim, Terence E., 21, 27n36, 99–111, 115–135, 140n8, 143n10
Friedman, Richard Elliott, 22, 27n37, 100–111, 115–135, 137

Geddes, Alexander, 12
Gnuse, Robert Karl, 3n4, 3n5, 5n8, 63n1, 63n2, 63n6, 64n7, 64n8, 66n10, 66n11, 68n18, 75n38, 77n42, 114n26, 139n6, 140n8, 142n9, 146n14
Gomes, Jules, 27, 36n21, 55n14, 73n29, 73n31, 73n33, 112n22
Gottwald, Norman K., 68
Goulder, Michael, 4, 5n6, 5n7, 69
Graf, Karl Heinrich, 12
Graupner, Alex, 24, 27, 35n18, 69, 82, 83, 86n9, 91, 94n24, 99–105,

Name Index

106–11, 115–121, 123–24, 126–27, 132n70, 134, 136
Gray, John, 50n8
Grottanelli, Christiano, 147n15
Guillaume, Philippe, 73n30, 73n31, 73n33
Gunkel, Hermann, 13

Hackett, Jo Ann, 63n3
Hahn, Herbert, 11n1
Hartford-Battersby, John, 13
Hayes, John H., 11n1
Heschel, Abraham Joshua, 140n8
Hoftijzer, Jacob, 63n3
Hölscher, Gustav, 13–14, 28
Holzinger, Heinrich, 13
Hupfeld, Hermann, 12
Hurowitz, Victor, 68n16, 73n32

Ilgen, Karl David, 12

Jaroš, Karl, 21–22, 27n37
Jenks, Alan W., 11n1, 11n2, 21, 27, 35n18, 44, 56n15, 57n16, 66–67, 76, 88n17, 90–91, 99–111, 115–135
Jones, Gwilym, 57n16

Kaiser, Otto, 28, 67
Kammenhuber, Annalies, 65n9
Kelle, Brad E., 71n28
Kim, Hyun, 114n25
Klein, Hans, 21, 27n37, 70
Knauf, Ernst, 73n31, 74n34, 90
Knight, Douglas A., 29n2
Knohl, Israel, 41n29, 128n59
Knoppers, Gary N., 71n28
Kooij, G. van der, 63n3
Kraus, Hans-Joachim, 11n1
Kuenen, Abraham, 12–13

Lang, Bernhard, 66n11
Lehnart, Bernhard, 45, 55n13
Levin, Christopher, 29n2, 30
Levine, Baruch A., 63n5, 73
Lichtenstein, Murray, 102n5
Lohfink, Norbert, 66n11

Luther, Martin, 11

Marquis, Liane, 133
Mayes, A. D. H., 29, 30n3
McCarter, P. Kyle, 63n3, 63n4, 63n6, 66n11
McEvenue, Sean, 22, 36, 87, 93n23, 100–111, 115, 116, 117–18, 120–21
McKenzie, Stephen L., 54, 55n13
Moore, Michael, 63n4, 71n28
Mowinckel, Sigmund, 14
Müller, Hans-Peter, 63n5
Myers, Ched, 149n17

Nicholson, Ernst, 13n3, 14n4, 49n7, 103n6, 129n61
Nigosian, S. A., 138n5
Noss, David, 138n5
Noth, Martin, 14, 16, 27, 99–111, 115–128, 132–33, 134

Oberman, Julian, 65n9
O'Brien, Mark A., 23, 99–111, 115–128, 132–34
Oppenheim, A. Leo, 64n8, 65n9

Pederson, Johannes, 14
Pfeiffer, Henrik, 73n30, 73n31
Pleins, J. David, 23, 28, 70n26, 80n2, 84n7, 87n12, 90n19
Procksch, Otto, 13, 76
Propp, William H. C., 24, 109–10, 117–124, 126–29, 134
Puech, Emile, 63n5

Rad, Gerhard von, 14
Redford, Donald B., 28, 114n25
Rendtorff, Rolf, 30
Reuss, Eduard, 12
Roberts, Kathryn, 39n25
Rose, Martin, 29, 30n3
Rouillard, Hedwige, 63n4
Rudolph, Wilhelm, 1, 29
Ruppert, Lothar, 15

Sasson, Jack M., 65n9

Name Index

Schmidt, Ludwig, 38
Schmitt, Hans-Christoph, 5, 24, 28, 29n2, 30n6, 70, 80, 100–111, 113, 115–19, 122n46, 123–27, 134
Schüpphaus, Joachim, 15–16
Schwartz, Baruch, 124
Sherman, Phillip Michael, 68n17
Silberman, Lou, 136
Smend, Rudolph, 27, 28n44
Smith, Mark S., 66n11, 67
Smolar, Leivy, 8n11, 49n6, 129n62
Snaith, Norman, 129n64, 131n67
Sommer, Benjamin, 8n10, 40n28, 97n25, 128n58
Spinoza, Baruch, 11
Stackert, Jeffrey, 26, 27
Sweeney, Marvin A., 8n11, 54, 129n62, 147n16

Tappy, Ron E., 71n27
Terrien, Samuel, 137

Van Seters, John, 1, 2n2, 29, 30n3, 31, 45, 78–79

Vater, Johann, 12
Vatke, Wilhelm, 12
Volz, Paul, 1, 29
Vörlander, Hermann, 66n11

Walsh, Jerome T., 57n16
Weisman, Z., 68
Wellhausen, Julius, 13, 61
Wenham, Gordon, 36n19
Wette, Wilhelm Leberecht de, 12
White, Marsha, 46n4, 51n9, 128n57, 145n13
Whybray, R. Norman, 15, 30n5, 30n6, 31–34, 80n1, 107n17
Winnet, Frederick, 29n2
Wolff, Hans Walter, 15–16, 27

Yoo, Philip, 135n78
Yoreh, Tzemah, 25, 27, 41n31, 78, 100–111, 114–128, 130n66, 132–34
Youn Ho Chung, 25, 40
Zertal, Adam, 71n27
Zimmer, Frank, 27
Zobel, Hans Jürgen, 27, 68